The Complete Book of
NATURE CRAFTS

The Complete Book of
NATURE CRAFTS

How to Make Wreaths, Dried Flower Arrangements, Potpourris, Dolls,
Baskets, Gifts, Decorative Accessories for the Home, and Much More

Eric Carlson, Dawn Cusick, and Carol Taylor

Rodale Press, Emmaus, Pennsylvania

Copyright © 1992 by Altamont Press, Inc.

Published by Rodale Press, Inc.
33 East Minor Street, Emmaus, PA 18098

Created and produced by Altamont Press, Inc.
50 College Street, Asheville, NC 28801

Printed in the United States of America on acid-free paper ∞

Executive Editor: Margaret Lydic Balitas
Editor: Cheryl Winters Tetreau
Horticultural Consultant: Nancy J. Ondra
Copy Editor: Laura Stevens
Art Director: Chris Colando
Production: Elaine Thompson, Chris Colando
Photography: Evan Bracken (unless otherwise noted)
Illustrations: Chris Colando
Cover Photography: Evan Bracken
Editorial Assistance: Roswitha Friedl

If you have any questions or comments concerning this book, please write:
    Rodale Press
    Book Readers' Service
    33 East Minor Street
    Emmaus, PA 18098

Library of Congress Cataloging-in-Publication Data
Carlson, Eric.
    The complete book of nature crafts : how to make wreaths, dried flower arrangements, potpourris, dolls, baskets, gifts, decorative accessories for the home, and much more / by Eric Carlson, Dawn Cusick, and Carol Taylor.
        p.   cm.
    Includes bibliographical references and index.
    ISBN 0–87596–141–X hardcover
    1. Nature craft. I. Cusick, Dawn. II. Taylor, Carol.
III. Title.
TT157.C272   1992
745.5–dc20   92–18563
                                     CIP

Distributed in the book trade by St. Martin's Press

2 4 6 8 10 9 7 5 3 1   hardcover

CONTENTS

INTRODUCTION

A stroll through any large craft store might well convince you that crafting originated with the invention of glue guns, silica gel, puff paints, and other intriguing inventions of the twentieth century. History, though, tells us otherwise. Early man recognized nature as the source of food and shelter and revered its power and beauty. Items made from natural materials were equally respected. And while function was clearly the goal of these early crafts, the repetition of making them day in, day out generated boredom, and the boredom inspired an awareness of creative alternatives. Color was added with dyes, new patterns and shapes were devised, and a worldwide tradition of natural crafting began.

This book explores the exhilarating variety of craft techniques that use materials provided by nature instead of a high-tech molding machine. You'll find projects made from flowers and herbs; fruits and vegetables; leaves and bark; wheat and grasses; sticks, saplings, and vines; seeds, seedpods, nuts, and cones; gourds; seashells, sand, and driftwood; cornhusks; and pine needles. Step-by-step instructions make it easy to duplicate your favorite project or to make substitutions that suit your taste and your access to materials.

We hope this book will both enhance your appreciation for the remarkable materials nature has provided and yield a bountiful collection of cherished nature crafts.

BASIC CRAFT
TOOLS AND TECHNIQUES

Almost by definition, nature crafts involve basic tools and simple techniques. For centuries, people with no particular training have been making wreaths and garlands, baskets and birdhouses, candles and Christmas tree ornaments.

To make almost all of the projects in this book, you'll need only a few tools and materials that are either already lying around the house or readily available in craft stores and discount marts. For some projects, simple hand tools—a handsaw, for example—are required. Occasionally, a common power tool, such as an electric drill, would be helpful. Aside from that, you'll need only common sense and a few tricks of the trade, which are revealed here.

TOOLS

Most of the tools and techniques described in this section originated with florists, who by the nature of their profession have need for quick, reliable tools that are inconspicuous in the finished project and do not cost a lot of money. You'll soon discover, though, that these same tools and techniques are well suited not only for flowers but also for materials such as leaves, evergreens, fruits, vegetables, shells, cornhusks, seedpods, nuts, vines, and grasses, just to name a few.

FLORAL PICKS

These versatile wooden picks come with a short length of fine-gauge floral wire attached. Floral picks are used to secure stems of flowers or foliage that are too weak to insert directly into a foam or straw base. As a time-saving technique, materials can be grouped into small bouquets of three to five stems and then attached to a floral pick. The end of the pick is precut at an angle to make perforation into the base easier.

To use a floral pick, position the pick against the stems so the pick extends about 1 inch

(2.5 cm) below the stems. Wrap the wire around the stems once or twice, then wrap and spiral the wire down around the stems and the pick, binding them together. Trim the stems where the wire ends. If the stems are especially fragile, you can add strength by wrapping the picked stems with floral tape. (See Figure 1.)

CRAFT PICKS

Craft picks are floral picks without the wire, and they're used primarily to attach materials such as fresh fruits and vegetables to a craft base. The sharp end of the pick easily perforates the fruit or vegetable, and then the protruding end is inserted into a foam, straw, or vine base.

FLORAL PINS

These curved pieces of wire look and work like old-fashioned hairpins. To use one, simply position the materials you're attaching against a straw or foam base, position the pin with its prongs on either side of the material, and press the pin at an angle into the base.

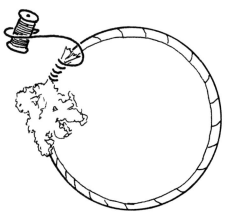

FIGURE 2

FLORAL TAPE

Floral tape comes in two varieties: a thick, strong tape (also known as adhesive floral tape) that resembles electrical tape, and a thinner, more elastic tape that's usually referred to simply as floral tape. The first variety is used to secure foam for arrangements in its container and can be substituted with any other strong tape, if desired. The second variety comes in several shades (such as brown and green) compatible with natural materials and is used to strengthen picked bouquets, or in conjunction with floral wire to lengthen and/or strengthen single floral stems. (For instructions on how to do this, see "Floral Wire" below.)

FLORAL WIRE

Floral wire comes in a variety of gauges, ranging from very thin and pliable (fine-gauge floral wire) to very thick (heavy-gauge floral wire). For large projects, such as covering a wreath base with miniature bouquets, you may wish to purchase the wire on a spool (often referred to as spool wire; see Figure 2). You can also use wire to create new

FIGURE 1

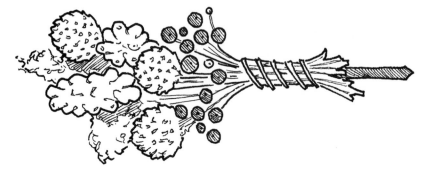

stems for blooms that are too short and/or too weak to otherwise use. To do this, simply place a length of wire against the stem so there's as much overlap as possible. Then secure the two by wrapping with floral tape. Always wrap the tape down the stem at an angle and stretch it slightly as you work for better adhesion. (See Figure 3.)

FLORAL TUBES

These clever little gadgets allow crafters to easily add fresh-cut flowers to dried projects. The tops of the small plastic tubes unscrew so the tube can be filled with water, and there's a slit in the top just large enough for a single stem to fit through. The tubes themselves are hot-glued in place, and as the flowers wilt, they can easily be replaced.

GLUE GUNS

Glue guns come in two varieties: hot melt and low melt. Hot melt glue guns have been around for years. They're fast, versatile, and the only challenge in using them is avoiding the painful burns they can cause. Low melt glue guns are relatively new to the market, and their glue melts at a temperature so low it can't cause burns. The only negative to low melt glue guns is that they require special glue sticks that tend to be more expensive than the regular glue sticks.

No matter which variety you choose, you will continually be amazed at how quickly glue guns work and at the endless number of items they will attach. Because they work so fast, though, it's important to play with angles and positions before you apply the first bit of glue.

WHITE CRAFT GLUE

This everyday white glue is sold under any number of formulas and brand names, so always read the label to be sure it will work with your materials. When a materials list calls for white craft glue, don't substitute hot glue.

MAKING BASES

Making your own craft bases can be fun and inexpensive, and it allows you to begin working on ideas as soon as you feel inspired instead of waiting until you can get to a craft store.

FOAM BASES

A serrated knife can be used to cut just about any shape or size of foam base out of the large foam blocks available at craft stores. Cutting your own bases costs significantly less than buying precut foam. Leftover foam scraps should never be thrown away because they often serve as inspiration for new projects. You should also consider cutting the precut foam shapes from craft stores to suit your needs. Foam balls, for instance, can be cut in half to create a base that makes a more rounded flower arrangement (see Figure 4), and foam wreath bases can be cut in half to make bases for curved garlands.

WIRE BASES

Wire bases are usually used for garlands and wreaths, and are made from heavy-gauge floral wire. The only tool you'll need is a pair of good wire cutters; you simply curve the wire into the desired shape. A great way to recycle wire coat hangers is to unravel them to form wire bases. (See Figure 5.)

VINE AND TWIG BASES

Like wire bases, vines and twigs are popular craft base choices because they can be curved into just about any shape. Vines and twigs, however, have the additional benefit of look-

FIGURE 3

ing very attractive in finished craft projects, so you don't have to cover the entire base. To form a base for a short swag, simply gather several stems together (the number depends on how much prominence you want the vines or twigs to have in the finished product) and wire them securely together at the center with medium- or heavy-gauge floral wire.

To make a vine wreath base, curve four to six fresh-cut vines together to form a circle allowing an overlap of about 2 inches (5 cm). (If fresh-cut vines aren't available, you can soak older vines in a tub of warm water until they soften.) Weave one or two more vines around the base to hold the vines together. (See Figure 6.)

STRAW BASES

Straw bases are used almost exclusively for wreaths. They're inexpensive to make and a good base choice if you're working with lots of dried materials with at least 3-inch (7 cm) stem lengths. To make a straw wreath base, hold a small handful of straw against a heavy-gauge wire base and secure the straw by wrapping fine-gauge floral wire around it and the base at 2-inch (5 cm) intervals. (See Figure 7.) Do not trim the wire. Continue adding handfuls of straw until the wire base is completely covered. Wrap the fine-gauge floral wire around the ending point three times to secure, then cut the wire. If you have lots of dried materials and desire an unusually thick wreath base, you can cover the straw base with another layer of straw, wiring it on in the same way as you did the first layer.

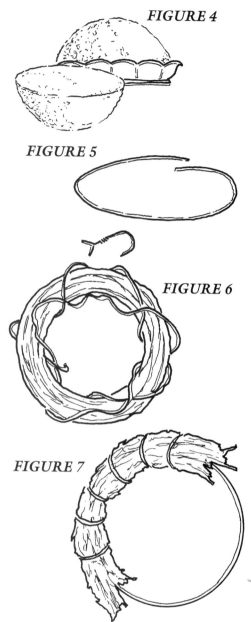

FIGURE 4

FIGURE 5

FIGURE 6

FIGURE 7

MAKING WREATHS

Wreathmaking is one of those wonderful crafts that can be as simple or as complicated as you choose. And as long as you're working with attractive materials, there's virtually no way to make an ugly wreath. The only rule to remember is never to judge an unfinished wreath— even the most beautiful wreath was probably not attractive at the halfway point.

The techniques involved in making a wreath are relatively simple, and which technique you choose should be determined more by the materials

you're using than by any personal preferences you may have. The basic techniques are discussed and illustrated below. Keep in mind that on a single wreath you may use more than one technique.

ATTACHING SINGLE BLOOMS

Because it would take a long time and a large quantity of materials, bases are rarely covered with just small blooms. Instead, single blooms are hot-glued into a background material such as 'Silver King'

artemisia, sweet Annie, or bay leaves. Care should be taken to position the blooms at different depths and angles for a more natural appearance. (See Figure 8.)

ATTACHING SMALL BOUQUETS

Spool wire is used to attach small bouquets of dried materials to metal ring and wire bases, while floral picks are used to attach bouquets to foam, straw, and vine bases. To wire a bouquet to a metal or wire base, position it against

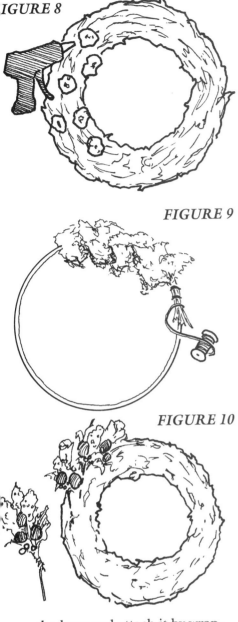

FIGURE 9

FIGURE 10

Grapevine Eucalyptus Wreath, see page 52

the base and attach it by wrapping several times around the bouquet and base with spool wire. (See Figure 9.) Position each successive bouquet to cover the stems of the previous bouquet. You can attach the bouquets with one continuous length of spool wire. The stems of the last bouquet should be neatly tucked under the blooms of the first bouquet to make the start and finish points indistinguishable in the finished wreath. Bouquets can be alternately positioned to the left, center, and right to create a fuller look, if desired. When

the base is completely covered with bouquets, examine the wreath for bare spots and fill them in by hot-gluing additional stems at the same angle as the bouquets.

To pick a bouquet into a foam, straw, or vine base, insert the pick into the base at an angle. (See Figure 10.) As with wiring, every bouquet after the first one is positioned to cover the stems (and pick) of the previous bouquet, and the

stems from the last bouquet should be neatly tucked under the blooms of the first bouquet to make the start and finish points indistinguishable. With foam and straw bases, you can work in three separate stages, first covering the inner edge of the base, then the outer edge, and then the center surface area. With vine bases, you may need to apply a dab of hot glue to the end of each pick before inserting it into the vines.

MAKING ARRANGEMENTS

One of the most creative parts of making an arrangement is choosing the container that will hold it. Anything that's stable and large enough to hold the materials will do—a basket, vase, mixing bowl, pitcher, mug, or bottle.

After choosing a container, the next step is to cut a piece of floral foam to fit it, using a serrated kitchen knife. Available at craft stores and discount marts, this rigid, fine-grained foam will support dried materials exactly where you want them. Tough-stemmed items, such as sprigs of evergreens, are cut at an angle and inserted directly into the foam. Flimsy stems must be attached to a floral pick first.

An invaluable material is "wet" foam—floral foam that will absorb and retain water for days. When working with fresh flowers or foliage, saturate the foam and insert the fresh materials. Check the foam every couple of days and add more water to prevent it from drying out.

Before inserting either fresh or dried materials, decide on an overall shape for the arrangement—round, for example, or oval, or triangular. It's usually helpful to establish the boundaries first—to insert the item that will provide the highest point, then those that will define the outer perimeter. With those boundaries to guide you, proceed to fill in the arrangement. When filling it in, try to add the heavy, bulky materials first, to avoid damaging the lighter, more delicate ones.

MAKING GARLANDS

By definition, a garland is long and thin—ready to drape over mirror or mantle, window or door. Creating one involves attaching materials to a long "spine"—anything strong enough to support the weight of the materials and flexible enough to be draped in graceful curves. Jute cord, the kind used in macramé, makes an excellent spine. Heavy-gauge floral wire also works well.

It's helpful to have a location in mind before you make the garland. Then you can measure how long the garland needs to be—the length of the mantle plus 10 inches on each end, for example, or the total distance up one side of a doorway, across the top, and down the other side. When you cut the spine, make it about 12 inches (30 cm) longer than the length you want the garland to be. This will allow you ample room to tie off each end after all the materials are attached. Most crafters just lay the spine on a table or on the floor and work there. Others tie the spine between two chair backs at a convenient working height.

To make the garland, form a small bunch of greenery or flowers—six to eight stems, all going in the same direction—and wire the stems together with fine-gauge floral wire. Then wire the bunches to the spine, again with fine-gauge wire (see Figure 11). Make sure the leaves or flowers of each bunch overlap and conceal the stems of the previous one. Continue until the spine is well covered.

The bunches should lie in a deliberate pattern. One possi-

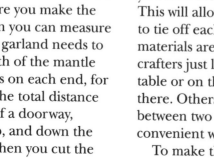

FIGURE 11

bility is to work from one end of the garland to the other, with the bunches all pointing in the same direction. A second option is to work from the center to one end, placing the bunches so that they all point outward, then repeat the process on the other side, creating a mirror image. A bow, knick-knack, or very full bunch of foliage or flowers can be wired or hot-glued to the center to cover the inevitable bare spot.

Bunches can be composed of a single material (pine needles, for example) and alternated with bunches of other materials, say, boxwood and baby's-breath. Alternatively, each bunch can be composed of a mixture of different materials.

After the spine is well covered, decorative accents can be hot-glued to the foliage—pinecones, berries, knick-knacks, or whatever befits the season. Ribbon is an attractive final touch. Wrap a ribbon loosely down the entire length of the garland, wire a bow to the center, or wire a bow at each end.

Making Swags

Swags are essentially arrangements of natural materials designed to hang vertically. The simplest is a collection of greenery, flowers, cones, or garlic bulbs wired together by their stems with medium-gauge floral wire. A bow or some other decorative accent, attached with fine-gauge floral wire, usually conceals the wired stems.

Somewhat more complex are horizontal swags. Divide the background material—for example, 'Silver King' artemisia—into two bunches and place them end to end, with their stems overlapping in the center. Wire the stems together with medium-gauge floral wire, then add additional materials with fine-gauge floral wire or hot glue. Finally, wire a bow or other accent in the center, to hide the means of attachment.

A third type of swag uses a found object for a base—a small broom, for example. Wire foliage and flowers to the broom with fine-gauge floral wire and hang your creation on the wall.

Yarrow and Sumac Spray, see page 41

MAKING BASKETS

Basketry is one of the oldest craft forms, predating both pottery and weaving. Every civilization throughout history has produced some form of basket, but because baskets were commonplace and made from plant fibers that deteriorated quickly, few examples of early basketry survive. Still, baskets dating to about 9000 B.C. have been unearthed from ancient granaries in Egypt, where the arid climate helped preserve them.

The first baskets were probably developed for lightweight carrying, a necessity for hunter-gatherer tribes. With the advent of farming, baskets became vital both for harvesting crops and as storage containers to preserve food for the winter. Evidence suggests that the use of mud-lined baskets for cooking led to the development of pottery. Basketry techniques have also been used for centuries to make fish and game traps, walls for huts, cradles, hats, and even boats.

Today bags, cans, boxes, and jars fulfill most of our carrying and storage needs, but the basket remains a popular alternative that is both functional and decorative. Whether stuffed in a corner as a simple trash receptacle or enshrined as a treasured keepsake, a basket lurks somewhere around most homes. Baskets can be made from anything easily bent or woven. While many of these materials can be easily gathered in the wild, most are also available through craft suppliers.

Bark can be peeled from trees and either torn into strips for weaving or sewn together in panels. (See page 86 for information on how to strip bark from a tree.)

Branches and twigs from willow, elder, birch, elm, and other trees are often supple enough for weaving into baskets.

Grasses can be wrapped or stitched together in bunches for use in coiled basketry. Some grasses are available commercially.

Leaves, such as cattail, palm, yucca, daylily, and other long, broad leaves, can be used whole, stripped into narrow lengths, or twisted into basket weavers.

Pine needles are easily gathered from the forest floor for making coiled baskets—the longer the better. If there are no longleaf pines in your area, they can also be ordered by mail.

Reeds, processed from a vinelike palm called rattan, are very popular for basket making, and are available flat or round and in a wide range of thicknesses. Reeds can be purchased in craft stores.

Roots from the sugar pine, cedar, spruce, cattail, and other plants can be used for weaving. Use them whole or split. (See "Gathering and Preparing Spruce Roots" on page 89.)

Vines like honeysuckle, grape, ivy, Virginia creeper (woodbine), and wisteria are easily gathered for use in woven or coiled baskets. Vine rattan can also be purchased through craft suppliers.

Wood splints can be stripped from ash, oak, hickory, elm, and other trees for weaving baskets. Most are also commercially available.

TYPES OF BASKETS

At first glance, the seemingly endless variety of baskets might seem confusing. While there are no hard-and-fast rules for

Plaited Market Basket, see page 115

classifying basket types, they can be roughly grouped according to four patterns of construction: spoked, plaited, ribbed, and coiled.

Spoked baskets take their name from the pattern formed by their supporting members, which radiate from the center of the circular base like the spokes of a wheel. The base is begun by stacking layers of spokes either in several crossed pairs or in a spiral pattern. The weavers, usually thinner and more pliable, are then woven over and under the spokes until the base is filled to the desired size. Then the spokes are upsett (bent upward) and the weaving continues to form the sides of the basket.

In laying out the crossed pairs of spokes for the basket base, you will naturally end up with an even number. In order for successive rows of weaving to fall on opposite sides of the spokes, you will need to either use a new weaver for each row or split one of the spokes to create an odd number.

Plaited baskets generally have weavers and stakes that are

Ribbed Egg Basket, see page 88

both flat and of equal strength so that neither one dominates the design. The base, usually square or rectangular, is formed by creating a mat of splints woven at right angles. Once the base reaches the desired shape and size, the splints are upsett to create stakes for weaving the sides of the basket.

As with the spoked basket, the base will naturally end up with an even number of stakes, requiring that you either weave each row independently or split one stake.

Ribbed baskets are made by first creating a sturdy framework that establishes the intended shape before weaving begins. Most start with two hoops lashed together at right angles to form a rim and a handle for the finished basket. Ribs are inserted into the hoop lashings to form arcs that outline the shape of the finished basket. Weavers are threaded over and under the ribs and back and forth between the rims. An uneven number of ribs is not required for continuous weaving because the weaver naturally changes sides between rows as it wraps around the rim. A second (and sometimes a third) set of ribs is usually added during weaving.

Coiled baskets are unique in that they are not woven. Instead, a long rope of fibers is tightly wrapped in a continuous coil of concentric circles or ovals, with each row stitched or nailed to the previous one. Straw, sweetgrass, willow rods, vines, and pine needles are commonly used to make coiled baskets. The stitching is usually done with rattan or thread.

Coiled Pine Needle Basket, see page 228

GLOSSARY OF TERMS

Base The bottom of a basket.

Cane The outer peel of the rattan vine, frequently used as a weaver on chair bottoms.

Coiling The technique of wrapping a foundation of fibers with thread or other material into a ropelike strand, which is then stitched in concentric circles to form a basket (see Figure 12).

Continuous Weave Weaving done over an odd number of stakes or spokes in a single, unbroken line, with new weavers added as the previous one runs out (see Figure 18).

Ear The lashing used to secure the intersection of the basket's rim and handle. Also the lashing into which the basket's ribs are inserted (see Figure 13).

Lasher The piece of reed that wraps around the rim, securing the rim to the top of the sides (see Figure 19).

Plain Weave The most basic form of basket weaving, in which the first row passes over, under, and over, and the next row passes under, over, and under (see Figure 14).

Reed The inner core of the rattan palm that has been cut into flat, round, oval, half-round, or half-oval shapes.

Rib A flat or round piece of wood or reed used to form the skeleton of a ribbed basket (see Figure 20).

Rim The top edge of a basket, or the pieces that fit inside and outside the top row of weaving (see Figure 15).

Spoke The equivalent of a stake, especially when arranged radially (as in the spokes of a wheel) for the base of a basket (see Figure 18).

Stake A woven piece of the base that is upsett to become one of the upright elements for weaving the sides of a basket (see Figure 21).

Twill A type of weaving in which the stakes and weavers pass over and under each other two at a time (see Figure 16).

Twining A method of weaving using two or more weavers, usually round, that twist around each other between each stake (see Figure 22).

Upsett To bend the basket's stakes up after the base is completed to create vertical elements for weaving the sides (see Figure 17).

Weaver The flexible fiber used to weave over and under the stakes, spokes, or ribs (see Figure 23).

FIGURE 12

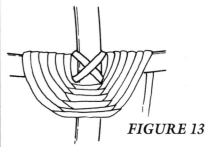

FIGURE 13

FIGURE 14

FIGURE 15

FIGURE 16

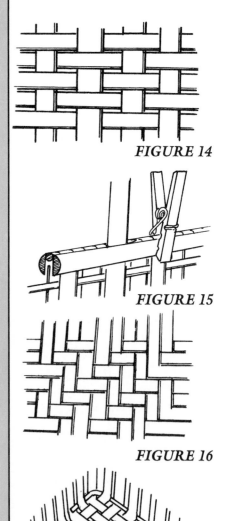

FIGURE 17

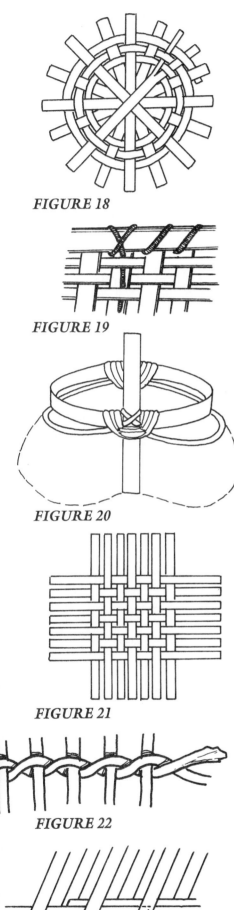

FIGURE 18

FIGURE 19

FIGURE 20

FIGURE 21

FIGURE 22

FIGURE 23

BASKETRY TECHNIQUES AND TIPS

Soaking

In most cases, basket materials must be soaked in water to make them pliable enough for weaving. Some fibers, such as narrow reed, take only about five minutes in warm water, while some wood splints may need to soak for several days. Test the materials frequently for flexibility. Ribs must be supple enough to bend into the desired arc. Test stakes, spokes, and weavers for flexibility by bending them in half over your finger. If they still crack, soak them some more. Once they're flexible enough, you can keep them in a damp towel.

Trueing the Base

Once you've woven the base of a staked basket, it's important to make sure all the weaving is even and the sides are square before upsetting the stakes. Measure and mark all four corners so you can check and readjust the base as you continue weaving.

Starting to Weave

Always begin the first row of weaving on the outside of a stake that has been upsett from beneath the last row of base weaving (see Figure 17). The other stakes will not be anchored by the base and will not stay in place if you start on the outside of them.

Ending a Row

When using individual weavers for each row, the end should be tucked behind the beginning to create an overlap. Cut the weaver so the end lies in the middle of a stake (see Figure 23). Turn the basket a quarter turn before beginning the next row, to prevent one side from building up with overlapped weavers. The same techniques for hiding ends can be used when adding new weavers in a continuous weave.

Dying Baskets

Colored weaving materials add another dimension to your basket making. You can either dye all the spokes and weavers before weaving or dip the finished basket in dye. (Keep in mind that machine-made hoops are likely to come unglued if soaked in a dye bath, so it is best not to dye such hoops.) You can also make intricate patterns by using several different colors of weavers.

There are numerous commercial dyes made specifically for basket fibers, or you can experiment with other varieties of dyes. Natural dyes are favored by many basket makers for their subtle, earthy tones. Multipurpose household dyes are inexpensive and available in a wide range of colors. The disadvantage of both these dyes is that they are not lightfast and will fade with age, unlike the fiber-reactive dyes made especially for basketry.

Follow the package directions for mixing your dye. Then simply dip your reeds into the dye bath. Keep dipping until the desired shade is achieved. You don't want to soak your reeds in boiling dye bath for a long period because this tends to dry them out, making them more likely to split and fray while you're weaving.

PROJECTS

FLOWERS AND HERBS

Flowers and herbs have been the pride of gardeners for centuries, and what better way to showcase their beauty than in the lovely variety of craft projects in this chapter? Fresh-cut flowers can be kept looking fresh in floral tubes (see page 11 for directions) or by using a floral foam known as wet foam, which absorbs enough water to keep the blooms fresh.

Dried flowers and herbs allow you to create craft projects that will last for years. You can purchase them in small bouquets at craft stores or dry them at home fresh from your garden. The paragraphs below explain the basic techniques for harvesting and drying flowers and herbs.

To start, you'll need to harvest a good selection of materials. Always do your cutting on a sunny day, after the morning dew has dried, and well after a rain shower. Avoid picking materials with insect damage, and keep in mind that most materials shrink as they dry.

Most materials can be dried with one of two air-drying techniques. The first of these techniques, known as hanging, involves grouping several stems of the same flower or herb together, securing them with raffia or a rubber band, and then hanging them upside down in a dark, dry location. The second air-drying method, known as screen or rack drying, involves spreading single blooms or leaves on a wire screen that has been placed so there is room to ventilate on all sides. Drying times will vary, depending on the type of plant and how moist it was when it was harvested. Five to 15 days is an average range.

Desiccant drying is a popular drying method for flower blooms. It involves layering blooms in a moisture-absorbing substance such as borax, kitty litter, sand, or silica gel. Silica gel is the most expensive of these desiccants, but its granules are lighter in weight than the other desiccants so they won't crush delicate blooms as easily. Check the progress of your blooms every few days to prevent overdrying. To prevent the blossoms from reabsorbing moisture, avoid leaving already-dry blooms in a moist area, such as the bathroom.

An interesting variation of desiccant drying involves using silica gel in the microwave oven to speed up the drying process. Cover the bottom of a microwave-safe container with a thin layer of silica gel. Arrange your materials in a single layer so their sides don't touch, and cover them with another thin layer of silica gel. Microwave on a medium setting for two-and-a-half minutes and allow a standing time of ten minutes. If your materials are overdried, start again with fresh materials and reduce the microwaving time by 30-second intervals until the materials do not overdry. If the materials are not dry enough, add time in 15-second intervals.

The chart below provides you with information for drying many of the most popular flowers and herbs used in crafts.

FLOWERS	DRYING INSTRUCTIONS
Baby's-Breath	Air-dry by hanging upside down in small, loose bundles.
Bee Balm	Air-dry on a rack or by hanging upside down. Harvest the blooms early in the blooming cycle.
Blue Sage	Air-dry by hanging upside down. Handle gently to prevent damage.
Cockscomb	Air-dry by hanging upside down after foliage has been removed. Harvest early in the morning to prevent matting.
Dusty Miller	Air-dry the foliage on a drying rack.
Globe Amaranth	Air-dry the blooms on a drying rack.
Larkspur	Air-dry by hanging upside down. Harvest when most of the flowers on a stalk have opened.
Love-in-a-Mist	Air-dry by hanging upside down. Harvest the seed heads before the first frost.
Rose	Air-dry by hanging upside down or dry in a desiccant. Harvest before the blooms are fully opened.
`Silver King' Artemisia	Air-dry by hanging upside down if straight lines are desired; air-dry by standing upright in a vase if curved lines are desired.
Statice	Air-dry by hanging upside down.
Strawflowers	Air-dry on a drying rack or by hanging upside down.

MINI TOPIARY

STEP THREE

Cover the uncut foam ball with Spanish moss, attaching it with floral pins (see page 10).

STEP FOUR

Insert the stick into the center of the foam base in the pot and hot-glue around the stick and foam.

STEP FIVE

Working in the order given in the materials list, hot-glue the herbs and flowers to the moss-covered ball, distributing each type evenly around the ball.

STEP SIX

Cover the top of the foam base with Spanish moss. Wrap the raffia several times around the top of the pot and tie the ends in a bow.

MATERIALS

Serrated knife
2 2-inch (5 cm) diameter
    foam balls
Glue gun
3-inch (7 cm) diameter clay
    pot, about 2-1/2 inches
    (6 cm) high
1/2-inch (1.3 cm) diameter
    stick, 7 inches (17 cm) long
About 2 ounces (57 g) of
    dried Spanish moss
Floral pins
24 small mint leaves
32 tiny dried pink rosebuds
17 dried heads of yellow
    yarrow
24 dried heads of pearly
    everlasting
14 dried heads of lavender
36-inch (90 cm) length
    of raffia

Wisps of Spanish moss interspersed with herbs and flowers lend an airy look to this topiary.

STEP ONE

Using the serrated knife, cut one of the foam balls in half. Hot-glue one of the halves into the clay pot, curved side down, with the flat surface even with the top of the pot. Save the other half for a future project.

STEP TWO

Insert the stick into the center of the other, uncut foam ball.

Basket Wall Arrangement

MATERIALS

12-inch (30 cm) diameter
   rattan mat
Water
Floral wire
Small bunch of green sheet
   moss
8 pieces of dried German
   statice, 4 trimmed to
   10 inches (25 cm),
   2 trimmed to 7 inches
   (17 cm), and 2 trimmed
   to 4 inches (10 cm)
6 stems of dried baby's-breath,
   2 trimmed to 10 inches,
   2 trimmed to 7 inches,
   and 2 trimmed to 4 inches
Glue gun
12 stems of dried pink
   peppergrass, 4 trimmed
   to 10 inches, 4 trimmed
   to 7 inches, and 4
   trimmed to 4 inches
7 stems of dried pink larkspur,
   4 trimmed to 10 inches
   and 3 trimmed to 4 inches
5 dried globe amaranths,
   3 trimmed to 10 inches
   and 2 trimmed to 7 inches
10 dried strawflowers,
   5 trimmed to 10 inches
   and 5 trimmed to 7 inches
8 stems of dried cockscomb,
   4 trimmed to 7 inches
   and 4 trimmed to 4 inches
3 dried roses, trimmed to
   7 inches
3 clusters of dried pepperberries, trimmed to 7 inches
18 sprigs of dried blue sage,
   10 trimmed to 10 inches,
   5 trimmed to 7 inches,
   and 3 trimmed to 4 inches
9 stems of preserved boxwood,
   trimmed to 10 inches
3 yards of 1-1/2-inch
   (4 cm) pink moiré
   wire-edged ribbon

This lovely dried flower arrangement uses a rattan mat folded like a taco shell to create a basket that will lie flat against the wall on a table or mantle.

STEP ONE

Soak the rattan mat in water until it's pliable, and bend it so one-third of the mat is turned up in front with two-thirds in back. Use three loops of wire between the front and back to hold the mat in this position, leaving 2 inches (5 cm) between front and back.

STEP TWO

Pack the inside bottom and sides of the mat with sheet moss. Starting along the inside back wall of the mat with the longest stems, insert the statice and baby's-breath in a fan shape, and glue the stems in place.

STEP THREE

Glue in the remaining dried flowers in a fan shape between the layers of mat and across the outside front. Use the longer stems in back and the short ones in front.

STEP FOUR

Make a bow with the ribbon and wire it to the bottom front of the mat.

HERBAL BROOM

Decorated brooms are found in almost every country house, on the well-founded theory that it's more fun to look at housework than to actually do it. This broom is decorated with herbs and flowers.

STEP ONE

To make a hanger, wrap one end of the wire around the broom handle, and twist the wire together close to the handle. Form the other end into a loop, and twist the pieces of the wire together.

STEP TWO

Make a miniature bouquet using half of the stems of mountain mint, artemisia, annual statice, blue sage, and wormwood.

MATERIALS

18-inch (46 cm) length of heavy-gauge floral wire
24-inch (60 cm) long country broom
6 stems of dried mountain mint, trimmed to 10 inches (25 cm)
6 stems of dried 'Silver Queen' artemisia, trimmed to 14 inches (36 cm)
10 stems of dried pink annual statice, trimmed to 10 inches
4 stems of dried blue sage, trimmed to 10 inches
2 sprigs of dried wormwood, trimmed to 10 to 12 inches (25 to 30 cm)
Brown yarn
7 feet (2 m) of wired ribbon
Fine-gauge floral wire

STEP THREE

Lay the bouquet on the broom as shown in the photo above, with the flower heads pointing downward and to the right, and tie the bouquet onto the broom by its stems with a piece of yarn.

STEP FOUR

Make a second bouquet using the remaining floral materials, and lay it on the broom with the flower heads pointing upward and to the left, so that it and the first bouquet make a diagonal line. If the second bouquet is too long, trim the stems. Tie it to the broom with yarn.

STEP FIVE

Cut a 25-inch (63.5 cm) length of ribbon. Wrap it around the handle and over the plant stems to hide the yarn, and tie it in a knot. Make a six-loop bow with the remaining ribbon and wire it on top of the ribbon knot. Arrange the loops and ribbon ends to form a pleasing shape.

SILVER HERBAL WREATH

This graceful wreath combines 'Silver King' artemisia, blue sage, yellow tansy, and pink globe amaranth for a colorful but restrained effect. Although the directions say to tie the flowers to the base with yarn, they can be picked in.

STEP ONE

Form a bouquet of four sprigs of artemisia, three stems of blue sage, three stems of tansy, and three stems of globe amaranth. Lay the bouquet on the wreath base and tie it on with a piece of yarn. Clip the yarn ends.

STEP TWO

Form eight more bouquets and tie them to the base, laying the bouquets in the same direction and overlapping the stems of one bouquet with the flowers and foliage of the next.

MATERIALS

- 36 stems of dried 'Silver King' artemisia, trimmed to 6 to 8 inches (15 to 20 cm)
- 27 stems of dried blue sage, trimmed to 6 to 8 inches
- 27 stems of dried tansy, trimmed to 4 to 6 inches (10 to 15 cm)
- 27 stems of dried pink globe amaranth, trimmed to 4 inches
- 11-inch (27 cm) diameter grapevine wreath base
- 9 6-inch pieces of brown yarn

HERBAL VINEGARS

Mild or hot, pungent or mellow, herbal vinegars have a variety of uses. Mix with a favorite oil to make an instant salad dressing. Stir into steamed green vegetables to bring out their flavor. Sprinkle on fresh, ripe fruit to add zest to an otherwise sweet dish. The six vinegars shown are, from left to right, Raspberry Vinegar, Lemony Herb Vinegar, Lemon Grass Vinegar, Hot Stuff, Oregano Chive Vinegar, and Rosemary Vinegar.

Raspberry Vinegar

STEP ONE

Gently wash and drain the raspberries and place them in the canning jar.

STEP TWO

Heat the vinegar in a non-aluminum pan until the first bubbles appear and add it to the jar, filling the jar to the top.

STEP THREE

Cover the jar with plastic wrap (to keep the acidic vinegar from rusting the screw ring), and twist on the screw ring. Store in a dark, cool place for six weeks.

STEP FOUR

Strain the vinegar through a strainer lined with the coffee filter. Pour it into a clean, decorative bottle, then cap.

STEP FIVE

Tie the netting around the neck of the bottle, position the artemisia and globe amaranth on the netting, and tie the decoration on with the raffia.

MATERIALS

Raspberry Vinegar

3 cups (708 ml) of fresh raspberries
1-quart (0.9 l) canning jar and screw ring
About 3 cups of white vinegar
Non-aluminum pan
Plastic wrap
Tea strainer or kitchen strainer
Paper coffee filter
Decorative bottle with cap, lid, or cork
3 × 6-inch (7 × 15 cm) piece of netting
3 sprigs of dried 'Silver King' artemisia, trimmed to 3 inches (7 cm)
1 dried pink globe amaranth, stem removed
12-inch (30 cm) length of raffia

MATERIALS

Lemony Herb Vinegar

1 cup (236 ml) of fresh lemon balm leaves
1 cup of fresh lemon verbena leaves
1-quart (0.9 l) canning jar and screw ring
Wooden spoon
4 cups (0.9 ml) of white vinegar
Non-aluminum pan
Plastic wrap
Tea strainer or kitchen strainer
Paper coffee filter
Decorative bottle with cap, lid, or cork
1 sprig each of fresh lemon balm and lemon verbena
1 dried red strawflower
2 small dried heads of white yarrow
12-inch (30 cm) length of raffia

Lemony Herb Vinegar

STEP ONE

Place the lemon balm and lemon verbena leaves in the canning jar and bruise them with a wooden spoon.

STEP TWO

Heat the vinegar in a non-aluminum pan until the first bubbles appear and add it to the jar, filling the jar to the top.

STEP THREE

Cover the jar with plastic wrap (to keep the acidic vinegar from rusting the screw ring), and twist on the screw ring. Store in a dark, cool place for six weeks.

STEP FOUR

Strain the vinegar through a strainer lined with the coffee filter. Pour it into a clean, decorative bottle, add a fresh sprig of each herb, and cap the bottle.

STEP FIVE

Position the strawflower and yarrow on the neck of the bottle, and tie the decoration on with raffia.

Lemon Grass Vinegar

STEP ONE

Place the lemon grass leaves in the canning jar and bruise them with a wooden spoon.

STEP TWO

Heat the vinegar in a non-aluminum pan until the first bubbles appear and add it to the jar, filling the jar to the top.

STEP THREE

Cover the jar with plastic wrap (to keep the acidic vinegar from rusting the screw ring), and twist on the screw ring. Store in a dark, cool place for six weeks.

STEP FOUR

Strain the vinegar through a strainer lined with the coffee filter. Pour it into a clean, decorative bottle, add a sprig of lemon grass and three pieces of lemon peel, then cap the bottle.

STEP FIVE

Position the lemon peel spirals on the neck of the bottle and tie them on with raffia.

MATERIALS

Lemon Grass Vinegar

1 cup (236 ml) of fresh lemon grass leaves
1-quart (0.9 l) canning jar and screw ring
4 (0.9 l) cups of white vinegar
Non-aluminum pan
Plastic wrap
Tea strainer or kitchen strainer
Paper coffee filter
Decorative bottle with cap, lid, or cork
Sprig of fresh lemon grass
3 pieces of lemon peel, cut 2 inches (5 cm) long
2 lemon peel spirals, cut 2 inches long
6-inch (15 cm) length of raffia

MATERIALS

Hot Stuff

1 clove garlic
Small saucepan
Clean 750-milliliter wine bottle, with cork
Rubber gloves
About 3 cups (708 ml) of fresh cayenne peppers
About 3 cups of white vinegar
Non-aluminum pan
12-inch (30 cm) length of twisted cord
1-inch (2.5 cm) length of fine-gauge floral wire
3 dried cayenne peppers

Hot Stuff

STEP ONE

Drop the garlic into a small pan of simmering water and blanch it for 1 minute, to kill any bacteria that could spoil the vinegar. Drop the blanched garlic into the wine bottle.

STEP TWO

Wearing rubber gloves, wash the fresh peppers and cut them in half lengthwise, up to the green top. Fill the bottle with the peppers.

STEP THREE

Heat the vinegar in a non-aluminum pan until the first bubbles appear and add it to the bottle, filling the bottle to the top. Cork the bottle and store it in a cool, dark place for six weeks.

STEP FOUR

Wrap the cord around the neck of the bottle and tie it in a bow. Wire the dried peppers to the bow.

Oregano Chive Vinegar

STEP ONE

Drop one clove of garlic into a small pan of simmering water and blanch it for 1 minute, to kill any bacteria that could spoil the vinegar. Drop the blanched garlic into the canning jar.

STEP TWO

Place the oregano leaves in the canning jar and bruise them with a wooden spoon. Add the chive leaves.

STEP THREE

Heat the vinegar in a non-aluminum pan until the first bubbles appear and add it to the jar, filling the jar to the top.

STEP FOUR

Cover the jar with plastic wrap (to keep the acidic vinegar from rusting the screw ring), and twist on the screw ring. Store in a dark, cool place for six weeks.

STEP FIVE

Strain the vinegar through a strainer lined with the coffee filter. Pour it into a clean, decorative bottle.

STEP SIX

Blanch the second clove of garlic and add it to the vinegar. Add the six chives and cap the bottle.

MATERIALS

Oregano Chive Vinegar

2 cloves garlic
Small saucepan
1-quart (0.9 l) canning jar and
   screw ring
1/2 cup (118 ml) of fresh
   oregano leaves
Wooden spoon
1/2 cup of fresh chive leaves,
   trimmed to 1 inch (2.5 cm)
4 cups of white vinegar
Non-aluminum pan
Plastic wrap
Tea strainer or kitchen strainer
Paper coffee filter
Decorative bottle with cap, lid,
   or cork
6 fresh chives

MATERIALS

Rosemary Vinegar

11 sprigs of fresh rosemary,
   trimmed to 6 inches (15 cm)
1-quart (0.9 l) canning jar and
   screw ring
Wooden spoon
4 cups of white vinegar
Non-aluminum pan
Plastic wrap
Tea strainer or kitchen strainer
Paper coffee filter
Decorative bottle with cap, lid,
   or cork
1 sprig of fresh mint, trimmed
   to 4 inches (10 cm)
1 sprig of fresh pennyroyal,
   trimmed to 4 inches
1 sprig of fresh annual statice,
   trimmed to 3 inches (7 cm)
1 stem of fresh globe
   amaranth, trimmed to
   2 inches (5 cm)
8-inch length of raffia

Rosemary Vinegar

STEP ONE

Place ten rosemary sprigs in the canning jar and bruise them with the wooden spoon.

STEP TWO

Heat the vinegar in a non-aluminum pan until the first bubbles appear and add it to the jar, filling the jar to the top.

STEP THREE

Cover the jar with plastic wrap (to keep the acidic vinegar from rusting the screw ring), and twist on the screw ring. Store in a dark, cool place for six weeks.

STEP FOUR

Strain the vinegar through a strainer lined with the coffee filter and pour it into a clean, decorative bottle. Add a sprig of rosemary and cap the bottle.

STEP FIVE

Position the sprigs of mint, pennyroyal, and annual statice with the globe amaranth on the neck of the bottle, and tie them on with raffia.

EGG BASKET TABLE ARRANGEMENT

MATERIALS

Block of wet floral foam
Serrated knife
Large egg basket
Plastic liner
9 stems of pink larkspur,
    2 trimmed to 18 inches
    (46 cm), 2 trimmed to
    16 inches (41 cm), 2
    trimmed to 14 inches
    (36 cm), 4 trimmed
    to 4 inches (10 cm)
3 stems of tesia, 1 trimmed
    to 18 inches and 2 trimmed
    to 14 inches
7 stems of 'Silver Queen'
    artemisia, 1 trimmed to
    16 inches, 3 trimmed
    to 14 inches, and
    3 trimmed to 4 inches
3 stems of pink daylilies,
    1 trimmed to 16 inches,
    1 trimmed to 12 inches,
    and 1 trimmed to 5 inches
    (12 cm)
4 stems of Queen-Anne's-lace,
    1 trimmed to 12 inches and
    2 trimmed to 4 inches
2 stems of cockscomb,
    trimmed to 4 inches
3 stems of miniature
    carnations, 2 trimmed
    to 12 inches and
    1 trimmed to 5 inches
3 stems of begonias,
    trimmed to 4 inches
3 stems of pink asters,
    1 trimmed to 14 inches
    and 2 trimmed to 5 inches
1 galax leaf

Varying hues of green, ivory, and red fresh flowers and foliage create a soft, elegant arrangement for a summer table.

STEP ONE

Cut the foam with the serrated knife to fit snugly inside the basket. Soak the foam in water, then blot with a towel. Place the plastic liner in the bottom of the basket and place the foam on top of the liner.

STEP TWO

Create the triangular outline of the arrangement by first inserting the longest larkspur stem and the longest tesia stem into the top center of the foam. Form the sides of the triangle with the remaining larkspur and tesia. Fill in the sides with 'Silver Queen' artemesia.

STEP THREE

Fill in the center of the arrangement with the daylilies and Queen-Anne's-lace, inserting the longest stems at the top and the shorter stems in the middle and bottom. Fill in the remaining space with the cockscombs, miniature carnations, begonias, and pink asters. Position the galax leaf at the center bottom of the basket and drape it over the side.

TUSSIE MUSSIES

These endearing small bouquets date back to the Victorian days, when they were filled with symbolic, fragrant flowers and herbs to create special messages. The bouquets were often carried in front of young ladies' faces to disguise unpleasant odors.

STEP ONE

Arrange the annual statice, Queen-Anne's-lace, zinnias, strawflower, rose, marigold, and nasturtium into three loose bouquets. Lengthen the stem portion of each bouquet to 4 inches with floral wire and wrap with floral tape. (See page 10 for instructions on extending stems with floral

wire.) Secure the stems of the three bouquets together with floral tape and gently tuck small pieces of Spanish moss into the spaces between the blooms.

STEP TWO

Arrange the stems of baby's-breath, German statice, and cedar around the outside of the bouquets and secure them in place by wrapping around the stems with floral tape. Hot-glue the three dried leaves and the rose into the center of the bouquet.

STEP THREE

Mark the middle point of the narrow ribbon, fold the two ends in to the mark, and then fold in half. Carefully tie the folded ribbon into a loose bow. Slip a 4-inch length of floral wire through the bow's knot, twist to secure, and add the bow to the bouquet with floral tape. Position the lace around the bouquet and hot-glue in place.

MATERIALS

For tussie mussie at right:
5 stems of dried annual statice
2 dried Queen-Anne's-lace blooms
2 dried zinnias
1 dried strawflower
1 dried rose
1 dried marigold
1 dried nasturtium bloom
Medium-gauge floral wire
Floral tape
Spanish moss
4 stems of dried baby's-breath, dyed pink and trimmed to 4 inches (10 cm)
5 stems of dried German statice, trimmed to 4 inches
10 stems of glycerin-preserved cedar, trimmed to 4 inches
Glue gun
3 dried leaves
1 yard (0.9 m) narrow satin ribbon
1 yard of 4-inch-wide lace, gathered

DECORATED SACHETS

Appreciated for their fragrance, potpourri sachets are usually tucked out of sight in clothing drawers or linen closets. With the addition of just a few sprigs and blooms of dried herbs, though, they become lovely decorations for bedrooms and bathrooms.

STEP ONE

For each sachet, fold the fabric in half, right sides together, to form a vertical rectangle. Sew the side and bottom seams and turn the bag right-side-out. Fold the top down inside the bag 2 inches and press down with a hot iron. Fill the sachet with the potpourri and tie closed with the ribbon. Tie the ribbon ends into a bow.

STEP TWO

Begin decorating the sachet by positioning the stems of the longest material at the center of the bow so the stems face each other, and hot-glue in place. Layer on any additional stems and hot-glue in place. Arrange single blooms or seed heads to cover the area where the stems meet, and hot-glue. Last, tuck the rose leaves under and around the arrangement, and hot-glue.

MATERIALS

For sachet at left:
6 × 22-inch (15 × 55 cm) piece of chintz fabric
1-1/2 cups (340 g) of potpourri of your choice
1/2 yard (46 cm) of narrow satin ribbon
Glue gun
2 stems of dried baby's-breath, trimmed to 2 inches (5 cm)
3 stems of dried larkspur, trimmed to 3 inches (7.5 cm)
1 dried strawflower bloom
2 large dried rose leaves

For center sachet:
6 × 22-inch piece of chintz fabric
1-1/2 cups of potpourri of your choice
1/2 yard of narrow satin ribbon
Glue gun
3 stems of dried pink peppergrass, trimmed to 3 inches
1 dried rosebud
2 love-in-a-mist seed heads
7 small dried rose leaves

For sachet at right:
6 × 22-inch piece of chintz fabric
1-1/2 cups of potpourri of your choice
1/2 yard of narrow satin ribbon
Glue gun
1 dried cockscomb bloom
1 dried strawflower bloom
1 dried rosebud
2 large dried rose leaves

GRADUATED COLORS WREATH

Subtle tone variations in an assortment of pink and peach flowers draw the eye down the sides of this wreath to the focal point, the bow, at bottom center.

STEP ONE

Working with two of the 24-inch stems at a time, position the 'Silver King' artemisia against the wire wreath base and twist it around the base, overlapping as needed. Secure the artemisia to the base by gently wrapping it with fishing wire in 2-inch (5 cm) intervals. Repeat this process until you've used all of the 24-inch stems.

MATERIALS

40 stems of dried 'Silver King' artemisia, 10 trimmed to 24 inches (60 cm) and 30 trimmed to 4 inches (10 cm)
12-inch (36 cm) diameter wire wreath base
Fishing line
Glue gun
15 stems of dried German statice, trimmed to 4 inches
2 spikes of dried larkspur, trimmed to 6 inches (15 cm)
12 dried globe amaranths, stems removed
12 stems of dried, dyed pink peppergrass, trimmed to 3 inches (7 cm)
4 dried hydrangea blooms
12 dried strawflower blooms
3 dried rosebuds
Large pink bow

STEP TWO

Starting at the top center of the wreath, hot-glue the 4-inch stems of 'Silver King' artemisia and the German statice into the artemisia base you created in Step 1. Set aside four or five stems of the artemisia for later use.

STEP THREE

Hot-glue the remaining flowers (except for the artemisia) down the sides of the wreath,

starting about 3 inches (7 cm) from the top center. Add the flowers in the order given in the materials list to create the effect of increasing fullness from top to bottom. Set aside one rosebud.

STEP FOUR

Hot-glue the bow to the bottom center of the wreath. Hot-glue the reserved stems of 'Silver King' artemisia to the center of the bow and top them with the remaining rosebud.

Yarrow and Sumac Spray

Muted autumn tones highlight this handsome spray made from wild plants that are easy to find in fields, vacant lots, or along roadsides. Gather them when in full color and hang them up to dry before use. Be aware that poison sumac has white berries. Gather only sumac with red berries.

Step One

Gather the yarrow in a bunch and secure temporarily with a rubber band around the stems.

Step Two

Arrange sumac, goldenrod, butterfly weed flowers, and angelica in the spray by sliding the stems under the rubber band. When you are pleased with the composition, secure the bundle with wire and remove the rubber band.

Step Three

Tie the ribbon in a bow. Thread a length of wire through the bow's loop and wire it to the spray, covering the wire that is securing the stems. Tie the raffia streamers to the bow.

MATERIALS

12 stems of dried yarrow, trimmed to 12 inches (30 cm)
Rubber band
8 stems of sumac, trimmed to 12 inches
3 stems of goldenrod, trimmed to 12 inches
4 butterfly weed flowers, trimmed to 12 inches
6 stems of wild angelica, trimmed to 12 inches
Medium-gauge wire
3 yards (2.7 m) of paper ribbon
3 yards of raffia, color matched to ribbon

HERB AND FLOWER BIRD CAGE

A bird in a gilded cage may get moody and restless. In a bird cage bedecked with herbs and flowers, it will settle down and sing.

MATERIALS

- 6 5-1/2-inch (13 cm) long twigs, about 1/2 inch (1.3 cm) in diameter
- 8-inch (20 cm) long twig, about 1/2 inch in diameter
- Heavy-gauge floral wire
- 9 × 18-1/2-inch (22 × 47 cm) piece of chicken wire
- 6 6-inch (15 cm) twigs, about 1/2 inch in diameter
- Glue gun
- 3-inch (7 cm) diameter clump of Spanish moss
- 2 artificial birds, about 2-1/2 inches (6 cm) from beak to tail
- 35 mountain mint leaves
- 1 dried pink rosebud
- 1 dried pink snapdragon, trimmed to 6 inches
- 7 dried burgundy strawflowers
- 3 dried purple strawflowers
- 3 dried white strawflowers
- 2 dried orange strawflowers
- 11 dried pink globe amaranths
- 7 clusters of dried tansies, about 1 inch in diameter
- 1 dried oxeye daisy
- 1 dried pink carnation
- 1 golden marguerite
- 5 stems of pink annual statice, trimmed to 2 inches (5 cm)
- 1 stem of white annual statice, trimmed to 2 inches
- 11 1-inch (2.5 cm) diameter clusters of pearly everlasting
- 10 dried purple Mexican bush sage blooms
- 7 sprigs of baby's-breath, trimmed to 2 inches

STEP ONE

To make the bird cage base, cross a 5-1/2-inch twig and the 8-inch twig, forming an X. The twigs should cross in the center of the shorter stick and 2-1/2 inches from one end of the longer one. Three inches (7 cm) of the longer twig will project from the cage to serve as a perch. Using the heavy-gauge floral wire, wire together the two twigs where they cross.

STEP TWO

Curve the chicken wire into a 5-inch (12 cm) diameter circle, 9 inches high, and place it on the base. Wire it to the twigs. Wire the remaining 5-1/2-inch twigs vertically to the outside of the chicken wire circle, spacing them evenly.

STEP THREE

Hot-glue a nest of Spanish moss to the center of the base, and hot-glue a bird in the nest.

STEP FOUR

At the top of the vertical twigs, bend and gather the chicken wire to form the sloping roof of the cage. Lay the 6-inch twigs on the wire so they radiate from the center of the roof, with each one projecting out between two vertical twigs. Wire them to the center of the roof.

STEP FIVE

Hot-glue 13 mountain mint leaves horizontally to the chicken wire near the base of the cage, using only a drop of glue at the base of each leaf. Glue the remaining mint leaves along the roof twigs, overlapping the leaves and pointing their tips downward. Glue the second bird to the roof.

STEP SIX

Glue the dried rosebud to the base, right by the perch. Glue the snapdragon to the center of the roof. Then glue the remaining flowers around the base of the cage and to the roof, spacing varieties and colors in an interesting fashion. Since the baby's-breath is the most fragile, glue it on last.

PRESSED-FLOWER PICTURE MATS

Bouquets of colorful pressed flowers are arranged to spill out from the corners of these decorative picture mats. The flowers and foliage were dried by arranging them between two sheets of porous paper and then placing the paper between the pages of a thick book for several weeks.

MATERIALS

For the Mat at Right:

12 pressed pink geraniums
5 pressed purple geraniums
8 pressed red sage blooms
12 stems of pressed fern, trimmed to 2 inches (5 cm)
White craft glue
Small paintbrush
Oval picture mat set
Aerosol resin

For the Mat at Left:

2 pressed Queen-Anne's-lace blooms
4 stems of pressed 'Silver King' artemisia, trimmed to 2 inches (5 cm)
8 stems of pressed fern, 2 trimmed to 2 inches and 6 trimmed to 3 inches (7 cm)
1 pressed pink flax bloom
1 pressed white flax bloom
White craft glue
Small paintbrush
Oval picture mat set
Aerosol resin

STEP ONE

Place all of the pressed blooms and foliage face down on a flat surface. Apply a thin coat of glue to each bloom or leaf with the paintbrush and gently press them onto the mat, using the photos as a guide.

STEP TWO

After the glue has dried completely (at least an hour), apply a thin, protective coat of spray resin, and allow it to dry completely before assembling the mat with a photograph and frame.

MEXICAN HAT ARRANGEMENT

A vibrant selection of fresh flowers and the interesting use of a hat for a container makes this arrangement the perfect party centerpiece.

STEP ONE

Place the hat right-side up on a flat surface and press the crown down as far as it will go. Cut the foam with the serrated knife to fit snugly inside the center of the depressed crown.

MATERIALS

Mexican hat
Block of wet floral foam
Serrated knife
Plastic liner
2 stems of larkspur,
    1 trimmed to 12 inches
    (30 cm) and 1 trimmed
    to 10 inches (25 cm)
2 stems of zinnias, 1 trimmed
    to 11 inches (27 cm) and
    1 trimmed to 4 inches
6 stems of miniature
    carnations, 1 trimmed
    to 8 inches (20 cm),
    1 trimmed to 6 inches
    (15 cm) and 4 trimmed
    to 4 inches (10 cm)
4 stems of Queen-Anne's-lace,
    2 trimmed to 7 inches
    (17 cm) and 2 trimmed
    to 4 inches
3 purple coneflowers,
    2 trimmed to 5 inches
    (12 cm) with the petals
    removed and 1 trimmed
    to 6 inches
4 stems of calendula,
    1 trimmed to 7 inches
    and 3 trimmed to 4 inches
4 stems of tree fern, trimmed
    to 5 inches
5 stems of variegated pittospo-
    rum, 1 trimmed to 7 inches
    and 4 trimmed to 4 inches

Soak the foam in water, then blot with a towel. Place the plastic liner inside the crown and place the foam on top of the liner.

STEP TWO

Insert the flower stems into the center of the foam, working first with the longest larkspur stems, then with the longest zinnia stem, the longest carnation stem, and the two longest stems of Queen-Anne's-lace. Then add the second larkspur stem, the longest coneflower stem, the longest calendula stem, the tree fern stems, and the 6-inch carnation stem. Take care to insert the flowers at various angles.

STEP THREE

Space the three remaining stems of calendula evenly around the front of the arrangement. Fill in the arrangement first with the remaining flowers and then with the variegated pittosporum.

LARKSPUR SWAG

Swags are a wonderful way to display the bounty of summer year-round. All of the natural materials in this lush swag are dried by simply arranging them in small groups and hanging them upside down in a dark place to dry for a week to ten days.

STEP ONE

Working on a flat surface, arrange each group of dried materials into a separate fan shape. Position the fan of artemisia on top of the eucalyptus fan and secure the two together about 1 inch (2.5 cm) from the top of the stems with one piece of the floral wire. Trim off any extra wire.

MATERIALS

8 stems of dried 'Silver King' artemisia, trimmed to 18 inches (46 cm)

8 stems of dried eucalyptus, trimmed to 20 inches (50 cm)

2 8-inch (20 cm) lengths of medium-gauge floral wire

14 stems of dried light blue larkspur, trimmed to 12 inches (30 cm)

7 stems of dried dark blue larkspur, trimmed to 8 inches (20 cm)

2 yards (2 m) of velvet ribbon
Glue gun

12 stems of dried blue sage, trimmed to 5 inches (12 cm)

STEP TWO

Layer the fan of light blue larkspur on top of the artemisia and then layer the fan of dark blue larkspur on top of the light blue. Use the second piece of floral wire to secure all four groups of stems together. Do not clip this wire.

STEP THREE

Tie the ribbon into a large bow. Attach the bow to the swag by threading the unclipped floral wire through the bow's loop and twisting the wire ends together several times. Last, hot-glue the stems of blue salvia into the bow's loop.

HERBAL TEA BAGS

People of virtually all cultures have been brewing herbal teas for centuries. Pressed into tea bags, the dried herbs from your garden will make welcome gifts.

STEP ONE

Select a dried herb that makes a good tea, used either singly or in combination with other herbs.

STEP TWO

Lay half of a tea bag on a firm, heat-proof surface and spoon about 1 tablespoon (15 ml) of dried herbs in the center.

STEP THREE

Place the other half of the tea bag over the herbs, matching up all four edges. Using a medium-hot iron, press around all four edges, fusing the halves together. Avoid pressing the herbs.

MATERIALS

Dried herbs, such as mint, chamomile, sage, lemon balm, lemon thyme, thyme, and scented geranium

Fusible tea bags, available at craft, gourmet, and health food stores

Iron

Opposite Page—
Top left: Pinecones (bottoms cut off), hemlock cones, twigs, canella berries, pampas grass, and orange peel.
Bottom left: Bay leaves, lemon verbena, cloves, orange peel, and spice basil.
Right: Rosebuds and rose petals, globe amaranths, annual statice, and lavender.

This Page—
Top: Lamb's-ear foliage and blooms, hydrangeas, money plant, red salvia, annual statice, plumed celosias, globe amaranths, and love-in-a-mist.
Bottom: Scented geranium leaves, yarrow, tiger lilies, black-eyed Susans, strawflowers, calendulas, and tansy blooms.

The ideal potpourri need contain only two things: dried materials that are fragrant (such as roses, lavender, evergreens, and rosemary) and dried materials that are pretty to look at (such as globe amaranth, money plant, strawflowers, and berries). Of course you can always replicate the potpourri recipes here, but creating your own "secret" recipes is fun and foolproof. If you get the fragrance right but the potpourri looks awful, just crumble up the dried materials and use them in a sachet. If the potpourri looks perfect but there's no fragrance, just add a few drops of your favorite essential oil and 1 teaspoon of a fragrance fixative, such as ground orris root, for every 1 cup of dried materials. If you want your potpourri to emit a very strong fragrance, place it in a brown paper bag after you've added the essential oil and fixative. Leave the potpourri in the bag for several weeks and shake it well every few days.

GRAPEVINE EUCALYPTUS WREATH

The rich, dark green of eucalyptus is a perfect backdrop for
brilliant red strawflowers, pale
globe amaranths, and white
baby's-breath.

STEP ONE

Twist the grapevine into a
wreath base 8 inches (20 cm)
in diameter or use a purchased
grapevine wreath base.

STEP TWO

Bend the eucalyptus sprays and
glue them all around the front
surface of the wreath base. Set
aside one strawflower and glue
on the rest, alternating strawflowers with globe amaranths.
Intersperse with bunches of
baby's-breath.

STEP THREE

Tie the ribbon in a bow, leaving streamers to dangle below
the bow. Thread a length of
floral wire through the bow's
loop and wire it to the base.
Glue a strawflower to the
center of the bow.

STEP FOUR

Glue the two pinecones to the
vine base beneath the bow.

MATERIALS

30 feet (9 m) of freshly cut
    grapevine, 3/16 inch
    (5 mm) in diameter (or
    an 8-inch [20 cm] diameter
    grapevine wreath base)
6 sprays of eucalyptus,
    12 inches (30 cm) long
Glue gun
7 dried strawflowers, stems
    removed
16 dried globe amaranths,
    stems removed
4 small bunches of dried
    baby's-breath
4 yards (3.7 m) of thin ribbon
2 small pinecones
Fine-gauge floral wire

POTPOURRI BASKET

Although people often think of potpourri as being made from crumbled flowers, the potpourri displayed in this basket demonstrates how beautiful large, whole blooms can be. (See page 24 for basic instructions on drying flowers and herbs.)

STEP ONE

Tie the paper ribbon into a simple bow and hot-glue it to the center front of the basket. Hot-glue a single bee balm bloom in the center of the bow and circle it with 1-inch (2.5 cm) stems of rose-colored yarrow.

STEP TWO

Fill the basket with the dried blooms and seed heads, saving several of the prettiest blooms for the top. Display the basket away from direct sunlight to prevent colorful blooms from fading.

MATERIALS

24-inch (60 cm) length of paper ribbon
Glue gun
Oblong fruit basket
Enough dried blooms and seed heads to fill the basket you've chosen (bee balm, rose-colored yarrow, Queen-Anne's-lace, roses, violets, petunias, teasels, dogwood, coneflowers, yellow yarrow, geraniums, coreopsis, and phlox are in the potpourri shown in the photo)

POTPOURRI PIE

A kitchen potpourri is a pleasant cover-up for the lingering traces of last night's cabbage soup and broiled scrod. With its fruit scent and pielike appearance, this one is a fitting choice.

STEP ONE

Fill the pie pan with the potpourri. Hot-glue the tulle net to the top of the pan, anchoring it with half a dozen drops of glue.

STEP TWO

To make the lattice "crust," hot-glue the two 7-inch strips of velvet ribbon perpendicular to each other across the center of

MATERIALS

5-1/2-inch (13 cm) metal
    pie pan
1 cup (236 ml) fruit-scented
    potpourri (see page 51)
Glue gun
6 × 6-inch (15 × 15 cm)
    square of cream-colored
    tulle net
2 7-inch (17 cm) lengths of
    1/4-inch (6mm) wide
    cream-colored velvet ribbon
4 6-inch (15 cm) lengths of
    1/4-inch wide cream-
    colored velvet ribbon
18-inch (46 cm) length of
    1-inch (2.5 cm) wide
    cream-colored velvet ribbon
Dry powder blush in
    cinnamon tone
2 mountain mint leaves
    2-1/2 to 3 inches (6 to
    7 cm) long, or other herb
    leaves that won't shrivel
    when dried
4 1-inch pieces of stick
    cinnamon
1 star anise

the pie. The ends should lap over the rim of the pan. Glue the 6-inch strips of ribbon to the sides, top, and bottom of the center ribbons. Trim the ribbon ends close to the pan.

STEP THREE

Glue the 18-inch length of ribbon around the rim of the pan, crimping (making small folds) as you go to make it fit. Keep half the width of the ribbon

above the rim and half below. It helps to apply a zigzag pattern of hot glue to 3 inches (7 cm) of the ribbon at a time and then press it onto the pan.

STEP FOUR

Glue two mountain mint leaves to the center of the pie, and glue the four pieces of cinnamon in an X over the mint. Glue the star anise over the center of the X.

OVERLAPPING TRIANGLES ARRANGEMENT

This triangular arrangement is unique because it is made up of four triangles of fresh materials, each created with a different flower, positioned to overlap one another for eye-pleasing continuity.

STEP ONE

Cut the foam with the serrated knife to fit snugly inside the bottom of the basket. Soak the foam in water, then blot with a towel. Place the plastic liner on the bottom of the

basket, and place the foam on top of the liner.

STEP TWO

Create the top triangle outline by inserting the stars-of-Bethlehem into the foam. Then create the next three triangles, working first with the tweedia, then with the pink yarrow, and then with the feverfew. Next insert the rose annual statice to add additional color around the arrangement.

STEP THREE

Fill in the arrangement with the greenery, working first with the variegated pittosporum and then with the sourgum. Arrange the two galax leaves on the lower front edges of the basket.

MATERIALS

Block of wet floral foam
Serrated knife
Low, square basket
Plastic liner
2 stems of star-of-Bethlehem, trimmed to 14 inches (36 cm) and 12 inches (30 cm)
3 stems of tweedia, 1 trimmed to 11 inches (27 cm) and 2 trimmed to 4 inches (10 cm)
10 stems of pink yarrow, 5 trimmed to 4 inches (10 cm) and 5 trimmed to 5 inches (13 cm)
5 stems of feverfew, 2 trimmed to 5 inches and 3 trimmed to 3 inches (7.5 cm)
6 stems of rose annual statice, 3 trimmed to 4 inches and 3 trimmed to 5 inches
5 stems of variegated pittosporum, 1 trimmed to 8 inches (20 cm), 1 trimmed to 7 inches (18 cm), 1 trimmed to 6 inches (15 cm), 1 trimmed to 5 inches, and 1 trimmed to 4 inches
4 stems of sourgum, trimmed to 4 inches
2 large galax leaves

BLOOMING CRYSTAL ORNAMENTS

Add the magic of natural beauty to your next Christmas tree by decorating it with these dried flower ornaments. You can use dried flowers in a single color scheme or mix and match. Use ornaments in a variety of shapes and sizes for visual interest.

STEP ONE

Fold the 6-inch length of ribbon in half and hot-glue the two ends to the center top of the ornament to form a hanger. Tie a simple bow from the 18-inch piece of ribbon and hot-glue it over the ends of the ribbon hanger. If you wish, you can use two smaller bows instead of one, positioning them back-to-back on either side of the loop.

STEP TWO

Hot-glue the largest of your dried materials on the top of the ornament. (With a larger ornament, you can drape the materials over the sides and hot-glue in place.) Hot-glue the remaining materials around and/or on top of the first materials and into the bow loops, if desired. Save the smallest, most delicate materials for last.

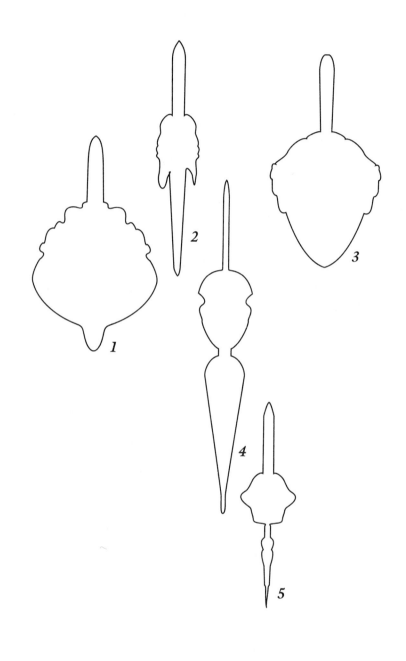

MATERIALS

For one ornament:

Clear glass ornament

Glue gun

2 lengths of narrow satin ribbon, 1 trimmed to 6 inches (15 cm) and 1 trimmed to 18 inches (46 cm)

Several sprigs and/or blooms of your favorite dried flowers and herbs

(1) Top left: Three dusty miller leaves, three sprigs of pepperberries, and two small rosebuds.

(2) Top center: Two stems of German statice trimmed to 3 inches (7 cm), two sprigs of pepperberries, and two rosebuds.

(3) Top right: Three sprigs of pepperberries and one small rosebud.

(4) Center: Four dusty miller leaves, two sprigs of pepperberries, and three sprigs of boxwood foliage.

(5) Bottom right: Two sprigs of pepperberries and one small rosebud.

56

ASYMMETRICAL TRIANGLE ARRANGEMENT

This arrangement combines small clusters of similarly shaped flowers with contrasting types of foliage. The trailing nature of the ivy makes it ideal material to help form the asymmetrical lines.

STEP ONE

With the serrated knife, cut the foam to fit snugly inside the center of the basket. Soak the foam in water, then blot with a towel. Place the plastic liner in the bottom of the basket and place the foam on top of the liner.

MATERIALS

Serrated knife
Block of wet floral foam
Low, round basket
Plastic liner
2 stems of pink roses, several
    blooms to a stem,
    1 trimmed to 16 inches
    (41 cm) and 1 trimmed
    to 8 inches (20 cm)
2 floral water tubes
3 stems of begonias, several
    blooms to a stem, trimmed
    to 10 inches (25 cm)
3 stems of African violets,
    several blooms to a stem,
    trimmed to 5 inches
    (12 cm)
2 large galax leaves
4 stems of trailing ivy,
    2 trimmed to 12 inches
    (30 cm) and 2 trimmed
    to 10 inches

STEP TWO

Cut the rose stems at an angle and insert them into water-filled floral tubes. Create the top focal point of the arrangement by inserting the rose tubes into the foam. Next, insert the begonias and the violets into the foam, using the photo as a guide for positioning.

STEP THREE

Fill in the area under the begonias with the galax leaves and fill in the areas in the middle and to the right of the arrangement with the trailing ivy.

Sweet Annie Wreath

This small, heart-shaped wreath is perfect for a bathroom, where steam from the shower will release the herbs' sweet scent.

Step One

Bend the sweet Annie into a heart shape approximately 6 inches (15 cm) high and 7 inches (17 cm) wide. Using the medium-gauge floral wire, wire the sprigs together in four places: at the center top, on each side, and at the center bottom.

Step Two

Thread the ribbon through the wire at top center. Tie a loop 1 inch from the end of the ribbon, to use as a hanger.

Step Three

Hot-glue the lavender stems evenly around the heart, pointing the blooms in the same direction.

Step Four

Hot-glue the rosebuds around the heart, using them to cover the stems of the lavender.

Step Five

Hot-glue the sprigs of baby's-breath evenly around the wreath.

MATERIALS

6 sprigs of dried, green-dyed sweet Annie, trimmed to 28 inches (70 cm)

4 6-inch (15 cm) lengths of medium-gauge floral wire

16 inches (41 cm) of 1/2-inch (1.3 cm) wide lavender velvet ribbon

Glue gun

13 stems of dried lavender, trimmed to 2 inches (5 cm)

35 dried pink rosebuds, 1/2 inch or less in diameter

13 sprigs of dried baby's-breath, trimmed to 1 inch (2.5 cm)

GRAPEVINE BOW

Wild grapevines are abundant and can be gathered in most semi-open woods. An alternative is to purchase a 12-inch (30 cm) grapevine wreath, remove any wires that are holding it together, and soak it a bucket of water overnight. The next morning, the vines will be loose enough to untangle and straighten.

STEP ONE

Lay the lengths of grapevine side by side. Treating them as one strand, form them into a bow with 19-inch (48 cm) loops and 14-inch (36 cm) streamers. Twist the heavy-gauge wire

around the center of the "bow" to hold it together. To make a hanger, form the excess wire into a loop and twist the wires together, close to the grapevine.

STEP TWO

Divide the mint sprigs into two equal bunches. Position one bunch on top of the bow, with the stems in the center and the foliage pointing to the left. Hot-glue the stems to the grapevine. Position the second bunch with the stems in the center of the bow and the foliage pointing to the right. Hot-glue the stems in place.

STEP THREE

Working in the order given in the materials list, attach the remaining six herbs, dividing each herb into two equal bunches and positioning them as described in Step 2.

STEP FOUR

Cut a 14-inch length of wired ribbon and trim a V-shape out of each end. Position it on the vine bow so that it slopes from upper right to lower left and wire it to the center of the bow with the fine-gauge floral wire.

STEP FIVE

Use the remaining ribbon to make a four-loop bow. Wire it on top of the first piece of ribbon with fine-gauge floral wire. Trim a V-shape out of the bow's ends.

MATERIALS

- 4 6-foot (1.8 m) lengths of grapevine
- 4-inch (10 cm) piece of heavy-gauge floral wire
- Glue gun
- 6 sprigs of mint, trimmed to 9 or 10 inches (22 to 25 cm)
- 2 stems of dried santolina, trimmed to 8 inches (20 cm)
- 6 stems of dried anise hyssop, trimmed to 6 inches (15 cm)
- 2 stems of dried cockscomb, trimmed to 6 inches
- 4 stems of dried lavender, trimmed to 6 inches
- 4 stems of dried pink globe amaranth, trimmed to 6 inches
- 4 stems of dried strawflower, trimmed to 7 inches (17 cm)
- 5 feet (1.5 m) of 2-inch (5 cm) wide wired ribbon
- Fine-gauge floral wire

HERB AND FLOWER WREATH

In the Victorian era, colorful wreaths like this one were often used as decorations at bridal receptions.

STEP ONE

Arrange the eucalyptus in bunches of five to six sprigs, mixing the colors, and attach to floral picks (see page 10). Pick the bunches into the wreath until the base is covered, inserting the picks at the same angle and overlapping the stems of one bunch with the foliage of the next.

STEP TWO

Hot-glue the flowers onto the eucalyptus, distributing each variety evenly around the wreath.

STEP THREE

Tie a bow with the ribbon and, holding the bow above the wreath, hot-glue the streamers to the back of the wreath for the hanger.

MATERIALS

12-inch (30 cm) foam
  wreath base
30 sprigs of red eucalyptus,
  trimmed to 2 inches (5 cm)
30 sprigs of green eucalyptus,
  trimmed to 2 inches
Floral picks
Glue gun
7 dried yellow strawflowers
10 dried pink strawflowers
12 dried red roses
24 dried miniature carnations,
  in assorted colors
12 dried pink roses
12 dried red-and-white
  variegated roses
12 dried Sweet William
  flower clusters, about 2
  inches in diameter
3 dried hydrangea flower
  clusters, 4 to 6 inches
  (10 to 15 cm) in diameter
12 sprigs of dried caspia,
  trimmed to 1 inch (2.5 cm)
12 stems of dried purple
  annual statice, trimmed
  to 1 inch
3-1/2 feet (1 m) of 2-inch
  wide burgundy velvet
  ribbon

CELOSIA TOPIARY

STEP FOUR

Cover the ball with Spanish moss, attaching it with floral pins (see page 10).

STEP FIVE

Divide the strawflowers into two piles and, working on half the ball at a time, hot-glue them randomly around the ball.

STEP SIX

Hot-glue the celosia to all areas not covered by straw-flowers. The ball should be completely covered.

STEP SEVEN

Fit the sheet moss into the pot, covering the plaster of paris.

MATERIALS

- 3-inch (7 cm) diameter clay pot, 3 inches high
- 12-inch (30 cm) piece of plastic wrap
- 2 cups (472 ml) of plaster of paris
- 1/2-inch (1.3 cm) diameter wooden dowel, 10 inches (25 cm) long
- 5-inch (12 cm) diameter foam ball
- Glue gun
- About 4 ounces (1.2 hg) of dried Spanish moss
- Floral pins
- 26 strawflowers
- 70 stems of celosia, about 1/2 to 1-1/2 inches (1.25 to 4 cm) wide and 1/2 inch long
- 3-inch-diameter circle of sheet moss

With its rich red celosia and bright strawflowers, this colorful topiary will enliven any decor.

STEP ONE

Line the clay pot with the plastic wrap, so the topiary can later be removed from the pot, if desired.

STEP TWO

Mix the plaster of paris according to package instructions and fill the clay pot. Insert the dowel upright in the center of the plaster, and allow the plaster to dry for two days.

STEP THREE

Center the foam ball over the dowel and press down to insert the dowel into the ball. Hot-glue around the dowel and foam.

Rainbow Floral Wreath

A lavish spectrum of color enlivens this lovely dried flower wreath. It can be displayed throughout the year against almost any background.

Step One

To form the wreath frame, shape the coat hanger into a 6-1/2-inch (16.5 cm) circle and secure with electrical tape.

MATERIALS

Wire coat hanger
Electrical tape
Fishing line
1-pound (.4 kg) bag of
　　Spanish moss
Large bunch of dried artemisia
Glue gun
8 dried strawflowers, stems
　　removed
16 stems of dried lavender,
　　trimmed to 4 inches
　　(10 cm)
8 daisies, trimmed to 4 inches
2 stems of dried larkspur,
　　trimmed to 4 inches
6 dried roses, trimmed to
　　4 inches
18 stems of dried blue sage,
　　trimmed to 4 inches
4 dried carnations, trimmed
　　to 4 inches
20 dried globe amaranths,
　　stems removed
2 stems of dried Queen-
　　Anne's-lace, trimmed
　　to 4 inches
2 bunches of dried blue
　　hydrangea, trimmed
　　to 4 inches
8 sprigs of dried baby's-breath

Step Two

Tie fishing line to the frame. Place a small bunch of moss around the frame and wrap with fishing line to secure. Add more moss and keep wrapping until the frame is covered, forming a base.

Step Three

Continue wrapping fishing line around the base, adding small bunches of artemisia as you go.

Step Four

Glue the flowers (except for the baby's-breath) into the artemisia in clusters around the base.

Step Five

Tuck in small bunches of baby's-breath at various points around the wreath.

SPRING FLING ARRANGEMENT

A simple triangle-shaped arrangement showcases the bright beauty of spring flowers. Many of the flowers and leaves in this arrangement will dry in place after a few weeks, although there will probably be enough shrinkage to require the addition of new materials.

MATERIALS

Serrated knife
Block of wet floral foam
Basket
2 stems of yellow freesia, several blooms to a stem, 1 trimmed to 18 inches (46 cm) and 1 trimmed to 14 inches (36 cm)
7 red roses, 1 trimmed to 13 inches (33 cm), 2 trimmed to 11 inches (27 cm), 3 trimmed to 7 inches (17 cm), and 1 trimmed to 4 inches (10 cm)
12 purple asters, 1 trimmed to 13 inches, 4 trimmed to 11 inches, 3 trimmed to 7 inches, and 4 trimmed to 6 inches (15 cm)
4 stems of purple larkspur, 1 trimmed to 11 inches, 2 trimmed to 7 inches, and 1 trimmed to 5 inches (12 cm)
10 stems of tree fern, 2 trimmed to 16 inches (41 cm), 2 trimmed to 14 inches, 2 trimmed to 12 inches (30 cm), 2 trimmed to 9 inches (22 cm), and 2 trimmed to 6 inches
8 stems of variegated pittsoporum, 4 trimmed to 9 inches and 4 trimmed to 4 inches

STEP ONE

With the serrated knife, cut the foam to fit snugly inside the basket. Soak the foam in water, then blot with a towel. Place the plastic liner in the bottom of the basket and place the foam on top of the liner.

STEP TWO

Create the top points of the triangle shape by inserting the freesia into the foam. Next, make the sides of the triangle with the roses, using the photo as a guide for positioning. Fill in the triangle with the asters and the larkspur.

STEP THREE

Insert the stems of fern on both outer edges of the triangle and then insert the variegated pittsoporum along the bottom edge and in the center of the arrangement.

Golden Horn Arrangement

A few inexpensive craft props—such as the horn and tray in this arrangement—dress up the simplicity of natural materials without detracting from them.

Step One

With the serrated knife, cut the foam to fit inside the tray and secure it to the tray with floral clay or floral wire. Using floral pins, cover the foam with Spanish moss and center the horn on top of the foam. Wire the horn in place and then secure with hot glue.

Step Two

Insert the magnolia leaves horizontally into the four sides of the foam block, as close to the tray as possible. Next insert the stems of Fraser fir, again on all four sides and about 2 inches (5 cm) up from the magnolia leaves. Attach one end of all three ribbons to one floral pick. Insert the pick into the foam under one side of the horn, letting the ribbon streamers flow out under the bell of the horn.

Step Three

Insert the eucalyptus and amaranth stems into the foam, taking care to position them at different angles and at different depths. For both pinecones, loop the wire from a remaining floral pick between the last two layers of petals and then insert the pick into the foam behind the horn. Last, hot-glue the pomegranates in a small cluster in front of the horn.

MATERIALS

Serrated knife
Block of floral foam, 3 inches
    (7 cm) thick
Large, square gold tray
Floral clay
Heavy-gauge floral wire
Floral pins
Spanish moss
Large, gold craft horn
Glue gun
20 glycerin-preserved
    magnolia leaves
10 stems of glycerin-preserved
    Fraser fir, trimmed to
    8 inches (20 cm)
3 lengths of gold ribbon,
    trimmed to 20 inches
    (50 cm)
3 floral picks
18 stems of dried eucalyptus,
    trimmed to 20 inches
8 stems of dried amaranth,
    trimmed to 8 inches
2 large pinecones
5 dried pomegranates

KITCHEN ARCH

The sage and garlic in this culinary arch will add wonderful fragrance to your kitchen. The cayenne peppers and pepperberries add color.

STEP ONE

If the wreath base has a green plastic wrapper, leave it on, to keep the straw from shedding. Using the handsaw, saw the base in half, and set one of the halves aside for a future project. Wrap the tulle around the other half, securing the fabric with floral pins.

STEP TWO

To make a hanger, wrap the heavy-gauge floral wire around the center of the base and twist the ends together. Form a loop in the excess wire and twist the wire ends together close to the base.

STEP THREE

Form 32 bunches of dried sage, each composed of three or four stems. Pin them to the base until it is completely covered. Outline the arch first, working from the center to each end and tucking the stems of each new bunch under the foliage of the previous bunch. Then fill in the front face of the arch, again working from the center outward.

STEP FOUR

Attach a floral pick to each bunch of pepperberries. Pick the pepperberries into the base, spacing them over the arch.

STEP FIVE

Attach a floral pick to each garlic bulb right next to the bulb. Pick the garlic into the base, spacing the bulbs evenly across the arch, with their stems trailing across the front of the arch.

STEP SIX

Cut the paper ribbon into seven 9-inch (22 cm) lengths. Form each length into a loop and attach each one to a floral pick. Cut two ribbon streamers 9 inches long, and attach one end of each to a pick. Pick the loops into the top of the base to form a bow. Then pick in the streamers, tucking their ends into the back of the arch.

STEP SEVEN

Hot-glue the peppers evenly across the arch.

MATERIALS

20-inch (50 cm) diameter straw wreath base
Handsaw
5 feet (1.5 m) of 6-inch (15 cm) wide tulle
42 floral pins
18-inch (46 cm) length of heavy-gauge floral wire
96 to 128 stems of dried sage, trimmed to 5 to 10 inches (12 to 25 cm)
19 floral picks
6 bunches of pepperberries, trimmed to 8 inches (20 cm)
4 bulbs of elephant garlic, 2 to 2-1/2 inches (5 to 6 cm) in diameter, stems trimmed to 7 inches (17 cm)
7 feet (2.1 m) of 5-inch (13 cm) wide white paper ribbon
6 dried cayenne peppers, stems trimmed to 1 inch (2.5 cm)

HERBAL WEDDING WREATH

Made with flowers and herbs whose symbolic meanings create a special wedding message, this wreath is a gift that will be cherished for years to come. The cockscombs and globe amaranths symbolize unfading affection; the carnations symbolize bonds of affection; the marjoram, joy and happiness; the rosemary, remembrance and fidelity; the lavender, love and devotion; the sage, domestic virtue; and the thyme, strength and courage.

MATERIALS

12-inch (30 cm) diameter wire wreath base
Fishing line
40 stems of dried 'Silver King' artemisia, 10 trimmed to 24 inches (60 cm), and 30 trimmed to 5 inches (12 cm)
Glue gun
26 stems of dried German statice, trimmed to 4 inches (10 cm)
8 stems of dried baby's-breath, trimmed to 4 inches
2 large dried cockscomb heads
16 dried globe amaranth blooms
8 dried carnation blooms
2 stems of dried marjoram, trimmed to 4 inches
4 stems of dried rosemary, trimmed to 4 inches
10 stems of dried larkspur, trimmed to 4 inches
20 spikes of dried lavender, trimmed to 4 inches
10 dried rosebuds
6 dried sage leaves
4 stems of dried thyme, trimmed to 4 inches
10 dried love-in-a-mist seed heads

STEP ONE

Working with two stems at a time, position the 24-inch lengths of 'Silver King' artemisia against the wire base and begin twisting them around the base, overlapping as needed. Secure the artemisia to the base by gently wrapping it with fishing wire in 2-inch (5 cm) intervals. Repeat this process until you've used all ten of the 24-inch stems.

STEP TWO

Hot-glue the 5-inch stems of 'Silver King' artemisia into the base. Set aside the ten stems of German statice and the baby's-breath. Mentally divide the wreath in half vertically. Working on the first half, arrange each material in small clusters and hot-glue the clusters into the base. Repeat the process in the same order on the other half of the wreath. Fill in any bare spots with the reserved German statice and baby's-breath.

VINE BASKET DRIED ARRANGEMENT

Tie the ribbon in a bow. Thread a length of floral wire through the bow's loop and wire it into the moss-covered foam at one end of the arrangement.

MATERIALS

10 × 7-inch (25 × 17 cm) vine basket
Block of floral foam
Sharp knife
Glue gun
Spanish moss
12 dried pale pink straw-flowers, stems removed
2 bunches of dried pink hydrangea, trimmed to 2 inches (5 cm)
3 stems of dried cockscomb, trimmed to 2 inches
2 large dried roses, stems removed
6 small dried roses, stems removed
4 dried pale-pink miniature carnations, trimmed to 2 inches
3 bunches of della robia blueberries with leaves
1 small della robia apple
6 stems of dried Queen-Anne's-lace, trimmed to 2 inches
2 stems of dried pink larkspur, trimmed to 2 inches
1 yard (90 cm) of 1-1/2-inch (4 cm) wire ribbon
Floral wire

This colorful arrangement of dried flowers and artificial fruits seems to pour over the sides of its rustic vine basket. The soft muted colors make it an ideal table adornment for any room in the house.

STEP ONE

Fit the foam block into the basket, shaping it with a sharp knife until the top of the foam is level with the basket rim.

STEP TWO

Glue Spanish moss to the foam until the surface is completely covered.

STEP THREE

Glue a grouping of straw-flowers across the moss beneath the basket handle.

STEP FOUR

Glue hydrangea to the moss on either side of the strawflowers.

STEP FIVE

Next glue the cockscomb, roses, carnations, della robia fruits, Queen-Anne's-lace, and larkspur until they cover the surface and spill over the basket rim.

71

Fruits and vegetables add a burst of excitement to wreaths, arrangements, topiaries, garlands, and much more. Their colors, shapes, and textures are a refreshing change from the usual floral materials, plus they're fun to work with.

Fruits and vegetables can be used in crafts in their fresh or dried states. Many craft stores now offer fruits and vegetables that have been freeze-dried. Using a dehydrator is also an option, or you can always air-dry materials such as sliced apples and mushrooms.

Working with fresh fruits and vegetables is a little more challenging, but well worth the effort. Be sure to select only the freshest materials. The chart that follows provides you with a list of inspiring fruits and vegetables, along with the best ways to secure them to a base and their average life expectancies in craft projects.

FRUIT OR VEGETABLE	WAYS TO SECURE	LIFE EXPECTANCY
Apple	Craft picks and hot glue	7-12 days before rotting
Artichoke	Craft picks and hot glue	5-8 days before turning brown
Broccoli	Craft picks and hot glue	3-4 days before turning brown
Grape	Floral pins for bunches	3-5 days before rotting
Lettuce	Craft picks when using the whole bunch; hot glue or floral pins for individual leaves	2 days before wilting; replace individual leaves as long as the rest of the project still looks nice
Mushroom	Craft picks	2-3 days before shrinkage begins; after shrinkage, the mushrooms will dry in place and last indefinitely
Onion	Floral picks and hot glue	5-8 days before rotting
Potato	Craft picks and hot glue	7-10 days before rotting
Radish	Craft picks and hot glue	2-3 days before shrinkage begins, although they're still attractive in this state
Squash	Floral wire and hot glue	Varies with variety; from several days to several months

DECORATED GARLIC BRAID

MATERIALS

14-inch (36 cm) long garlic braid
Glue gun
17 to 25 dried bay leaves
8 to 12 sprigs of dried hydrangea blooms
9 to 12 love-in-a-mist seed heads

The simple braids of garlic available at most farmers' markets make a wonderful base for adding colorful natural materials, and add a distinctive, culinary decorating flair to any kitchen. Some attractive alternatives to the materials shown here include globe amaranths, rosemary sprigs, chili peppers, oregano blooms, and rosebuds.

STEP ONE

Working on the back side of the braid, arrange and hot-glue the bay leaves down each side, positioning them so they overlap at an angle and protrude about 1-1/2 inches (4 cm) on the front side of the braid.

STEP TWO

Working on the front side of the braid, hot-glue the hydrangea into the crevices between garlic bulbs, and then hot-glue the love-in-a-mist seed heads randomly around the braid at various angles. Last, add color to the top of the braid by hot-gluing several bay leaves sideways between the stems.

FRUIT, VEGETABLE, AND FLORAL ARRANGEMENT

MATERIALS

Block of wet floral foam
Serrated knife
Low, oval basket
Plastic liner
Floral tape
19 craft picks
1 large artichoke
10 stalks of asparagus,
    trimmed to 10 inches
    (25 cm)
4 apples
4 mushrooms
5 stems of larkspur,
    1 trimmed to 19 inches
    (48 cm), 3 trimmed to
    14 inches (36 cm), and
    1 trimmed to 10 inches
7 stems of fern, 1 trimmed
    to 16 inches (41 cm),
    2 trimmed to 12 inches
    (30 cm), and 4 trimmed
    to 5 inches (12 cm)
10 stems of German statice,
    5 trimmed to 12 inches
    and 5 trimmed to 9 inches
    (22 cm)
10 stems of annual statice,
    4 trimmed to 7 inches
    (17 cm) and 6 trimmed
    to 5 inches
3 tulips, 1 trimmed to
    15 inches (39 cm),
    1 trimmed to 10 inches,
    and 1 trimmed to 7 inches
3 roses, 1 trimmed to
    14 inches, 1 trimmed
    to 10 inches, and
    1 trimmed to 5 inches
2 lilies, 1 trimmed to
    12 inches, and 1 trimmed
    to 9 inches
2 large clumps of red grapes
4 floral pins
7 galax leaves
Spanish moss

This exuberant arrangement adds a burst of excitement to everyday dinner tables as well as to the most formal buffet tables. To extend the arrangement's life span, be sure to store it in the refrigerator when not in use.

STEP ONE

Cut the foam with the serrated knife to fit snugly inside the basket. Soak the foam in water, then blot with a towel. Place the plastic liner in the bottom of the basket. Place the foam on top of the liner and secure it in place with several strips of criss-crossing floral tape. Prepare the vegetables and fruit by inserting craft picks into the artichoke, asparagus, apples, and mushrooms.

STEP TWO

Position the artichoke in the front right of the arrangement. Next, create the outline of the arrangement by inserting the stems of larkspur, fern, German statice, and annual statice into the foam. Insert the tulips, asparagus, roses, lilies, and apples into the foam, following the photo as a guide for positioning them.

STEP THREE

Insert the mushrooms into the base. Then arrange the grapes so they spill over the side of the basket and secure them with floral pins. Insert the galax leaves so they fold over the side of the basket. Last, tuck in small clumps of Spanish moss to hide any bare spots.

Bay Leaf Swag and Wreaths

This decorative culinary set adds fragrance and color to the kitchen. The 4-foot (1.2 m) long swag is a perfect size for draping over a window or doorway. The small wreaths will enliven walls or cabinets.

Swag

Step One

Using the drill and 1/10-inch bit, drill a hole through each pomegranate, nutmeg, and cinnamon stick, drilling side to side rather than end to end.

Step Two

To prevent the materials from falling off the swag, make a small loop in one end of the wire by wrapping it around a pencil. Using wire cutters, snip the other end of the wire into a point.

Step Three

Thread the swag materials onto the pointed end of wire, wiring the bay leaves in groups of 20, the cinnamon sticks in groups of five, and the nutmeg in groups of four. Intersperse the pomegranates among the grouped materials as shown in the photo above.

Step Four

When all the materials are strung, blunt-cut the pointed end of the wire and make a small loop in the wire, as close as possible to the materials, as described in Step 2.

MATERIALS

Swag

Electric drill with
    1/10-inch bit
5 dried pomegranates
16 whole nutmegs
50 cinnamon sticks, 2-1/2 to
    3 inches (6 to 7 cm) long
4-1/2-foot (1.4 m) length of
    heavy-gauge floral wire
Pencil
Wire cutters
400 bay leaves

Wreath

STEP ONE

Using the drill and 1/10-inch bit, drill a hole through each pomegranate and cinnamon stick, drilling side to side rather than end to end.

STEP TWO

Make a small loop in the end of the heavy-gauge wire by wrapping it around a pencil. Using the wire cutters, snip the other end of the wire into a point.

STEP THREE

Thread the materials onto the pointed end of the wire, wiring the bay leaves in groups of 20 and the cinnamon sticks in groups of two. Intersperse the pomegranates evenly among the materials, as shown in the photo at right.

STEP FOUR

When all the materials are strung, blunt-cut the pointed end of the wire and tie that end into a knot, as close as possible to the materials. Bend the wired fruit into a circle, twist the wire ends together, and clip off any excess wire.

STEP FIVE

Thread the raffia through the twisted loop, draw the ends up evenly, and tie it in a double knot close to the wire.

STEP SIX

Make a six-loop bow from the homespun ribbon and tie it tightly against the raffia knot, using fine-gauge wire or heavy string. Tie the raffia in a knot

close to the ends, to make a large loop to hang the wreath by. Trim the ends.

VARIATION

Replace the cinnamon sticks with small lime pomanders.

Insert whole cloves into three limes until they're well covered and thread the resulting pomanders on the wire, interspersing them with groups of bay leaves and the pomegranates.

MATERIALS

For one wreath:

Electric drill with
   1/10-inch bit
3 dried pomegranates
6 cinnamon sticks, 2-1/2 to
   3 inches (6 to 7 cm) long
18-inch (46 cm) length of
   heavy-gauge floral wire
Pencil

Wire cutters
140 bay leaves
14-inch (36 cm) length
   of raffia
1 yard (0.9 m) beige
   "homespun" ribbon
   1-1/4 inches (3 cm) wide
Fine-gauge floral wire or
   heavy string

POMEGRANATE WREATH

This bright red and pale green wreath combines pomegranates, hydrangeas, roses, and celosias.

STEP ONE

Attach one bunch of artemisia to the wire base by wrapping monofilament around the base and the stems. Add a second bunch so that its foliage overlaps the stems of the first and secure with the monofilament. Continue in this fashion around the base, using one continuous piece of monofilament to attach the bunches, until the base is completely covered.

MATERIALS

50 bunches of dried 'Silver King' artemisia, 4 inches (10 cm) long and 1 inch (2.5 cm) in diameter at the stem ends
12-inch (30 cm) diameter wire wreath base
2 yards (1.8 m) of mono-filament fishing line
Glue gun
6 dried pomegranates
14 lemon leaves, about 4 inches long
6 dried blue hydrangea flowers, 3 to 4 inches in diameter
7 dried pink hydrangea flowers, 3 to 4 inches in diameter
10 dried red roses, trimmed to 1 inch
4 love-in-a-mist seedpods
7 bunches of dried red celosia, 2 to 3 inches (5 to 7 cm) wide
3-inch length of heavy-gauge floral wire

STEP TWO

Hot-glue the other materials onto the artemisia in the order given in the materials list, spacing each variety evenly around the wreath.

STEP THREE

To make a hanger, bend the heavy-gauge floral wire into an inverted U-shape and twist each end onto the wire base at the back of the wreath.

Beans and Herbs Wreath

The simple materials in this small wreath can be found in almost any kitchen, and the finished wreath looks lovely hanging over a spice rack.

Step One

Coat the top surface area of the wreath base with a thick layer of adhesive spray and quickly sprinkle on the green and yellow split peas or beans. Press gently in place.

Step Two

Fill in any bare spots on the wreath by applying dabs of craft glue and pressing the saffron, parsley, and dehydrated green peas into the glue. Allow to dry completely.

Step Three

Holding all of the raffia strands together, wrap them loosely around the wreath and tie in a loose bow at the top. Hot-glue in position as needed.

MATERIALS

7-inch (17 cm) foam wreath base
Adhesive spray
8-ounce package of green and yellow split peas (a package of assorted beans may be substituted)
White craft glue
Small amounts of dried saffron and parsley
Dehydrated green peas
3 lengths of raffia, trimmed to 22 inches (56 cm)
Glue gun

STORAGE JAR BONNETS

Everyone likes to save attractive jars for storing things. These dried fruit-and-flower bonnets transform ordinary canning jars of dried mint, peppers, and candy sticks into delightful kitchen decorations.

STEP ONE

Cut an apple (stem-end up) into slices 3/16 inch (1.5 mm) thick. Mix the lemon juice and salt together. Soak a few apple slices at a time in the solution for three minutes. Shake off the excess juice and dry on a rack in a warm oven (150°F) for four to five hours.

STEP TWO

Sew the lace around the outer edge of the fabric circle. Sew the elastic strip around the underside of the circle 5/8 inch (1.6 cm) from the edge of the fabric. Set aside.

STEP THREE

Holding all of the raffia strands together, tie them into a bow and glue on the sprigs of box-wood, statice, and yarrow with stems toward the center. Glue on the cinnamon stick at an angle and glue a dried apple slice over the cinnamon. Glue the pinecones, the sweet-gum ball, and the strawflowers to the sides of the apple.

STEP FOUR

Slip the cloth bonnet over the jar lid and glue the decoration to the front. It helps if you stretch the elastic at the attachment point before gluing on the decoration and hold it there until dry.

MATERIALS

For one bonnet:

Apple
Knife
2 cups (500 ml) of lemon
　juice
2 tablespoons (28 g) of salt
3/8-inch (1 cm) wide lace,
　21 inches (53 cm) long
6-1/2 inch (16.5 cm) diameter
　circle of cotton fabric
1/8-inch (3 mm) wide elastic,
　9 inches (22 cm) long
7 lengths of raffia, trimmed
　to 36 inches (90 cm), and
　1/8 inch wide

Glue gun
Sprig of boxwood, trimmed
　to 4 inches (10 cm)
3 stems of statice, trimmed
　to 4 inches
Stem of yarrow, trimmed
　to 4 inches
Cinnamon stick
2 small pinecones
Sweet-gum ball
2 strawflowers, stems removed
Standard 1-quart (0.95 l)
　canning jar, with lid

Radish Topiary

Step Two

Press the bottom center of the foam ball down over the top of the twig about 1 inch (2.5 cm). Remove the ball, fill the hole with hot glue, and replace over the twig. Prepare the radishes by inserting a craft pick into the bottom of each one.

Step Three

Insert the radishes into the foam ball until it's completely covered. Tuck small pieces of Spanish moss between the radishes to prevent any bare foam from showing.

Step Four

Decorate the base of the topiary by arranging several radicchio leaves around the twig. Secure the leaves with floral pins. Insert a craft pick into the bottom of the apple and then insert the other end of the pick into the foam base.

This free-spirited topiary makes the perfect conversation piece for a barbecue centerpiece or a more formal social gathering.

Step One

Cut the block of foam with the serrated knife so that it fits snugly inside the clay pot. Insert the twig about 2 inches (5 cm) into the center of the foam. Remove the twig, fill the hole with hot glue, and replace the twig. Cover the foam with Spanish moss and use floral pins to hold the moss in place.

MATERIALS

Block of floral foam
Serrated knife
5-inch (12 cm) clay pot
1/4-inch (6 mm) diameter
    twig, 20 inches (50 cm)
    long
Glue gun
Spanish moss
10 to 15 floral pins
4-inch (10 cm) foam ball
35 to 45 radishes
36 to 46 craft picks
3 to 5 radicchio leaves
1 apple

A tree's accoutrements—its leaves or needles and its inner and outer bark—are among its most beautiful elements. For centuries people have been creating useful and decorative objects from them, from coconut leaf baskets to bark canoes, from cattail hats to reed backpacks.

LEAVES

For functional items, clearly a leaf's individual traits must be matched to the project. A basket can't be woven from a leaf that can't bend without tearing. For purely aesthetic projects—such as wreaths and swags—try to vary the colors, textures, and shapes. Evergreens come in an amazing array of colors—all called green, all distinctly different in hue. Leaves vary from the hand-shaped sassafras to the feather-shaped black locust.

Preserved with glycerin, leaves and evergreens will retain much of their color. Make several diagonal cuts in their stems and stand them in a mixture of three parts warm water to one part glycerin. The leaves will absorb the glycerin in about two weeks.

BARK

A variety of trees produce the kind of smooth, flexible bark that is good for making things: birch, tulip poplar, white ash, basswood, quaking aspen, cedar, and juniper, to name a few. The bark is easiest to strip in late spring or early summer.

Since stripping a significant piece of bark off a tree will kill it, it makes sense to fell the tree, remove all the usable bark, and make more than one project. If possible, choose a tree in a crowded area or one that's about to be cleared. Young, fast-growing, second-growth trees 3 to 5 inches (7 to 12 cm) in diameter are best. The stripped wood dries quickly and makes excellent firewood.

The bark is most flexible and workable when it first comes off the tree. Don't let it sit around for more than a day or two before beginning the project.

FIGURE 1

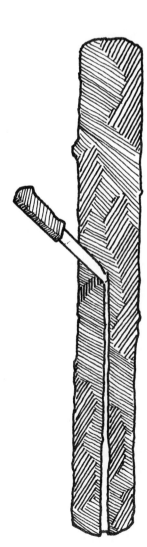

FIGURE 2

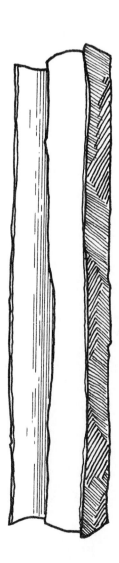

FIGURE 3

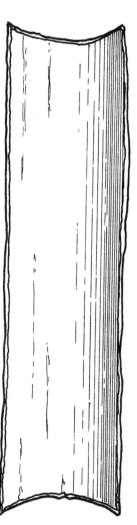

Fell the tree, using a handsaw or an axe. Select a smooth area on the trunk that's free of branches, and mark off the length of bark you need, using a pen or scratching with your knife.

With a sharp knife, cut around the tree trunk at the top and bottom of the marked area, cutting through the bark and into the sapwood. Then make a cut up one side of the marked area (see Figure 1). Use the knife or axe blade to pry under the bark along the cut, and carefully peel off the entire piece around the whole circumference of the trunk (see Figure 2). If all goes well, you'll be left with a flexible, untorn piece ready for a craft project (see Figure 3).

MAKING BARK LACING

The inner bark of a young tree is a tough, pliable material for lacing pieces of a project together or for weaving baskets. Hickory and basswood are especially flexible and durable, but other species will also work.

To make bark lacing, first fell a tree 3 to 5 inches in diameter. Using a knife or axe blade, pry up a piece of bark about 1 inch (2.5 cm) wide at the bottom of the trunk, and pull it firmly toward the top of the tree (see Figure 4) until it breaks off. Continue in this fashion until you have removed all the usable bark. Some strips may be only 1 to 2 feet (30 to 60 cm) long; others may be as long as the entire tree. The longer the better.

Peel each strip apart, separating the inner bark from the outer layer. This is best done by hand (see Figure 5), although a sharp knife is sometimes useful for the initial prying apart. Save the outer pieces for another craft project.

Using a sharp knife, cut the pieces of inner bark into narrow strips usable for lacing or weaving—anywhere from 1/8 to 1/2 inch (3 mm to 1.25 cm) wide, depending on the project. For best results, anchor one end of the strip under your foot and hold it taut while you cut up or down its length from the other end (see Figure 6).

The lacing can be used immediately or coiled and stored for future use. If it is stored, it must be soaked in a bucket of warm water for about 30 minutes before being used.

FIGURE 4

FIGURE 5

FIGURE 6

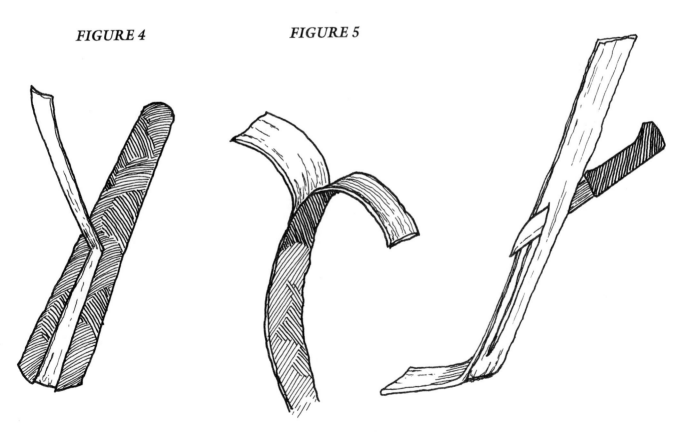

EGG BASKET

MATERIALS

20 to 40 feet (6.1 to 12.3 m) of dried honeysuckle vine

20 to 40 feet of hickory-bark lacing, 1/8 to 1/4 inch (3 to 6 mm) wide (see "Making Bark Lacing" on page 87)

20 to 30 feet (6.1 to 9.1 m) of spruce roots, 1/8 to 1/4 inch in diameter

30 feet (9.2 m) of round reed, 1/4-inch in diameter

Large bucket full of water

2 8-inch (20 cm) diameter round hoops

4 clothespins

Sharp knife

Pencil

Pocketknife or pencil sharpener

One of the most popular ribbed baskets ever made, the traditional egg basket can be woven from a variety of materials. This one is made from honeysuckle vine, hickory bark, and spruce roots.

STEP ONE

Soak the honeysuckle, hickory bark, spruce roots, and round reed in a large bucket of water until they are pliable, about 30 minutes.

STEP TWO

To make the basket's handle, stand one hoop vertically on the work table. To make the rim, center the second hoop horizontally inside the first hoop (see Figure 1 on page 90). Fasten clothespins to each of the intersections to temporarily hold the hoops in this position. Set aside.

STEP THREE

Using a sharp knife, cut the round reed into ten pieces: four 14 inches (36 cm) long, two 15-1/2 inches (40 cm) long, two 16-1/2 inches (42 cm) long, and two 18 inches (46 cm) long. Use the pencil to number two 14-inch pieces #1, two 14-inch pieces #5, two 15-1/2-inch pieces #2, two 18-inch pieces #3, and two 16-1/2-inch pieces #4. These numbered pieces will be the primary ribs of the basket. With the pocketknife or pencil sharpener, sharpen both ends of each rib (see Figure 2 on page 90).

STEP FOUR

Choose a piece of honeysuckle vine at least 8 feet (2.5 m) long, and begin the ear—the lashing that holds the handle to the rim. Starting at the dot in Figure 3 on page 90, wrap the vine around the junction in an X-shape, following the numbers. At position #4, take the vine behind the handle to position #1 and repeat the wrap three times. Use a clothespin to clip the free end of the vine in place. Using another piece of honeysuckle vine, make the ear on the other side of the basket and clip the free end in place.

DESIGNER'S TIP

GATHERING AND PREPARING SPRUCE ROOTS

Although the roots of other conifers can be used for weaving, those of the spruce tree are far superior. For the best roots, go to a forest where the spruce trees are large and grow thickly.

The soil in a spruce forest is usually a soft, peatlike duff. Using a stick or your hand, probe into the soil around a spruce tree until you find a root 1/16 to 1/2 inch (1 mm to 1.3 cm) in diameter. Gently pull the root up out of the earth, following its path along the forest floor. As you unearth the first root, it will inevitably lead to others that you can gather later. When you can pull no more out, cut it with a knife or small garden clippers. Fear not for the tree. Considering the root system of a good-size spruce, the tree will merely chuckle at your presumption.

When you have gathered a bundle of roots, strip off their outer bark, using a pocketknife or your fingers. Some roots will also need to be split before being used. Very small roots—those under 1/4 inch (6 mm) in diameter—can be used as they are. Medium-size roots (1/4 inch in diameter or so) should be split in half lengthwise (see Figure 1 below). Roots larger than 1/2 inch in diameter should be quartered and the inside corner cut off with a pocketknife (see Figure 2 below). For all roots that need to be split, start the split with your fingernail or knife, carefully dividing it in half. Then, if necessary, divide each half in the same way.

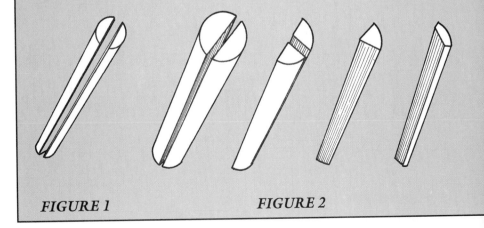

FIGURE 1   *FIGURE 2*

STEP FIVE

Remove the clothespin and, following the numbers in Figure 4, continue with the first ear, weaving the vine over the rim and around the back of the handle hoop. Repeat the weave, moving from one side of the handle to the other, until you have six rows on each side (see Figure 5). Don't cut the weaver; fasten it to the rim with a clothespin. Repeat on the ear on the opposite side of the basket.

STEP SIX

Insert one end of a #1 rib into the right side of one ear and the other end of the rib into the left side of the other ear. Insert the other #1 rib, mirroring the position of the other rib (see Figure 6). Insert the remaining pairs of ribs in numerical order, following the numbers pencilled onto them (see Figure 7).

STEP SEVEN

Working with one of the pieces of honeysuckle you pinned to the rim in Step 5, weave over and under the ribs (see Figure 7), making an ever larger semicircle. Each time you come to the rim, take the vine over it and back down the other side, continuing the over-and-under pattern. Continue the weaving until there is about 1 inch of vine on each side of the handle. (Measure along the rim.) Then repeat the process on the opposite side of the basket with the other piece of honeysuckle.

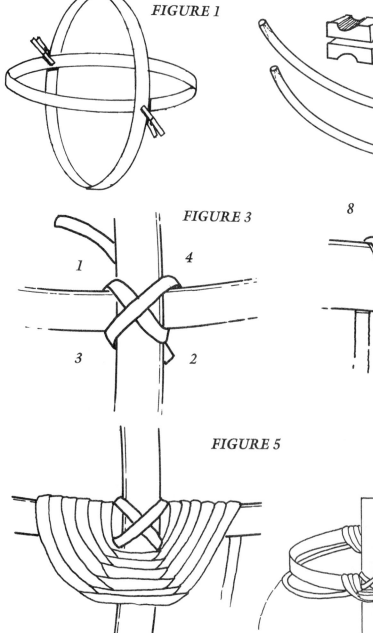

FIGURE 1

FIGURE 3

FIGURE 5

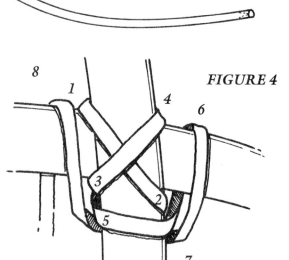

FIGURE 2

FIGURE 4

FIGURE 6

STEP EIGHT

Using a sharp knife, cut the round reed into eight pieces: two 12 inches (30 cm) long; two 14 inches long; two 15 inches (39 cm) long; and two 13 inches (33 cm) long. Use the pencil to label the 12-inch pieces A, the 14-inch pieces B, the 15-inch pieces C, and the 13-inch pieces D. These lettered pieces will be the secondary ribs of the basket. With the pocketknife or pencil sharpener, sharpen both ends of each rib (see Figure 2).

Insert the secondary ribs into the first available piece of vine, rather than all the way into the ear (see Figure 8). Rib A goes above #1; B goes above #2; C goes below #4; D goes below #5.

If any two ribs look too far apart, cut off a long piece of reed, make another rib, and insert it in the gap. Trim it to fit.

STEP NINE

Continue weaving on one side of the basket under and over all the ribs with the honeysuckle vine until there are about 2 inches of vine along the rim on each side of the handle. Repeat on the opposite side of the basket. Note: If a piece of honeysuckle vine ends in the middle of the basket, leave it behind a rib (inside the basket). Lay a new piece of vine behind the same rib, overlapping the ends for about 1 inch, and continue weaving with the new vine (see Figure 9).

STEP TEN

Starting on one side of the basket, weave in the hickory-bark lacing, again going under and over the ribs. Start the new weaver on the inside of the basket, leaving a 2-inch (5 cm) "tail." When you have woven two

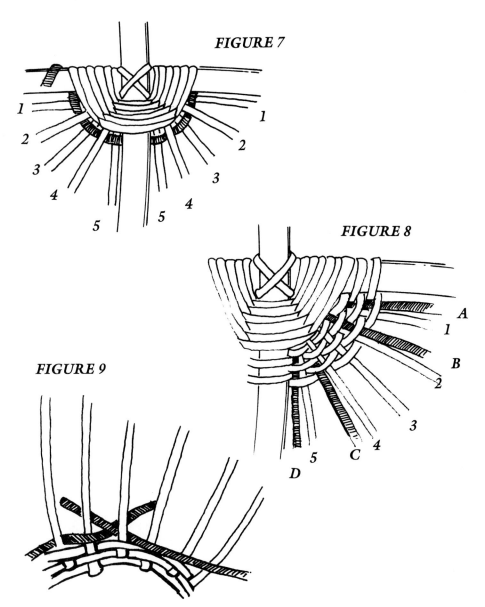

FIGURE 7

FIGURE 8

FIGURE 9

or three rows of bark, tuck the tail under them. Weave with the bark lacing until there are about 2 inches of bark lacing along the rim on each side of the handle and touching the honeysuckle vine. Repeat the process on the opposite side of the basket.

STEP ELEVEN

Weave with the spruce roots in the same manner on each side of the basket until you've filled in the center of the basket and there's no more room left along the rim. The spruce roots will cover about 4 inches (10 cm) of the rim on each side of the basket.

STEP TWELVE

Because of an egg basket's interesting shape (it's often called a fanny basket), there are occasionally some open spaces left on the bottom. If yours has such spaces, just select an extra weaver that matches the surrounding material, and weave over and under the ribs until the space is filled in.

Bark Bowl

A simple birch bark bowl can hold everything from dried flowers to fresh fruit. Left empty, it offers an interesting contrast between its smooth, tan interior and its peeling, white outer walls.

MATERIALS

15 × 20-inch (39 × 50 cm) piece of birch bark
Sharp, pointed knife
Ruler or tape measure
Pencil
Awl, gouge, or rotary leather punch
21 feet (6.5 m) of bark lacing, 1/8 to 3/16 inch (3 to 5 mm) wide (see "Making Bark Lacing" on page 87)
Scissors
5-foot (1.5 m) length of vine, about 1/4 inch (6 mm) in diameter

STEP ONE

Lay the bark on a flat surface, with the outer bark facing down. Cutting with the knife, round off the corners, creating an oval shape.

STEP TWO

At each "corner," measure about 4 inches (10 cm) into the piece of bark, and mark the point lightly with a pencil (see Figure 1). Cut from each pencil mark to its corresponding corner, cutting all the way through the bark.

STEP THREE

Using the awl, gouge, or rotary punch, make a row of holes around the perimeter of the bark, 3/4 inch (2 cm) from the edge and 1-3/4 inches (4.5 cm) apart. Then punch three holes down each side of the corner slits: the hole farthest into the bowl, 1/2 inch

FIGURE 1

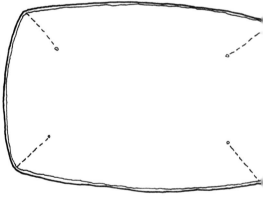

FIGURE 2

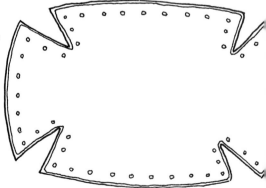

(1.25 cm) from the edge of the slit; the middle hole, 1 inch (2.5 cm) from the edge of the slit; and the hole closest to the bowl's rim, 1-1/2 inches from the edge of the slit. Make sure that the pairs of holes are opposite each other (see Figure 2).

STEP FOUR

With the outer bark on the outside, draw the two sides of a corner together and overlap them so that the holes align.

Using the bark lacing, lace them up (from top to bottom) as you would a shoe (see the photo), lacing from the outside of the bowl to the inside. When the corner is laced, tie a knot on the outside of the bowl and clip off the ends, using the scissors. Repeat for the other three corners.

STEP FIVE

On one short end of the basket, lay the vine against the outside rim. Note where

the vine will round the corner, and start lacing the vine to the rim there. (The tail will hang loose temporarily.) Thread the bark lacing through the holes and around the vine. When you return to the first end of the basket, lace over both the vine you're working with and the original tail. At the last hole, tie the lacing in a knot on the outside of the basket, right up against the wall.

ROSE LEAF SWAG

The rich colors in leaves make them an ideal base for wreaths, garlands, and swags. Note how well the pepperberries, fungi, and flowers contrast with the dark green foliage.

STEP ONE

Measure and mark the middle point of the coat hanger. Using the medium-gauge floral wire, begin wiring stems of rose leaves to the coat hanger, working from opposite ends so the

stems face the center point. Position each new stem of leaves so that its leaves cover the previous stems. When the entire length of coat hanger is covered, spray the leaves well with a coat of clear acrylic spray and allow to dry completely.

STEP TWO

Position a single large mushroom in the center of the swag to conceal the area where the stems meet and hot-glue it in

place. Space the remaining large and small mushrooms along the swag and hot-glue them in place. Arrange the pepperberries along the swag so their stems face in the same direction as the leaf stems and hot-glue them in place. Last, hot-glue the starflowers along the swag.

MATERIALS

1 metal coat hanger, unbent
20 to 30 stems of dried rose leaves, several leaves to a stem
Medium-gauge floral wire
Clear acrylic spray
3 large dried mushrooms
10 small dried mushrooms
Glue gun
15 stems of dried pepperberries, trimmed to 3 inches (7 cm)
32 dried starflower blooms

Evergreen Wreath and Garland

The holiday season has not arrived until evergreens perfume the house. This wreath and matching garland decoration combines three types of conifers for varying textures, scents, and shades of green.

Wreath

Step One

Attach the greenery to the vine base, mixing the four types randomly around the wreath and wedging, hot-gluing, and/or wiring the branches in place as needed. Keep adding greenery until the wreath looks plump and full.

Step Two

Make a bow with the plaid ribbon and wire it into place at the top of the wreath. Run a streamer of ribbon down each side of the wreath as shown in the photo, attaching the streamers with glue or wire as needed.

Step Three

Space the lotus pods evenly around the wreath, attaching them with wire or hot glue, as needed. Hot-glue the pieces of lichen evenly around the wreath.

MATERIALS

Wreath

1 peck (8.8 l) of pine branches, 12 to 20 inches (30 to 50 cm) long
12 juniper branches, 10 to 18 inches (25 to 46 cm) long
12 cedar branches, 6 to 8 inches (15 to 20 cm) long
5 holly sprigs, 6 inches long
18-inch (46 cm) diameter vine wreath base
Glue gun
Fine-gauge floral wire
5 yards (4.6 m) of 3-inch (7 cm) wide plaid ribbon
6 lotus pods
8 pieces of lichen, 2 to 3 inches (5 to 7 cm) in diameter

MATERIALS

Garland

Fine-gauge floral wire
1 bushel (35.2 l) of pine branches, 10 to 12 inches long
10-foot (3 m) length of heavy-gauge floral wire
10 juniper branches, 10 to 20 inches long
1 peck (8.8 l) of cedar branches, 6 to 12 inches long
20 holly sprigs, 6 to 10 inches long
7 yards (6.5 m) of 3-inch (7 cm) wide plaid ribbon
Glue gun
4 lotus pods
6 pieces of lichen, 2 to 3 inches (5 to 7 cm) in diameter

Garland

Step One

To make the garland, use the fine-gauge wire to attach the pine branches to the heavy-gauge wire "spine." Start by wiring the end of one branch to the center of the spine. Slide the end of the second branch under the needles of the first branch, and wire it to the spine. Continue wiring branches on in this manner until you reach the end of the spine. Then start at the center of the spine and wire on branches from it to the other end. The spine will be completely covered by branches when you are finished.

Step Two

Wire the juniper and cedar branches to the garland with the fine-gauge wire, spacing them evenly down its length.

Step Three

Make five to seven bunches of holly sprigs, with three to four sprigs per bunch. Wire the holly bunches evenly along the garland.

Step Four

Wrap the ribbon around the garland, in a spiral pattern, hot-gluing in place where necessary. Hot-glue the lotus pods and lichens evenly along the garland.

CATTAIL HAT

Light, airy, and rakish, a cattail hat is superb protection from spring rains and summer sun.

MATERIALS

60 dried cattail leaves
Garden hose with spray
    setting
Spray mister
Ruler or tape measure
Hat stand or wig form
Lazy Susan (optional)
Size J crochet hook (optional)

STEP ONE

Six to 12 hours before you plan to weave, wet the dried leaves down with a garden hose, using a gentle spray setting, and cover them with a towel, to make them flexible enough to weave with. Keep a spray mister filled with water close at hand while you weave, so you can keep the leaves moist at all times.

STEP TWO

Lay eight cattail leaves side by side, about 1 inch (2.5 cm) apart, on a flat surface. Alternate the butt (wide) and tip (narrow) ends (see Figure 1).

STEP THREE

Select eight more leaves to weave through the center of the first group, to make a square mat that will be the top of the hat. Again, alternate the butt and the tip ends. You can use a simple over-and-under weave (see the three cattails at the top of Figure 1) and have a very good hat. Or you can try a twill weave.

A twill weave is simply an over-two-and-under-two weave (see Figure 2). In order to produce the stair-step look, each horizontal weaver must start out differently before it goes into its over-two-and-under-two pattern. Here's the pattern (see Figure 1):

Weaver #1 starts *over two*, then goes under two, over two, under two, and so on.

Weaver #2 starts *over one*, then goes under two, over two, under two, and so on.

Weaver #3 starts *under two*, then over two, under two, and so on. Weaver #4 starts *under one*, then over two, under two, and so on.

The fifth weaver repeats the pattern of weaver #1. The sixth repeats the pattern of weaver #2, and so on.

FIGURE 1

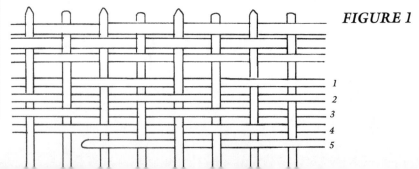

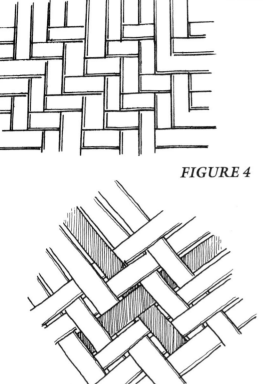

FIGURE 2

FIGURE 3

FIGURE 4

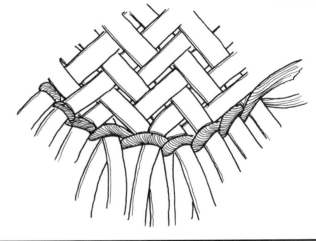

FIGURE 5

STEP FOUR

As you weave, push all the weavers together so you have a nice, tight weave. Weave until your flat, woven mat measures about 6 × 6 inches (15 × 15 cm). The dimensions are less critical (head sizes vary) than the shape. Measure it; if it's not square, add an extra weaver on one side or take one out on the other to square it up. The ends of these cattails will be the "spokes" around which you weave the rest of the hat. Be sure the leaves are still moist.

STEP FIVE

Now "twine" around your square mat, to hold the weave together. Twining is done with a weaver that's folded in half, to make two shorter weavers. They go over one and under one, crossing between each pair of spokes (see Figure 3). When you twine with cattails, the process of twisting the weavers

DESIGNER'S TIP

GATHERING AND PREPARING CATTAIL LEAVES

Mature, full-size cattail leaves are the most suitable for weaving. They mature in mid-to late summer in most temperate regions, where- upon their tips usually turn tan or brown.

To gather cattail leaves, wade fearlessly into the swamp (or along the drainage ditch or duck marsh), armed with a sharp knife and some string. Cut each cluster of leaves at or below the water level, and carefully lay them in neat piles on the bank (or on other cattails), trying not to bend or break the leaves. When you have gathered 30 clusters—enough for a hat— tie them into a neat bundle,

wrapping them along their entire length with string, taking care not to bend or break the leaves.

When you get home, separate the leaves. A cluster usually has a couple of older, brown outer leaves, a couple of tender, young inner leaves, and two to six leaves in between—your future weavers. Carefully spread these mature leaves out to dry in a warm, dry, airy place, and leave them for two weeks. Move them about a few times during this peri- od to ensure even drying.

When the leaves are dry, carefully bind them together loosely until you're ready to use them.

between the spokes makes the weavers look narrow and round (see the photo on page 96).

As you twine around the perimeter of your woven mat (either clockwise or counterclockwise), round off the corners. To round off the corners, count three spokes back from a corner in each direction (see Figure 4 on page 97). Then join pairs of corner spokes, twining around them in three sets of two (see Figure 5 on page 97). Twine once more around the woven top.

When a weaver runs out, insert the ends into previously twined rows (see Figure 6). Start the new weaver by looping it around the adjacent spoke.

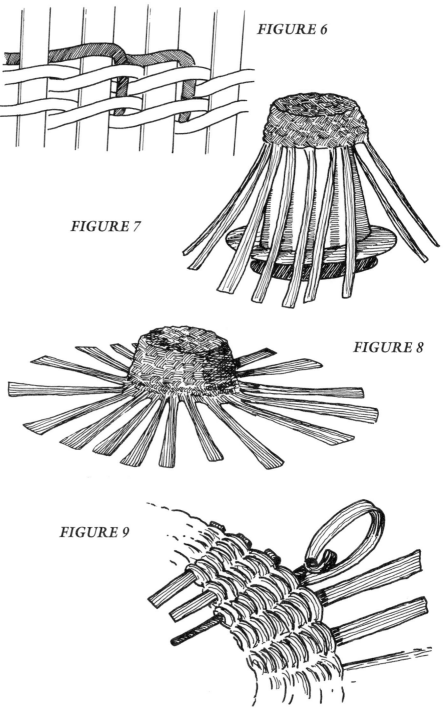

FIGURE 6

FIGURE 7

FIGURE 8

FIGURE 9

STEP SIX

To weave the rest of the crown and the brim, put the hat on a hat stand or wig form. It's convenient, but not essential, to put the stand on a lazy Susan, so you can turn the hat as you weave (see Figure 7).

Cut the long "spokes" radiating from the top of the hat to about 20 inches (50 cm), and fold them down around the form. Twine two more rows, then add a row of the flat over-and-under weave with an unfolded cattail leaf, if you like. Resume twining with a new cattail.

STEP SEVEN

Check the fit occasionally by trying the hat on. If it's too large, tighten the weave by twining over and under two spokes instead of one. If it's too small, spread the corner pairs of spokes—the ones you joined earlier at the corners—and start weaving them as individuals. Continue twining until the crown is the desired height. (Try it on. How does it look?) Use the spray mister to keep the leaves moist.

STEP EIGHT

Set the hat on a flat surface, and spread the spokes out (see Figure 8). Continue twining until the brim is the desired width. Then trim the spokes so that their remaining ends are about 1 inch (2.5 cm) longer than the width of the brim, and insert the ends back through the twined brim (see Figure 9). You can use the crochet hook to help pull the spokes through.

STEP NINE

While the hat is still wet, shape the brim into the desired style, bending and folding it. The hat will hold its shape when it dries. If, in the cold light of morning, you realize the shape was a fashion error, just rewet and reshape the hat.

Coconut Frond Basket

Wherever coconut palms grow, people make baskets from them. Lightweight and easy to weave, palm baskets are valued from southern Florida to the South Seas. When harvesting coconut fronds, avoid stressing the palm tree; harvest only one frond per tree. Don't cut a second frond from the same palm until several new fronds have appeared.

STEP ONE

Using the large knife, lopping shears, or pruning saw, cut a young frond from the center of the palm tree.

STEP TWO

Using the large knife, split the midrib (the central vein of the frond) in half all the way down its length, starting at the tip of the frond. Set half of the frond

FIGURE 1

aside. From the half you're going to use, cut a 16-inch (41 cm) long section of midrib, taking it from the central section where the leaflets are about equal in length. Using the carving knife, shave the midrib until it is thin and flexible (see Figure 1).

STEP THREE

Using the carving knife, cut two

MATERIALS

Large, sharp knife, lopping
   shears, or tree-pruning saw
Palm frond, with leaflets
   attached
Carving knife
String
Rubber bands (optional)
Clothespins
Scissors

pairs of notches at each end of the midrib (see Figure 2). Make sure the notches at each end are the same distance apart— between 1 and 2 inches (2.5 and 5 cm). Bend the midrib into a circle, with the leaflets on the outside, and overlap the ends so that the notches are aligned. Using the notches to anchor the string, tie the two ends together (see Figure 3). The hoop formed by the midrib will be the "foot" of the basket.

STEP FOUR

To weave the walls of the basket, place the hoop so that the rib of each leaflet is facing up. Choose one leaflet on the side away from you and, weaving in the direction in which the "weaver" leaflet is pointed, weave it under the adjacent leaflet, over the second one, under the third, then under the midrib and up inside the hoop.

STEP FIVE

Continue around the circle in the direction the leaflets are pointing, weaving each succeeding leaflet as you did the first (see Figure 4), until they are all neatly woven. Check to see that you have woven each leaflet in order, and pull gently on each one to tighten the weave (see Figure 5). Then go around the walls several times, pulling each leaflet and gently forcing the walls into a bowl shape.

FIGURE 2

FIGURE 3

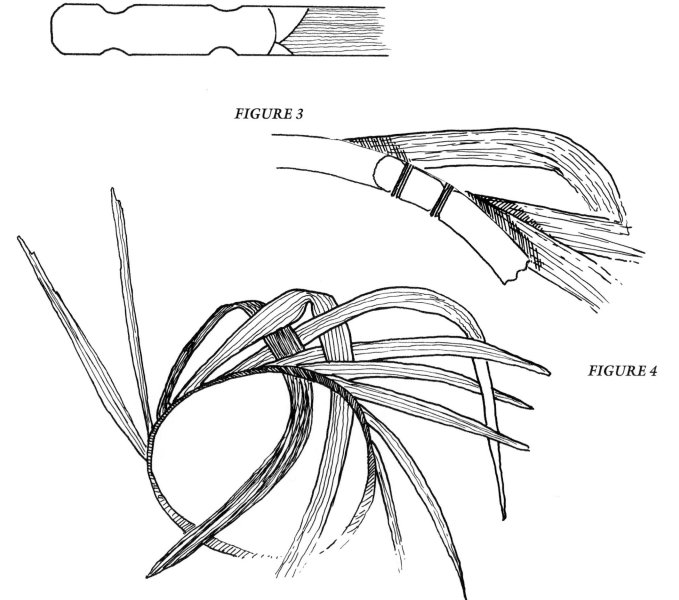

FIGURE 4

STEP SIX

To make the bottom of the basket, pick up the leaflets one at a time and hold them upright and parallel. When you have half of them, fasten them together with a rubber band or a piece of string. Gather and fasten the other half of the leaflets. (If you have an odd number, there's no problem. When you weave the bottom, start weaving with the smaller bundle.)

STEP SEVEN

Begin weaving the bottom of the basket with a leaflet on the far side of a bundle. Pull the leaflet loose from the rubber band and bring it over all the leaflets in the second bundle except the last; weave it under that last leaflet, and hold it in place by clipping it to the midrib with a clothespin.

Now return to the first bundle, select the leaflet adjacent to the one you just wove, and bring it over the leaflets in the second bundle, weaving it under the next-to-the-last leaflet in the second bundle. (Figure 6 shows the basic sequence.) Continue in this sequence until the first bundle is woven, then weave the second bundle through the first in the same manner.

STEP EIGHT

After all the leaflets are woven, tighten the weave by pulling on the loose ends one at a time until the leaflets are flat. Check again to see that they are all lying flat and untwisted and that they were woven in order.

STEP NINE

Weave the end of each leaflet around the foot of the basket, if there are any holes in the weave, or up into the sides.

Follow the weave and end the weaver leaflet on the inside of the bowl. Clip off any excess ends with scissors.

FIGURE 5

FIGURE 6

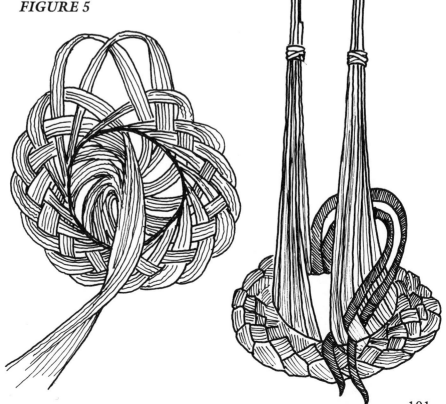

Bark Box

With its snugly fitting and almost invisible lid, this simple bark box is a marvelous project for a craftsperson with a few power tools. Since both unfinished bark and sanded surfaces will be visible, look for wood with interesting bark and an attractive grain. Most important, the wood must be seasoned well enough that it will not shrink or check (that is, split or crack) any further. Used fenceposts are excellent sources. In their absence, look for old piles of firewood or standing dead trees. (The box in the photograph is made of Rocky Mountain bristlecone pine.)

Step One

Choose one end of the wood to be the bottom of the box and flatten it on a table sander. Then, using a fence on the band saw, saw the other end of the wood (the top) so it is parallel to the bottom.

Step Two

Cut a 1/2-inch (1.25 cm) thick slice from the bottom and a 3/4-inch (2 cm) slice from the top. With the table sander, sand the cut surfaces of all three pieces smooth.

Step Three

Stand the body of the box on its bottom and choose a check or prominent section of grain that's straight and vertical. At that point, saw into the side of the body about 1/2 inch with the band saw. Then turn the cut as sharply as possible, and cut around the inside perimeter of the body, leaving extra wood in weak areas. When you return to your entrance point, exit through it.

Step Four

Remove the center plug of wood and saw off a 3/8-inch (2 cm) slice from the top.

Step Five

Apply a thin line of wood glue along the cut in the side of the body and force the glue inside the cut with the putty knife or spatula. Use the band clamp or other strong clamp to hold the cut closed. Wipe any excess glue from the inside and the outside with a clean rag, and allow to dry. If there are other deep checks in the wood, repair them at the same time in a similar fashion.

Step Six

Position the body upside down on the lid—the 3/4-inch-thick

MATERIALS

5-inch (12 cm) length of seasoned wood, about 4 inches (10 cm) in diameter
Table sander
Band saw
1/4-inch (6 mm) four-tooth, skip-tooth band saw blade
Wood glue
Small putty knife or spatula
Band clamp or other strong clamp
Clean rag
40-, 80-, 100-, 120-, 180-, and 320-grit sandpaper
Orbital sander
Semigloss lacquer and lacquer brush, or Danish finishing oil
Soft cloth

slice you cut in Step 3—matching the grain of the two pieces. Spread a thin layer of glue on the sanded side of the 3/8-inch slice you cut from the center plug in Step 5 and drop it down the center of the body onto the lid, glue-side down. Remove the body from the lid and clamp the slice to the lid,

being careful not to move it. Allow to dry. Glue the bottom to the body and allow to dry.

STEP SEVEN

Using the table sander and 40-grit sandpaper, round off the edges of the top and bottom, producing rounded curves. Then sand the top and bottom smooth. Sand with 80-, then 120-grit paper on the table sander. Then, for glassy smoothness, sand with the orbital sander, using 100-, then 180-, then 320-grit sandpaper.

STEP EIGHT

If the wood is porous—cedar, aspen, or basswood, for example—apply a coat of lacquer with a lacquer brush and rub off the excess with a soft cloth. If the wood is dense—oak, walnut, or hickory, for instance—apply a coat of Danish finishing oil, using a soft cloth.

BARK BASKET

Bark containers are light, attractive, and easy to make. Depending on their size, they can serve as backpacks, fruit baskets, waste baskets, purses, or clothes hampers. The small one shown here makes an excellent wall pocket for holding dried flowers.

STEP ONE

Lay the bark flat, with the outer side facing up. Using the pencil, draw the centerline 8 inches from each short end. Using this line as a reference point, draw a curved line on each side of it, creating an elongated football shape 2 inches (5 cm) wide in the center and tapering to a point on each end (see Figure 1). The "football" will be the bottom of the basket.

MATERIALS

Piece of bark, about 16 inches (41 cm) long and 8 inches (20 cm) wide
Pencil
Sharp knife
Felt-tip pen
Gouge, awl, or rotary leather punch
2 32-inch (80 cm) lengths of bark lacing, 1/16 inch (1 mm) wide (see "Making Bark Lacing" on page 87)
1/2-inch (1.3 cm) diameter piece of flat reed or wood splint, 18 to 19 inches (46 to 48 cm) long
3-foot (0.9 m) length of bark lacing, 1/16 inch wide
2 4-inch (10 cm) lengths of bark lacing, 1/16 inch wide (optional)

STEP TWO

Using the knife, score along the two curved lines, cutting just through the outer bark. Turn over the piece of bark so the outer side is down. Carefully fold the bark along the two curved lines, with the inner bark on the inside, creating a front and back (see Figure 2).

FIGURE 1

FIGURE 2

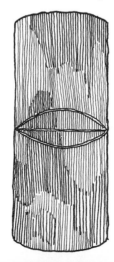

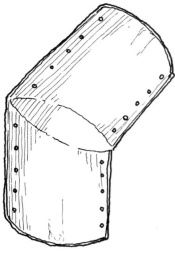

FIGURE 3

STEP THREE

In order to lace the front of the basket to the back, you'll need five pairs of holes opposite each other, on the right and left sides of the basket. Lay the bark flat again and, using the felt-tip pen, mark where the holes will go. Make sure the holes on the front piece and those on the back piece line up, and that the holes are about 1 inch (2.5 cm) in from the edge. Then use the gouge, awl, or punch to make the holes where marked (see Figure 3).

STEP FOUR

To make holes for the lacing around the top of the basket, mark and then punch a row of holes 1 inch apart and 3/4 inch (2 cm) from each end of the piece of bark in the same manner as before.

STEP FIVE

Fold the basket together, so that the back piece is slightly overlapping the front. Using a 32-inch piece of lacing, lace up one side as you would a pair of shoes (see Figure 4). Repeat with the second piece of 32-inch lacing on the other side. Tie a knot at the top of each side, on the inside of the basket.

STEP SIX

Using the knife, whittle the rim of the basket until it's smooth. Bend the flat reed into an oval shape and fit it inside the rim of the basket. Whipstitch the 3-foot piece of lacing through the holes and around the reed to hold the reed in place (see Figure 5). Finish with a knot inside the basket. If desired, mark and punch a pair of holes on each side of the basket and lace a 4-inch piece of lacing through each pair, knotting each end inside the basket, to serve as loops for a strap.

FIGURE 4

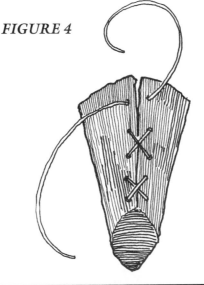

FIGURE 5

LEAF PRINT

MATERIALS

2 pieces of construction paper
    or sketch pad paper
Leaves in a variety of shapes
Flowers in a variety of shapes
    and colors
Pencil
Flat, 1-inch (2.5 cm) wide
    paintbrush
Tempera or poster paints in
    the same colors as the leaves
    and flowers
Box of tissues
Artist's paintbrush with
    pointed tip
Scissors
About 1-1/2 yards (1.4 m)
    fabric
Iron
Glue gun
Needle and thread or sewing
    machine

If you have ever longed to transfer the transitory beauty of leaves and flowers directly onto paper, a leaf print will let you do that. The one shown here displays ferns, beech leaves, and bay leaves to good advantage, along with dogwood blossoms, pansies, and daisies.

STEP ONE

On one of the pieces of paper, lay out the leaves and flowers in an arrangement that pleases you. If the foliage gets the paper dirty or damp when you do this, make the finished print on the second sheet.

STEP TWO

To give you a rough guide to follow, use the pencil to lightly draw a circle on the paper.

(Tracing around a dinner plate is helpful.) Pencil a dot at the top and bottom of the circle.

STEP THREE

Using the flat paintbrush, brush paint onto the surface of a leaf, and place it carefully on the circle. Take care not to move it around, or the paint will smudge and blur the shape. Cover the leaf with a tissue and lightly smooth it down with your hand. Lift the tissue and peel off the leaf.

STEP FOUR

Repeat the process described in Step 3 with the other leaves and flowers, working your way around the circle. It is simpler to print only the petals of the flowers. When the paint is dry, you can go back and paint the center with the pointed artist's brush. Feel free to print some items on top of others–for example, a pansy over the base of a fern. Make sure that the first color is dry before you overprint a second one.

STEP FIVE

Using the flat paintbrush, fill in any areas that did not print or did not print well.

STEP SIX

If desired, make a fabric frame for the print, along with a set of matching napkins. Using the scissors, cut four 1-1/2-inch (4 cm) wide strips of fabric on the bias. Cut two of the strips the length of the paper and two strips 2 inches longer than the width.

Wrong sides together, fold each strip of fabric in half down its length and press it closed, to create a crease down the middle. Reopen the strip, then fold under each long side so the edges fall on the middle crease. Press closed. Sandwich each of the folded strips down one side of the paper and hot-glue it in place. Cover the shorter sides of the paper first and wrap the extra inch of fabric around the edge. Then glue on the long strips.

Use the remaining fabric to make four napkins. Cut four pieces of fabric to the dimensions desired, either square or rectangular. Make a double hem by folding under 1/4 inch (6 mm) on all four sides, then folding 1/4 inch under again. Hand sew or machine stitch in place.

LEAF DESK SET

Leaves that have been preserved with glycerin are supple enough to arrange into any number of lovely shapes and patterns. An interesting variety of glycerin-preserved leaves is available in larger craft stores.

STEP ONE

Gently remove the leaves from their stems and experiment with their placement on the object you plan to decorate. When you're happy with the design, brush a thin layer of glue onto the backs of the leaves and gently press them in place.

STEP TWO

Add color to the leaf design by gluing on small pieces of red plaid ribbon. If the object you're decorating will not be protected with glass or plastic, apply a protective layer of clear acrylic spray.

MATERIALS

Glycerin-preserved leaves
Objects to decorate (a picture frame, address book, note paper, and wooden trinket box are shown here)
White craft glue
Small paintbrush
Narrow red plaid ribbon (optional)
Clear acrylic spray (optional)

Sticks, Saplings, and Vines

Gathering sticks, saplings, and vines is simplicity itself. Sticks litter the forest floor, vines hang from trees and fences, young saplings spring up where you don't want them to flourish. Just get out your hand clippers and pruning shears, and clear.

The only harvesting requirement is to match the materials to the project. If you're planning a rigid wreath base of twigs, don't gather limp little limbs. If you want to curl vines into a round, graceful wreath base, don't gather dry, aged vines that can't bend without breaking. For most projects, saplings and vines should be worked with when fresh, while they're still pliable. If you're gathering grapevine for a wreath base, leave those curly tendrils on the vine—they add grace and charm.

One note of caution: There's poison ivy out there, and if you're allergic to it, you will react to the vines much as you react to the leaves. It's prudent to note the locations of this nasty plant in the summer, when its leaves will warn you away. In winter you might want to leave anonymous vines alone. Otherwise, you may itch for a handsome vine wreath—literally.

ENGLISH VINE TRELLIS

This remarkably simple project provides splendid support to flowering vines or climbing roses.

STEP ONE

Lay two of the sticks on a flat surface, parallel to each other and about 20 inches (50 cm) apart. Lay the other two sticks at equal intervals between them, so you have four sticks lying about 7 inches (18 cm) apart.

STEP TWO

To create temporary spreaders, nail the pieces of wood lath to the four sticks, one across the top and one across the bottom, with each lath about 2 inches (5 cm) from the ends of the sticks.

STEP THREE

Working in a 10-inch (25 cm) wide strip across the middle, weave the vines over and under the sticks, using a loose, ran-

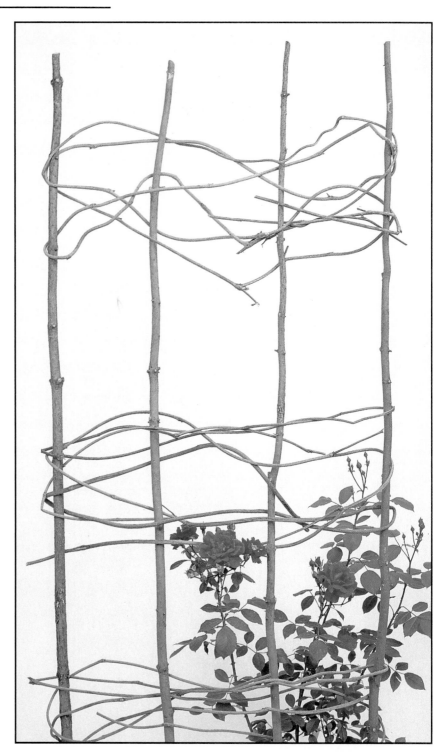

MATERIALS

4 fairly straight 5-foot (1.5 m) long sticks, 1 to 1-1/2 inches (2.5 to 4 cm) in diameter
Hammer
24 3/4-inch (2 cm) headless finishing nails
2 3-foot (0.9 m) pieces of wood lath
About 50 feet (15.4 m) of green vines, such as honeysuckle or wild grape, 1/4 to 1/2 inch (6 mm to 1.3 cm) in diameter

dom pattern, until you have woven from side to side five or six times. Weave similar areas across the bottom and the top of the sticks.

STEP FOUR

Nail a few of the vines to the four sticks where they intersect them and remove the laths. Your trellis is now ready for the garden.

RUSTIC TWIG PLANTER

STEP THREE

Nail one 4-inch twig horizontally to the two vertical 4-inch twigs at each end of the planter. Place a 14-inch twig horizontally on each side and nail to the vertical 4-inch twigs.

STEP FOUR

Press pieces of sheet and sphagnum mosses into the vertical spaces between the twigs and hot-glue as needed. Arrange the mushrooms around the planter and hot-glue in place. Lower three potted plants into the planter and pack the areas around their stems with moss.

FIGURE 1

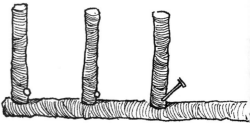

MATERIALS

4 twigs, 1/2 inch in diameter, trimmed to 14 inches (36 cm)
12 twigs, 1/2 inch (1.3 cm) in diameter, trimmed to 4 inches (10 cm)
Small nails
Hammer
Glue gun
2 handfuls of sheet moss
Sphagnum moss
Several dried mushrooms
3 small potted plants (daffodils are shown in the photo)

Designed to hold three small potted plants, this versatile twig planter can be used indoors or out, and the flowers can be changed with the seasons.

STEP ONE

Place two of the 14-inch twigs parallel to each other and 4 inches apart on a flat surface. Nail a 4-inch twig at each end, connecting the two 14-inch twigs. This is the base of the planter.

STEP TWO

Position a 4-inch twig in a vertical position on top of one of the 14-inch twigs at either end and every 3-1/2 inches (8 cm) and nail in place (see Figure 1). Turn the planter around and repeat the process on the other 14-inch twig and 4-inch twigs.

WOVEN BACKPACK

Weaving a backpack of ash splints is a traditional craft that flourished in the Adirondack Mountains and elsewhere in the northeastern United States. This backpack is woven of flat reed, available from any craft store that carries basket-weaving or chair-caning supplies. The well-padded, detachable shoulder straps can be purchased from a camping supplies store.

MATERIALS

14 5-foot (1.5 m) lengths of 3/4-inch (2 cm) flat reed
142 feet (44 m) of 1/2-inch (1.3 cm) flat reed
4-1/2-foot (1.4 m) length of 1-inch (2.5 cm) flat reed
4-1/2-foot length of 3/4-inch flat reed
24-foot (7.4 m) length of 1/4-inch (6 mm) flat reed
Bucket
Warm water
Hammer
7 8-penny nails
8 × 11-inch (20 × 27 cm) board, 1 inch thick
2 11 × 21-inch (27 × 53 cm) boards, 1 inch thick
5 × 7-inch (12 × 17 cm) board, 1 inch thick
String
Pocketknife
2 4-foot (1.2 m) lengths of hickory bark lacing, 3/4 inch wide (see "Making Bark Lacing," on page 87)
1 pair of detachable canvas shoulder straps
3 feet (0.9 m) of 1-inch-diameter nylon webbing (optional)

STEP ONE

Soak all the reeds in warm water for about 30 minutes, or until they are moist and flexible.

STEP TWO

For easiest weaving and best results, weave the backpack over a form. To make the form, nail the 8 × 11-inch board atop the two 11 × 21-inch ones (see Figure 1).

STEP THREE

Lay eight of the 5-foot lengths of reed—the struts—parallel to, and about 1/4 inch away from, each other. (In the illustrations, the spaces between the pieces of reed have been exaggerated in order to show the weave.) Weave the other six struts through them in an over-and-under pattern (see Figure 2), starting about 2 feet (60 cm) down from the top of the 5-foot reeds. Make sure to stagger the weave so that two successive weavers do not go over (or under) the same strut. The woven area—which will become the bottom of the backpack—should be about 8 × 11 inches.

STEP FOUR

Lay the woven area on top of the form and nail the 5 × 7-inch board on top of the woven area, making sure the nail goes between, not *through*, two struts (see Figure 3). The board will hold the woven bottom of the backpack in place while you weave the sides. Don't hammer the nail all the way in, or it will be difficult to remove later.

STEP FIVE

Bend all of the struts down the side of the form, and tie them temporarily in place with string (see Figure 4). To produce an

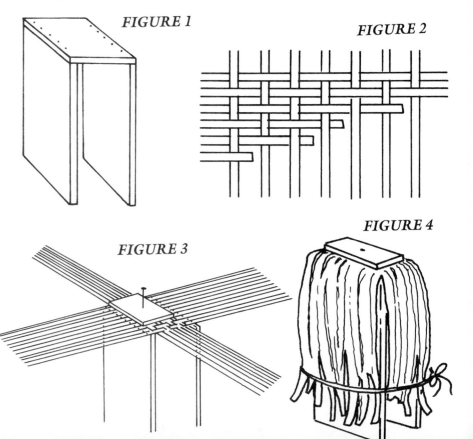

FIGURE 1

FIGURE 2

FIGURE 3

FIGURE 4

you want a shorter backpack, of course, stop sooner.) When the sides of the basket are woven, discard the string and remove the backpack from the form. Bend the tops of the struts to the inside and tuck them into the woven area.

STEP EIGHT

To make the rim of the basket, lay the 4-1/2-foot length of 1-inch reed along the upper edge of the outside of the backpack; lay the 4-1/2-foot length of 3/4-inch reed on the inside, with the backpack sandwiched between the reeds. Wrap the 24 feet of 1/4-inch reed around the inner and outer rims, threading the reed between every two struts, slanting the wraps in the same direction (see Figure 6 on page 114). When the rim is wrapped in one direction, turn the reed around a strut, reverse directions, and wrap back around the rim, creating a series of X's.

STEP NINE

Using the pocketknife, cut a 2-foot piece of 1/2-inch reed and taper both its ends. About 3 inches from the top of the basket, weave one end of the reed under and over four or five struts on what will be the back of the pack. Lay the reed over five or six struts, then weave the other end as you did the first (see Figure 7 on page 114), to make an anchor for the straps.

STEP TEN

Starting in the center of the anchor reed, wrap the hickory lacing around the anchor reed and the basket weaver it is lying on top of, wrapping from the center about 6 inches to the left (see Figure 8 on page 114).

odd number of struts, select one near a corner and split it from its end to the woven area, using the pocketknife.

STEP SIX

Insert one end of a piece of 1/2-inch reed behind a strut, right next to the woven bottom of the backpack. Select a strut that's about 1 inch from a corner. Weave the 1/2-inch reed horizontally, taking the weavers over and under the struts.

Weave continuously up the sides, rather than making separate rows. When a weaver is 2 or 3 inches (5 or 8 cm) from its end, lay a second weaver on top of it and weave both of them over and under, treating them as one weaver. This tucks both the old and new weavers neatly into the basket (see Figure 5 on page 114).

STEP SEVEN

Weave until there are 3 or 4 inches of struts left bare. (If

Then weave the lacing diagonally down the side of the basket toward the left front corner, passing the lacing under horizontal weavers as you go (see Figure 9). When you reach the left front corner, weave the lacing diagonally across the bottom to the right back corner (see Figure 10). At the back right corner, form the lacing into a loop about 2 inches in diameter, wrap the lacing several times around the closest strut, and tie a knot on the end. The bottom of the shoulder straps will attach to this loop.

STEP ELEVEN

Repeat Step 10 for the other side of the basket. Starting in the center of the anchor reed, wrap the lacing about 6 inches to the right. Then weave the lacing diagonally down the side of the basket toward the right front corner, then diagonally across the bottom to the left back corner, and end the lacing by forming a 2-inch-diameter loop. Secure this loop in the same manner as you did the first loop.

STEP TWELVE

Attach the shoulder straps to the anchor reed at the top and to the loops at the bottom, using the nylon webbing streamers and metal buckles that come on the straps. If you're feeling exuberant, wrap a colorful length of nylon webbing around the pack. You can tie a few extra items to the webbing while you're hiking.

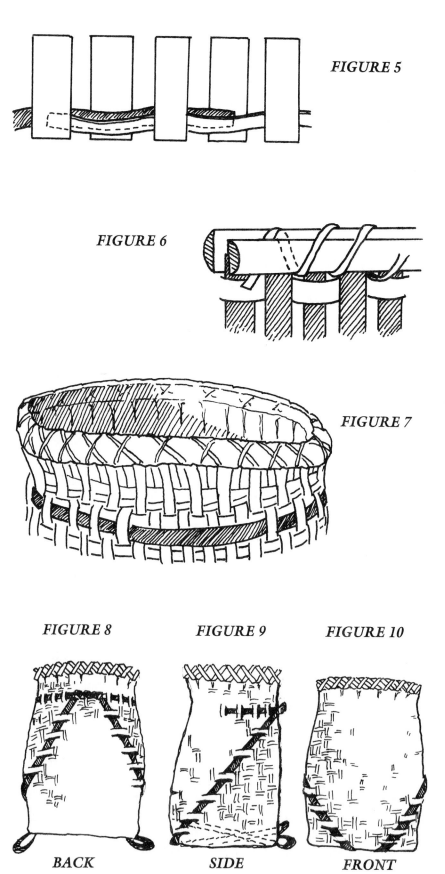

FIGURE 5

FIGURE 6

FIGURE 7

FIGURE 8   *FIGURE 9*   *FIGURE 10*

BACK   *SIDE*   *FRONT*

MARKET BASKET

Baskets are among the most useful and the most well-loved handcrafted items. At first glance their construction looks indecipherable, but in fact, basket weaving is an orderly, logical craft. Learning to make a basket is a most satisfying skill to master.

STEP ONE

In the bucket, mix the blue fabric dye according to the package directions, and dye a 9-foot (2.7 m) long piece of 5/8-inch flat reed a deep blue. Rinse and set aside.

STEP TWO

Cut 14 27-inch (68 cm) long pieces of 1-inch flat reed with the scissors. These are your stakes. With a pencil, mark the centers of two stakes with an X on the wrong side. (The wrong

MATERIALS

Large bucket
Blue liquid fabric dye
1 hank of 5/8-inch (1.5 cm) flat reed
1/2 hank of 1-inch (2.5 cm) flat reed
Scissors
Pencil
Tape measure or ruler
46-inch (1.2 m) length of 1/2-inch (1.3 cm) flat reed

Notched basket handle with a 10-inch (25 cm) span
2 45-inch (1.2 m) lengths of 5/8-inch flat oval reed
Small plane or pocketknife
4 to 6 clothespins
43-inch (1.1 m) piece of sea lyme grass
11-foot (3.4 m) length of 1/4-inch (6 mm) flat reed
Awl (optional)

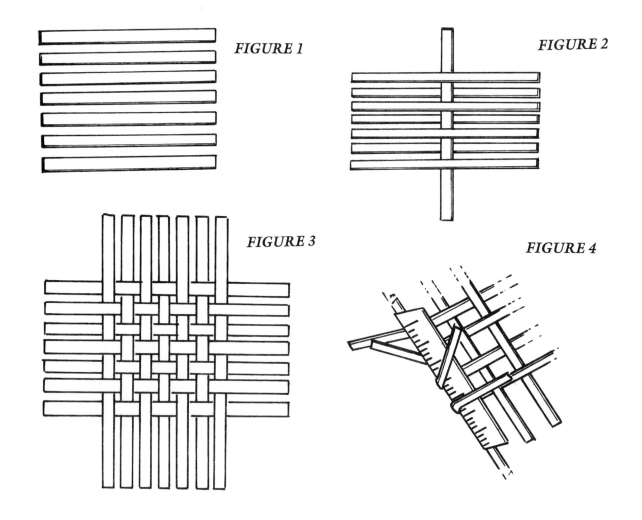

FIGURE 1

FIGURE 2

FIGURE 3

FIGURE 4

side is the rough side.) Soak all 14 stakes for 1 or 2 minutes in a bucket of cool water.

STEP THREE

Lay seven of the stakes horizontally on a flat surface, about 3/8 inch (1 cm) apart, with a marked stake in the middle (see Figure 1). Weave the other marked stake over and under the first seven, going up the middle and matching the two center marks (see Figure 2). Weave the remaining six stakes over and under in a similar fashion, with three on each side of the middle one, being certain the weaving alternates with every row. That is, two adjacent stakes must not go over or under the same horizontal stake (see Figure 3). You have now woven the bot-

tom of the basket. With a tape measure or ruler, check to see that it is square. It will be about 9 × 9 inches (22 × 22 cm).

STEP FOUR

To "upsett" the sides of the basket—that is, to make the stakes stand upright—bend each stake all the way over on itself, to form a permanent crease in the stake right next to where it meets another stake. It is helpful to press the stakes over a ruler to make the creases (see Figure 4).

STEP FIVE

Soak a long strip of 5/8-inch flat reed for 1 to 2 minutes in a bucket of cool water. This is your first "weaver." Place one end of the wet weaver on the

outside of one of the stakes on the bottom of the basket that originate from under the weaving as you look down into the bottom (see Figure 5). (The advantage of beginning here is to hold the bottom stakes upright first. The next row of weaving will pick up all the other stakes.) Weave with the smooth side of the weaver on the outside of the basket, and weave under and over the stakes. When you have woven all the way around the basket, weave over the original weaving for four more stakes, and cut the weaver behind the fourth stake (see Figure 6).

STEP SIX

Soak seven more long pieces of 5/8-inch flat reed for one to two minutes in a bucket of cool water. Take one piece and begin weaving the next row, as described in Step 5, starting on a different side of the basket to prevent one side from ending up too thick. Continue weaving the other six wet weavers, starting each on a different side of the basket. Make sure the rows alternate their over-and-under pattern around the stakes, and push each completed row down snugly against the previous one. Then weave a row with the dyed weaver in the same fashion. Finally, weave in one row of 1/2-inch flat reed—the "false weaver" that will lie underneath the rim.

STEP SEVEN

When you finish weaving, you will note that half of the stakes are under the last weaver and half are over it. Wet the top part of the stakes again. Cut the stakes that are under the last weaver so they are even with the weaver. Then cut the stakes that are over the last weaver so they taper to a point. Bend the pointed stakes to the inside of the basket and tuck them into the weaving (see Figure 7). Be sure each pointed end is hidden behind a weaver.

STEP EIGHT

Insert the basket handle into the weaving on the inside of the basket. Make sure the two sides of the handle are in front of two middle stakes on opposite sides of the basket. The handle should go over the false weaver, colored weaver, and one more weaver, then go under alternate rows of weaving (see Figure 8). Align the notch with the bottom of the false weaver. The rim will "sit" on the notch and prevent the handle from pulling out.

FIGURE 5

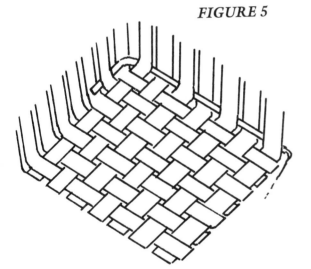

FIGURE 6

FIGURE 7

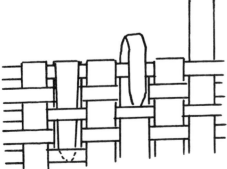

FIGURE 8

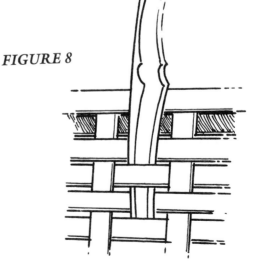

STEP NINE

Soak the two pieces of flat oval reed for one to two minutes in a bucket of cool water. Wrap one strip around the inside top edge of the basket, covering only the false weaver. This is the inside rim. Overlap the ends by about 3 inches (8 cm) and cut. Using the small plane or pocketknife, shave some of the thickness from the over-lapped area. Hold the reed in place with clothespins. Then wrap the second piece of 5/8-inch flat oval reed around the outside of the basket, so that it lies over the false weaver. Again, overlap the ends by about 3 inches and cut. Position the overlapped area near, but not on top of, the overlapped area of the inside rim. Hold both rims in place with the same clothespins (see Figure 9). Shave the over-lapped ends of the outside rim as before. Lay the piece of sea lyme grass between the two rim pieces, allowing the ends to overlap 1-1/2 inches (4 cm). When you come to the han-dles, take the sea lyme grass to the outside of each handle, then back between the rims.

FIGURE 9

FIGURE 10

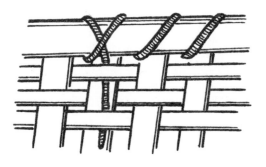

STEP TEN

Soak the piece of 1/4-inch flat reed for one to two minutes in a bucket of cool water. Lash all the rim pieces together with the 1/4-inch reed (see Figure 10). If necessary, use an awl to open a space for the lasher just under the rim, between the stakes. Tuck the ends into the weaving or between the rim pieces, so that the lashing does not pull out.

RUSTIC CHILD'S CHAIR

All sorts of useful and attractive furniture can be made out of sticks, saplings, logs, roots, and even stumps. This simple chair project will show you the basics of stick joinery using the mortise-and-tenon (or peg-in-hole) method. This works best with sticks that have been set aside to dry for several months. But you can also build from fresh-cut wood by using nails or screws. The most important rule to follow when "going rustic" is to let your materials guide your design.

STEP ONE

Secure one of the back posts in a vise and make pencil marks along the stick in a straight line at points 4 inches (10 cm), 8 inches (20 cm), 11 inches, and 21 inches (47 cm) from the bottom end. Drill 1/2-inch (1.3 cm) holes 1/2 inch deep at each mark. Do the same with the other back post.

MATERIALS

2 sticks for back posts, 22
   inches (55 cm) long and
   1 inch (2.5 cm) in diameter
Vise
Pencil
Electric drill with 1/2-inch and
   3/8-inch drill bits
4 sticks for back rungs, 10-1/4
   inches (26 cm) long and 3/4
   inch (2 cm) in diameter
Sharp carving knife
Wood glue
Twine
Scrap stick
2 sticks for front posts,
   13 inches (33 cm) long
   and 1 inch in diameter
2 sticks for front rungs,
   13-1/2 inches (34.25 cm)
   long and 3/4 inch in
   diameter
4 sticks for side rungs,
   8-3/4 inches (22 cm)
2 sticks for arms, 12 inches
   (30 cm) long and 1 inch
   in diameter
Scrap twig
Mallet
2 slender forked twigs, about
   11 inches (27 cm) long
50 feet (15.25 m) of cloth seating tape, 5/8 inch
   (1.5 cm) wide
Small tacks

FIGURE 1

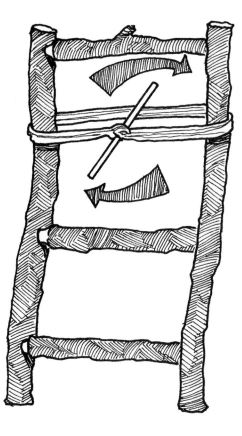

STEP TWO

Use the knife to whittle tenons (pegs) 1/2 inch long and 1/2 inch in diameter on both ends of the four back rungs. The tenons should not be tapered and should fit tightly in the 1/2-inch holes drilled in the back posts.

STEP THREE

When all the tenons fit snugly, glue them into the holes on the two back posts to create the ladderlike structure that will form the back of the chair. Make a "tourniquet" clamp by wrapping a piece of twine several times around the two posts, tying the ends together, and tightening it with a stick used as a winder (see Figure 1). Set the back aside to dry.

STEP FOUR

Secure one of the front posts in a vise and make pencil marks along the stick in a straight line at points 3 inches (7.5 cm) and 8-1/4 inches (21 cm) from the bottom. Drill 1/2-inch holes 1/2 inch deep at each mark. Do the same with the other front post.

STEP FIVE

Use the knife to whittle tenons 1/2 inch long and 1/2 inch in diameter on both ends of the two front rungs. The tenons should not be tapered and should fit tightly in the 1/2-inch holes drilled in the front posts.

STEP SIX

When all the tenons fit snugly, glue them into the holes on the two front posts. Secure with a tourniquet clamp and set aside to dry.

STEP SEVEN

When all the joints have dried, lay the back assembly on a work table. Make pencil marks on the front side of each post at 4-1/2 inches (12.25 cm) and 8-1/2 inches (21.25 cm) from the bottom and drill 1/2-inch holes 1/2 inch deep.

STEP EIGHT

Lay the front assembly on a work table and make pencil marks on the back side of each post at 4 inches (10 cm) and 9 inches (22 cm) from the bottom. Drill 1/2-inch holes 1/2 inch deep.

STEP NINE

Use the knife to whittle tenons 1/2 inch long and 1/2 inch in diameter on both ends of the four side rungs. The tenons should not be tapered and should fit tightly in the 1/2-inch holes drilled in the front and back posts. When all the tenons fit snugly, glue the chair together and secure with tourniquet clamps in both directions.

STEP TEN

Use the knife to whittle tenons 1/2 inch long and 1/2 inch in diameter on one end of each of the chair arms. (Notice that the maker of the chair in the photo has chosen arms with a natural crook that fits around the front posts.)

STEP ELEVEN

Position one of the arms as you would like it to look, with the tenon butting against the chair back. Make a mark where the tenon should go and drill a 1/2-inch hole 1/2 inch deep at the proper angle. Fit your tenon in the hole, trimming the tenon if necessary. Lay the other end of the arm against the outside of the front post at the desired position and drill a 3/8-inch hole through the arm and about 1/2 inch into the post.

STEP TWELVE

Glue the arm tenon into its hole on the back post. Use the knife to whittle a peg 2 inches long and 3/8 inch in diameter from a piece of twig. Apply a dab of glue to the peg and use the mallet to drive the peg through the arm until it protrudes from the other side. Put a dab of glue in the hole on the side of the arm and front post. Insert the protruding peg into the hole and drive it home. Trim the peg flush with the arm.

STEP THIRTEEN

Repeat Steps 11 and 12 to attach the other chair arm.

STEP FOURTEEN

To decorate the back of the chair, lay the two forked twigs in position. Mark and drill holes in the back to accommodate the twig ends and glue the twigs into place.

STEP FIFTEEN

Almost anything—sticks, slabs of wood, rattan, rope, even old rags—can be used to make seats for rustic furniture. This chair uses cloth seating tape. Begin by tacking one end of your weaving material to the rear underside of the seat frame. Bring the other end up and outside the rail and wrap it around and around across the front and back rails until the surface is full, then tack it under the frame (see Figure 2). This will form the "warp" of the seat.

FIGURE 2

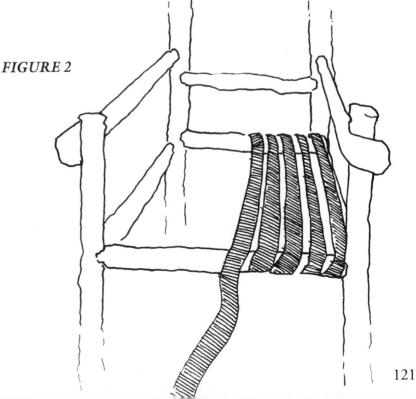

STEP SIXTEEN

Part the warp slightly and tack the end of the "woof" to the underside center of the rear seat rail. Bring it under the first row, over the second, under the third and so on to the side rail. Bring your material up and over the side rail and weave the top the same way (see Figure 3). Continue back across the bottom warp, this time weaving over the first row, under the second, and so on. Keep going until the seat is full. Tack the end somewhere on the bottom.

FIGURE 3

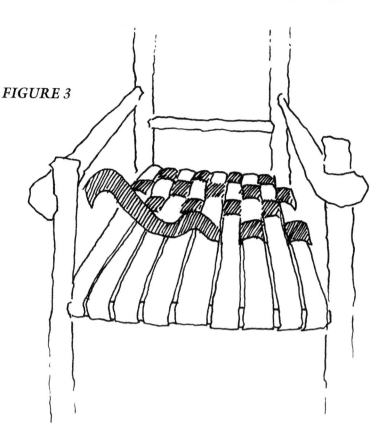

HICKORY SCRUB BROOM

Appalachian mountaineers used hand-carved brooms to scrub the wooden floors of their log cabins. First they sprinkled sand and ashes on the floor, then scrubbed away with their homemade brooms. It was serious work, they'll tell you, but those floors were *clean*.

STEP ONE

Using the knife, skin all the bark from the pole.

STEP TWO

Working from the larger end of the pole, shave a layer of slivers about 10 inches (25 cm) long and 1/8 inch (3 mm) thick all the way around the pole. Leave the slivers attached at the top. After the first layer is complete, make a second layer underneath it, then a third underneath that, and so

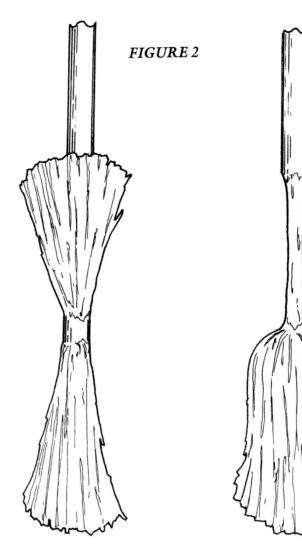

FIGURE 1   *FIGURE 2*   *FIGURE 3*

on until you reach the center. The bottom 10 inches of the pole should be a mass of shavings (see Figure 1).

STEP THREE

Measure up about 2 feet (60 cm) from the shaved end of the pole, and shave down to within 1 or 2 inches (2.5 to 5 cm) of where you stopped on the previous, upward strokes, again making slivers 10 inches long and 1/8 inch thick. Keep moving around the pole, carving one sliver after another, until the pole in the center is the size of a broom handle, or about 1 inch in diameter (see Figure 2).

STEP FOUR

Fold the top bunch of shavings

down around the bottom bunch (see Figure 3), and tie with string to hold them temporarily in place.

STEP FIVE

Tie the strip of hickory bark to two or three shavings at the top of the bundle—preferably to inner shavings, rather than to those on the outermost row. Weave the bark through the top layer of shavings, using an over-and-under pattern, for about ten rows. End the weaving by circling the entire broom and tying the lacing to two or three inside shavings. Trim the outer layer of shavings—the one through which you've woven the bark—just below the bark tie.

STEP SIX

Carve the handle to a comfortable, uniform width, and remove the string.

MATERIALS

Large, sharp knife
Straight, fresh-cut hickory
   pole (either limb or
   sapling), about 5 feet
   (1.5 m) long and 3 inches
   (7 cm) in diameter
String
5-foot strip of hickory bark
   lacing, 1/2-inch (1.3 cm)
   wide (see "Making Bark
   Lacing," on page 87)

COILED VINE BASKET

MATERIALS

Hand clippers or pruning
    shears
25-foot (7.7 m) length of
    1/2-inch (1.3 cm) diameter
    grapevine
Pocketknife
2-inch (5 cm) thick slice of
    log, 7 to 8 inches (17 to
    20 cm) in diameter
75 1-1/2-inch (4 cm) nails
    with heads
Hammer
12-foot (3.4 m) length of
    1/4-inch (6 mm) diameter
    grapevine

Every child has rolled a thin
"snake" of clay, then coiled it
around on top of itself to create a simple clay pot. This
grapevine basket works on
exactly the same principle.
For easier coiling, work with
freshly cut vines.

STEP ONE

With the hand clippers or
pruning shears, cut a 21-foot
(6.5 m) length of the 1/2-inch-
diameter grapevine. Use the
pocketknife to taper 2 inches
of one end, doing all of the
shaving on one side of the
vine (see Figure 1).

STEP TWO

Lay the log slice on a flat working surface and place the
tapered end of the vine along
the rim, shaved-side-up. Nail
the vine to the log slice (now
the base of the basket).

STEP THREE

Coil the vine around the rim of
the base, nailing it to the base
when necessary. Nails should
not be closer than about 6
inches (15 cm). The goal is
not perfect symmetry.

124

Step Four

Continue to coil the vine around the rim, gradually increasing the diameter of each circle, until you have five complete rows. As you coil, nail the vine to the previous row as necessary, using as few nails as possible to hold the rows together.

Step Five

Coil three more complete rows, splaying them outward at a much greater angle, to create a lip on the basket. Cut off the end of the vine at an angle.

Step Six

Cut a 26-inch (65 cm) length of the 1/4-inch-diameter grapevine and wrap it around the very bottom of the base, nailing it in place as necessary. To make the handle, cut a 45-inch (1.2 m) length of 1/2-inch-diameter vine and arc it over the basket from one side to the other. Nail one end to the base directly above the circle of 1/4-inch-diameter vine, and nail it again at the top of the base. Nail it in a similar fashion on the other side. Finally, nail each side of the handle to the top coil of the basket.

Step Seven

Cut a 28-inch (70 cm) length of 1/4-inch-diameter vine, bend it into a V-shape, and place it upside down under the handle on one side of the basket with its ends on the outside of the basket. Nail it to the base (see Figure 2). Cut another 28-inch length of 1/4-inch-diameter vine and attach it to the other side of the basket in the same manner.

FIGURE 1

FIGURE 2

Step Eight

Cut a 5-foot (1.5 m) length of 1/4-inch-diameter vine. Twist it around the handle and nail each end to the base, right next to the handle.

CONTORTED FILBERT WREATH

Contorted filbert is named for its growth habit—it avoids straight lines at any cost. Bent into a round or square shape, young saplings of contorted filbert make a striking, rustic wreath base, especially if the seedpods remain on the wiry branches.

MATERIALS

3 6-foot (1.8 m) untrimmed lengths of contorted filbert, or other twisty saplings
4 12-inch (30 cm) lengths of medium-gauge floral wire
Glue gun
5 magnolia seedpods
8 sweet-gum seedpods
6 clumps of garden moss, 3 inches (7.5 cm) in diameter

12 pieces of mushroomlike tree lichen, 2 inches (5 cm) in diameter
6 clumps of fuzzy lichen, 2 inches in diameter
6 dried heads of cockscomb
7 dried red roses
5 dried red miniature carnations

STEP ONE

Lay the three lengths of filbert side by side. Holding them as one long bundle, bend them into a roughly square shape, and wire them together at the corners.

STEP TWO

Hot-glue the plant materials to the base in the order given in the materials list. In the wreath shown in the photo, the materials are clustered in the corners and across the top of the base.

RUSTIC VINE WREATH

STEP THREE

Create the smaller arrangement near the top of the wreath by hot-gluing the reserved single large fungus onto the wreath base and hot-gluing the reserved two pieces of cockscomb, a stem of pepperberries, and a stem of sorghum around it.

MATERIALS

16-inch (41 cm) diameter vine and moss base
Glue gun
1 stem of dried purple larkspur, trimmed to 6 inches (15 cm)
4 stems of dried pink larkspur, trimmed to 6 inches
2 stems of dried pepperberries, trimmed to 3 inches (7 cm)
7 stems of dried sorghum, trimmed to 3 inches
5 stems of dried German statice, trimmed to 4 inches (10 cm)
3 sprigs of dried acacia
5 stems of dried eucalyptus, trimmed to 4 inches
3 dried Queen-Anne's-lace blooms
3 dried fungi
6 dried cockscomb heads
2 dried globe amaranths, 1 pink and 1 red, stems removed

The contrast between the rustic vine base and the colorful, delicate flowers in this wreath enhances the beauty of each.

STEP ONE

Set aside two pieces of cockscomb, one stem of pepperberries, one stem of sorghum, and one large fungus. Arrange the remaining stems of larkspur, pepperberries, and sorghum on one side of the wreath as shown in the photo and hot-glue them in place. Layer the stems of statice, mimosa, and eucalyptus on top of the first stems and hot-glue in place.

STEP TWO

Arrange the Queen-Anne's-lace, fungi, cockscomb, and globe amaranth on top of the previously placed stems, positioning them with care to cover areas where stems meet, and at varying angles for a more natural look.

PAN PIPES

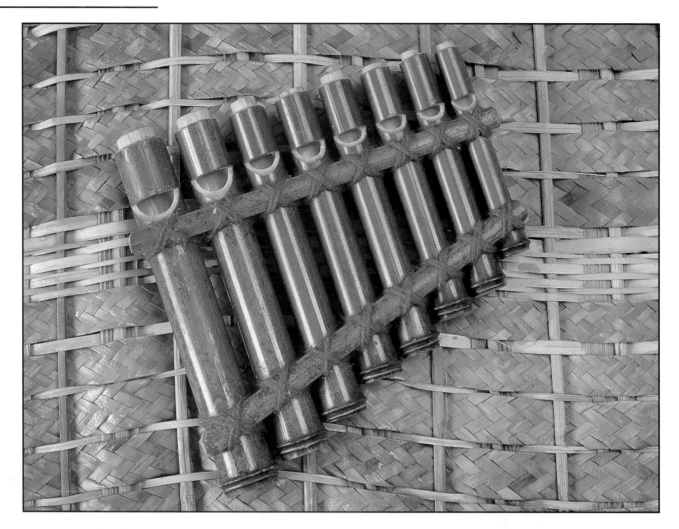

These woodland pipes are a series of bamboo cane whistles fastened together. Any number of whistles can be used: three, four, six, or the eight shown in the photo above. Since cane varies from stalk to stalk, you'll need to adjust the length of each pipe to get the musical note you want.

STEP ONE

Saw off a piece of bamboo 7 to 8 inches (17 to 20 cm) long. Be sure it's a complete joint—that is, it must have one open end and one end blocked by a tough "membrane" (see Figure 1).

STEP TWO

Using the pocketknife, cut a steep notch 1 inch (2.5 cm) from the open end. The notch should be cut into the hollow part of the bamboo, about one-third of the way through the whole stalk (see Figure 2).

STEP THREE

Saw off a 1-1/2-inch-long (4 cm) piece of the 1-inch-diameter dowel, and whittle a wooden plug to fit into the open end of the bamboo. Carve one side flat. The plug must fit snugly but not split the bamboo (see Figure 3).

STEP FOUR

Spread some glue on the plug and push it into the bamboo until the leading edge just reaches the edge of the notch.

MATERIALS

2 to 5 lengths of bamboo about 5 feet (1.5 m) long
Small saw or hacksaw
Pocketknife
1-inch (2.5 cm) diameter dowel or stick, 8 inches (20 cm) long
1/2-inch (1.3 cm) diameter dowel or stick, 8 inches long
White craft glue
11 yards (10 m) of yarn or raffia

The flat side should be on top—the side with the notch (see Figure 4).

STEP FIVE

Blow into the whistle—the end with the plug—and move the plug in and out until you get a good sound and the right note.

STEP SIX

Repeat the process seven more times, making each whistle 1/2 inch to 1 inch shorter than the previous one. Cut the plugs from the smallest dowel that can fill the bamboo.

STEP SEVEN

Lay your eight whistles side by side with the notches aligned, leaving 1/2 inch to 1 inch between them, and measure how wide the completed pan pipes will be. Add 1/2 inch—that's the length of your con-necting strips. In the photo on the opposite page, the strips close to the notches are 8-1/4 inches (21 cm) long. The strips tied at an angle near the other end are 8-1/2 inches (22 cm) long.

Split an 8-1/2-inch piece of bamboo lengthwise into four strips, and tie them one at a time to the front and back of the whistles, using the yarn or raffia.

FIGURE 1

FIGURE 2

FIGURE 3

FIGURE 4

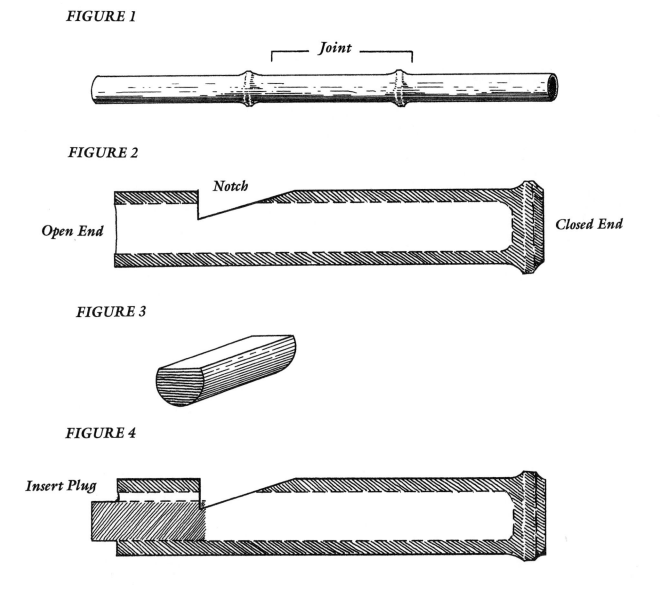

Pussy Willow Wreath

The interesting variety of shapes and textures in this wreath's materials creates a special visual allure.

MATERIALS

Metal coat hanger
Wire cutters
50 stems of dried pussy
  willow, trimmed to
  4 inches (10 cm)
Spool wire
Glue gun
10 dried rosebuds
18 assorted seedpods

STEP ONE

Form the wreath's base by bending the coat hanger into a circle and trimming off the hook with wire cutters. Position a single stem of pussy willow against the base and secure by wrapping several times with spool wire.

STEP TWO

Continue wiring stems of pussy willow to the base until it's completely covered, positioning each new stem so it covers the wired portion of the previous stem. Fill in any bare spots by hot-gluing additional stems of pussy willow in place, taking care to position them at the same angle as the surrounding stems.

STEP THREE

Embellish the completed wreath by hot-gluing on rosebuds and small seedpods.

Rustic Cooking Tools

Don't throw away old kitchen utensils with cracked or broken handles. They can be easily transformed into twig-handled cooking tools. Although these implements suggest an outdoor barbecue, they are handsome enough for the best of kitchens.

Step One

Separate the cooking utensils from their plastic or wooden handles by smashing the handles with a heavy hammer or maul. The handles will break, leaving you with a metal tool and its metal shaft.

Step Two

For each tool, select a stick to serve as a handle. Working with green wood is helpful; it will shrink as it dries and thus make a tighter bond. Rinse the twigs under running water and allow to dry. Saw straight across both ends of the stick, making sure you end up with the

desired length. A slotted spoon for indoor use needs a handle about 4 to 6 inches (10 to 15 cm) long. A fork for outdoor barbecuing works best with a 9- to 10-inch (22 to 25 cm) handle.

Step Three

Using the pocketknife, bevel each end of the stick by carving away a 1/4 inch (6 mm) strip of bark and a little of the wood itself. Otherwise, the end of the bark might snag on clothing or cooking pans.

Step Four

Measure the diameter of the utensil's metal shaft and select a drill bit the same size or just a fraction of an inch larger. Drill a hole about 1 to 2 inches (2.5 to 5 cm) deep into one end of the stick.

Step Five

Squeeze a thin coating of glue over the bottom inch of the

utensil's metal shaft and insert it into the hole in the stick. Allow to dry.

Step Six

If desired, use the pocketknife to carve designs in the stick handles.

MATERIALS

Stainless steel cooking utensils
Heavy hammer or maul
3/4-inch (2 cm) diameter fresh-cut sticks, 4 to 10 inches (10 to 25 cm) long (one for each cooking utensil)
Handsaw
Pocketknife
Electric drill with various-size bits
Tube of Super Glue or other super-strong glue

Twig Wreath

A wire coat hanger and a basketful of dry twigs make a striking wreath base. For extra fullness, select twigs that are branched and curved on their narrow ends.

Step One

Bend the coat hanger into a circle. Straighten the curved hook, then bend it so it follows the curve of the wire circle but protrudes enough to form a loop for hanging. Wrap the end of the wire around the circular frame.

Step Two

Gather the twigs into 15 bundles of four to five twigs each, and secure them with rubber bands close to their wide ends.

Step Three

Starting at the base of the hook, attach the twig bundles to the wire frame by holding a bundle parallel to the frame and wrapping fine-gauge floral wire around the bottom of the bundle and the frame. Lay a second bundle so that its top overlaps the bottom of the first, hiding the rubber band, and secure with the floral wire. Continue around the frame, either wrapping one continuous piece of fine-gauge wire to secure the bundles or clipping off an individual piece of wire for each bundle. Make sure the coat-hanger frame is completely covered.

Step Four

Hot-glue the lichens and flowers to the twig base in the order given in the materials list, spacing each type evenly around the wreath.

MATERIALS

Wire coat hanger
60 to 75 twigs, 3 to 5-1/2 inches (7 to 13 cm) long and 1/8 to 1/4 inch (3 to 6 mm) in diameter
15 rubber bands
Fine-gauge floral wire
Glue gun
13 mushroom-type tree lichens, 1 inch (2.5 cm) wide
12 clumps of dried lichens, 2 inches (5 cm) wide
24 dried pink roses, trimmed to 1 inch
6 dried orange roses, trimmed to 1 inch
20 magenta globe amaranths
14 dried yellow button mums
14 stems dried purple annual statice, trimmed to 1 inch

GOURDS

Gourds are often called nature's pottery. Since prehistoric times these fast-growing fruits of the calabash vine have been hollowed out and used for all manner of containers and utensils. Gourd bottles dated to 7000 B.C. have been found in ancient cave dwellings of Mexico. Tombs of the Egyptian pharaohs were stocked with gourd containers to keep the departed supplied for the journey to the great beyond. For thousands of years the Indians of Peru have used gourds as floats for their fishing nets. In Japan, intricately carved and lacquered gourds were used to store sake, while in Russia and Burma similar containers were inlaid with silver. Native Hawaiians used huge basket gourds for storing seeds. Throughout Africa and India gourds have been used for drums, rattles, sitars, and other musical instruments.

Nowadays gourd crafting remains a flourishing art form throughout the world. Since gourds are readily cultivated in a wide range of climates, most crafters find that growing gourds can be as much fun as using them. Others simply buy gourds (at very reasonable prices) at flea markets or roadside vegetable stands.

Though some crafters prefer the small ornamental varieties, most use some form of *Lagenaria* or hard-shell gourd. These come in an amazing variety of shapes and sizes, from the long, slender "dipper gourd" to the large, bulbous "basketball gourd." Like their relatives the squash, cucumber, melon, and pumpkin, gourds grow on long, running vines. They thrive best under full sunlight in rich, well-drained mounds of soil spaced 5 to 10 feet (1.5 to 3 m) apart. When the fruit are developing, they require lots of water.

In fact, gourds are made up almost entirely of water and so must be dried, or cured, before use. Huge, 100-pound (45 kg) gourds weigh only a few pounds when cured. The green skin hardens to a woody, water-proof shell that can be carved, burned, sanded, painted, and finished much like wood.

To cure gourds, simply place them on a rack or a series of boards (indoors or out) where air can freely circulate, and turn them occasionally. Lagenerias are dry when they turn off-white, beige, or brown and their seeds rattle when shaken, usually in about three to six months.

GOURD DIPPERS

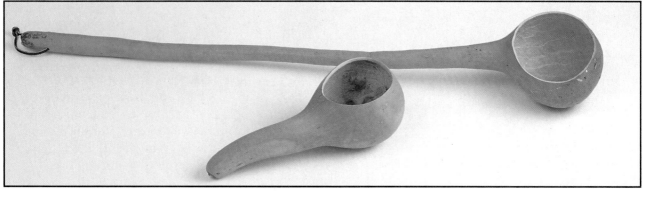

One of the oldest uses for a gourd, dating back to prehistoric times, is as a dipper, ladle, or spoon. In some cultures, the constellation Ursa Minor, which we call the "Little Dipper," is known as the "Drinking Gourd." Just about anyone who grows gourds also makes dippers because they are easy, useful, and decorative. Today the traditional use has lent its name to these gourds, commonly known as long-handled or short-handled dipper gourds.

STEP ONE

Soak the gourd in soapy water for 20 minutes and use the steel wool to scrub off all dirt and mold. Allow to dry completely.

STEP TWO

Cut a large hole in the ball of a long- or short-handled dipper gourd. Remove all seeds and pulp and scrub out the inside with soapy water and steel wool. Allow to dry completely.

STEP THREE

Sand the rim of the hole and the inside surface of the dipper.

STEP FOUR

If you have chosen a long-handled dipper gourd and plan to put your dipper to use, you may want to insert a cork into the neck to prevent liquid from flowing down the handle.

STEP FIVE

If you plan to hang the dipper on the wall, drill two small holes on either side of the gourd neck. Insert a length of rawhide lacing and knot to form a hanging loop.

MATERIALS

Long- or short-handled dipper gourd, cured
Soap
Water
Steel wool
Fine-toothed saw
Sandpaper
Bottle cork (optional)
Electric drill with 3/8-inch bit (optional)
Rawhide lacing (optional)

GOURD DISH

A bowl for chips or pretzels can be crafted from a round, symmetrical gourd of any size. The one in the photograph is 10 inches (25 cm) in diameter.

STEP ONE

Soak the gourd in soapy water for 20 minutes and use the steel wool to scrub off all dirt and mold. Allow to dry completely.

STEP TWO

With the pencil, draw a line around the gourd where you want the top of the bowl to be. To make a level line, put the gourd on a table, hold the pencil with the point against the gourd (brace your little finger against the table), and turn the gourd.

STEP THREE

Pierce the gourd with the sharp, pointed knife on the drawn line, creating a slit long enough for the fine-toothed saw blade to enter. Saw off the top.

STEP FOUR

Remove all the pulp and seeds and clean the inside with soapy water and steel wool. Let the gourd dry completely.

STEP FIVE

Draw the petal shapes around the top of the gourd, and cut them out with the hacksaw. Whittle off any jagged edges with a craft knife, and sand the edges smooth.

STEP SIX

In the enamel dishpan (or other dye-proof container large

enough to hold the gourd bowl), mix red fabric dye according to the package instructions. For the bowl in the photo a ratio of 4 ounces (118 ml) of liquid dye to 2 gallons (7.5 l) of water was used. Place the bowl upside down in the dye and weight it down with a brick to keep it from floating. Leave the gourd in the dye until it is slightly darker than you want it—about 15 minutes—and remove it. Wipe the outside with a paper towel, to prevent drip marks, and allow to dry.

STEP SEVEN

Draw the lines of the petals inside the dish and engrave over them with the wood-burning tool.

STEP EIGHT

Wax the outside of the gourd with the shoe polish.

MATERIALS

Hard-shell gourd, cured
Soap
Water
Steel wool
Pencil
Sharp, pointed knife
Fine-toothed saw
Hacksaw
Craft knife
Sandpaper
Enamel dishpan
Red liquid fabric dye
Brick
Wood-burning tool
Brown paste wax shoe polish

DYED TURQUOISE BOWL

An attractive gourd bowl makes an excellent plant container (place a waterproof pot inside it) or a handsome decoration for mantle or end table.

STEP ONE

Soak the gourd in soapy water for 20 minutes and use the steel wool to scrub off all dirt and mold. Allow to dry completely.

STEP TWO

With the pencil, draw a line around the gourd where you want the top of the bowl to be. To make a level line, put the gourd on a table, hold the pencil with the point against the gourd (brace your little finger against the table), and turn the gourd.

STEP THREE

Pierce the gourd with the knife on the drawn line, creating a slit long enough for the saw

MATERIALS

Hard-shell gourd, cured
Soap
Water
Steel wool
Pencil
Sharp, pointed knife
Fine-toothed saw
Wood-burning tool
Light-tan leather dye
Turquoise leather dye
Paintbrush
Awl
Soft rag
Brown paste wax shoe polish
Large-eyed sewing needle
Waxed linen
Several dozen dried long-
  leaved pine needles

blade to enter. Saw off the top.

STEP FOUR

Remove all the pulp and seeds and clean the inside with soapy water and steel wool. Let the gourd dry completely.

STEP FIVE

Draw your design in pencil on the outside of the gourd and engrave over the lines with the wood-burning tool.

STEP SIX

Using the paintbrush, paint the inside of the gourd with light-tan leather dye. Then use the tan and turquoise dyes to paint the areas on the outside that you want to color. Apply

two coats to the outside. Since the dye dries quickly, the second coat can be applied immediately.

STEP SEVEN

With the awl, punch a row of holes around the gourd 1/8 inch (3 mm) from the top and 3/4 inch (2 cm) apart.

STEP EIGHT

With the soft rag, rub brown paste wax shoe polish over the entire gourd. Let it dry, then buff.

STEP NINE

Thread the sewing needle with the waxed linen and tie a knot in one end. Pull the needle through one of the holes from the inside to the outside. Form a bunch of approximately six pine needles, and lay them next to the threaded hole on the rim of the bowl. Sew them on by whipstitching over the rim and through the holes. Add new bunches of needles end to end in this manner, until the rim is covered. Then add a second layer of needles, whipstitching through the same holes and over the top of the first needles.

SEED NECKLACE

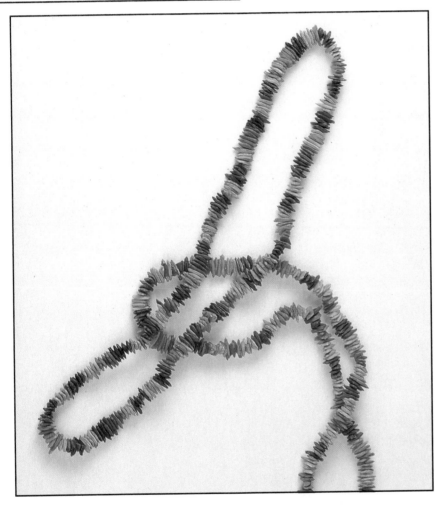

When you clean out gourds for the gourd projects, you'll end up with more seeds than you can sanely plant. Use the leftovers to make this unique jewelry.

STEP ONE

Pull any remaining flesh off the seeds and soak them for 20 minutes in a mixture of 1/2 cup bleach to 1 quart (0.9 l) water. Rinse and let dry.

STEP TWO

In a stainless steel pan, mix 1 pint (473 ml) of water and the red dye. Bring to boiling, remove from the heat, and add 70 seeds. Leave the seeds in the dye until they're slightly darker than the desired color, then remove them and allow to dry.

STEP THREE

Dye 70 seeds purple, using the technique described in Step 2.

The remaining seeds should be left undyed.

STEP FOUR

Thread the needle and knot the thread. String the seeds, piercing them in the middle of a flat side, in groups of five purple, then five natural, five red, five natural, then five purple. Continue with this color pattern until all the seeds are strung. For easier piercing, brace the needle upside down on a hard, flat surface, lay the seed on top of the pointed end, and force the seed down over the needle.

STEP FIVE

When all the seeds are strung, tie a knot in the thread against the last seed. Tie the two ends of the thread together and clip the ends.

MATERIALS

275 gourd seeds
1/2 cup (118 ml) household
   bleach
Water
Stainless steel pan
1 teaspoon (5 ml) red
   powdered fabric dye
1 teaspoon purple powdered
   fabric dye
36-inch (90 cm) length
   of strong thread
Heavy sewing needle

GOURD PENGUINS

MATERIALS

For one penguin:

2 dipper gourd necks, cured
Penguin gourd, cured
Scrap pieces of other gourds,
  cured
Soap
Water
Steel wool
Sharp knife
Glue gun
Fine-grit sandpaper
Acrylic paints
Paintbrush
Clear acrylic spray

Painted animals are a favorite subject for gourd crafters, and probably no creature is more appreciated than the penguin. In fact, the type of gourd used to make them is commonly known as the penguin gourd. The ones shown in the photo have been painted to resemble several different species.

STEP ONE

Soak the gourd necks, gourd, and gourd scraps in soapy water for 20 minutes and use the steel wool to scrub off all dirt and mold. Allow to dry completely.

STEP TWO

To make legs for your penguin, use a sharp knife to cut 1- to 2-inch (2.5 to 5 cm) long cylinders from the necks of dipper gourds and shape them to fit flush against the bottom front of your penguin gourd. Glue into place.

STEP THREE

Cut feet from flat scraps of gourd and glue these to the bottom of the legs.

STEP FOUR

Cut a tail from another scrap gourd and glue it to the lower back to create a third support for the penguin.

STEP FIVE

Cut long flippers from the sides of the other dipper gourd necks and glue these to the sides of the penguin.

STEP SIX

Lightly sand the penguin. Paint with two or more coats of acrylic paint. Finish by spraying on a coat of clear acrylic.

GOURD MASKS

This is a fun and easy gourd project for children. The incredible variety of gourd shapes will offer endless ideas for creatures to be made. Let the kids choose a gourd and an animal to make from it. After an adult cuts out the parts, the young ones can paint the faces and tie the masks together.

STEP ONE

Soak the gourd in soapy water for 20 minutes and use the steel wool to scrub off all dirt and mold. Allow to dry completely.

STEP TWO

Using a pencil, draw the desired face of your finished mask on the gourd, using its neck as the creature's nose.

STEP THREE

Drill a starter hole, then, using the saw, cut the mask shape out of the gourd and cut eye holes in the face. If you want to add ears or other parts to your mask, cut these out, too. Clean the pieces with soapy water and steel wool. Let dry.

STEP FOUR

If you plan to have floppy ears or other parts laced to the mask, drill holes and tie the pieces on with rawhide or strong twine. Drill holes for the rawhide or twine strap.

STEP FIVE

Paint your mask the appropriate colors and use marking pens to add details.

STEP SIX

Measure the circumference of your child's head, to determine how long the mask's strap should be. After the paint on the mask has dried, attach the proper length of rawhide or twine as a strap.

MATERIALS

For one mask:

Animal-shaped hard-shell
   gourd, cured
Soap
Water
Steel wool
Pencil
Electric drill with 3/8-inch bit
Fine-toothed saw
Rawhide lacing or twine
Acrylic paints
Marking pens

GOURD VASES

Whatever the shape of your wild-flower bouquet, a gourd vase can be made to hold it. All three containers shown here are deco-rated with a wood-burning tool. The bowl-shaped vase on the far left was left its natural color and shape. The other two vases have added stands, for stability, and a gloss that comes from a wood stain with added polyurethane.

Unpolished Bowl

Hard-shell gourd, cured
Soap
Water
Steel wool
Pencil
Sharp, pointed knife
Fine-toothed saw
Wood-burning tool with
  narrow and wide tips

Unpolished Bowl

STEP ONE

Soak the gourd in soapy water for 20 minutes and use the steel wool to scrub off all dirt and mold. Allow to dry completely.

STEP TWO

With the pencil, draw a line around the gourd where you want the top of the bowl to be. To make a level line, put the gourd on a table, hold the pencil with the point against the gourd (brace your little finger against the table), and turn the gourd.

STEP THREE

Pierce the gourd with the knife on the drawn line, creating a slit long enough for the saw blade to enter. Saw off the top.

STEP FOUR

Remove all the pulp and seeds and clean the inside with soapy water and steel wool. Let the gourd dry completely.

STEP FIVE

Draw your design in pencil on the outside of the gourd. To create the lines and define the contours of the dark spaces, engrave over the lines with the wood-burning tool, using a narrow tip. Then burn in the dark expanses with a wide tip.

Vase with Stand

STEP ONE

Soak the gourd and gourd neck in soapy water for 20 minutes and use the steel wool to scrub off all dirt and mold. Allow to dry completely.

STEP TWO

With the pencil, draw a line around the gourd where you want the top of the vase to be. To make a level line, put the gourd on a table, hold the pencil with the point against the gourd (brace your little finger against the table), and turn the gourd.

STEP THREE

Pierce the gourd with the knife on the drawn line, creating a slit long enough for the saw blade to enter. Saw off the top.

STEP FOUR

Remove all the pulp and seeds and clean the inside with soapy water and steel wool. Let the gourd dry completely.

STEP FIVE

From the gourd neck, cut out a ring to hold the finished vase and glue it to the bottom of the vase.

STEP SIX

Draw your design in pencil on the outside of the gourd. To create the lines and define the contours of the dark spaces, engrave over the lines with the wood-burning tool, using a narrow tip. Then burn in the dark expanses with a wide tip.

STEP SEVEN

Using the shellac brush, paint the vase with polyurethane stain.

Vase with Stand

Hard-shell gourd, cured
Bottle gourd neck, cured
Soap
Water
Steel wool
Pencil
Sharp, pointed knife
Fine-toothed saw
White craft glue
Wood-burning tool with narrow and wide tips
Shellac brush
Oak-colored polyurethane stain

FANTASY BIRDHOUSES

Birds are naturally attracted to nest in the cozy confines of a hollow gourd. But you can also embellish your gourd birdhouses to create backyard decorations that will please humans as well. The shingles on these storybook birdhouses are as functional as they are fanciful, assuring that rain will be diverted from the entrance.

STEP ONE

Soak the gourd in soapy water for 20 minutes and use the steel wool to scrub off all dirt and mold. Allow to dry completely.

STEP TWO

Cut a hole in the side of the gourd appropriate to the size bird you would like to attract, generally between 1 inch (2.5 cm) and 1-1/2 inches (4 cm).

MATERIALS

Medium-size bottle gourd, cured
Soap
Water
Steel wool
Sharp knife or fine-toothed craft saw
Bottle gourd neck, cured
Pocketknife or carving knife
Waterproof glue
Small spatula or putty knife
Wood dough
Scrap pieces of other dried gourds
Sandpaper
Marker or wood-burning tool (optional)
Wood stain (optional)
Acrylic varnish
Paintbrush

Remove all pulp and seeds. Clean the inside with soapy water and steel wool. Let the gourd dry completely.

STEP THREE

To make a stand for the birdhouse, cut a ring from the gourd neck large enough to fit nicely on the bottom of the bottle gourd, using the fine-toothed saw. If necessary, carve the top of the ring with the pocketknife or carving knife until the bottom of the bottle gourd fits smoothly into it. Glue the ring to the bottom of the bottle gourd and allow to dry. Using the small spatula or putty knife, apply wood dough to the joint between the birdhouse and the stand. Scrape off any excess and sand smooth when dry.

STEP FOUR

To make a perch, cut a piece of scrap gourd stem about 1-1/2 inches long. Cut a hole of the same diameter about 3/4 inch (2 cm) below the entrance and glue the perch into the hole.

STEP FIVE

Make an arched porch roof by cutting a piece from the bottom of a scrap gourd neck and trimming it to fit above the entrance. Glue into place.

STEP SIX

Cut shingles roughly 1 × 1-1/2 inches from scrap gourds. Vary the size to give a random look. It is best to cut shingles from parts of the scrap gourd that correspond with the area of the birdhouse you wish to cover. You will need 40 or more shingles to create the roof.

STEP SEVEN

Beginning at the widest part of the birdhouse, glue a row of shingles side by side around the gourd, staggering them vertically to give an uneven look. Continue adding rows of shingles, overlapping to leave about 1 inch of the previous layer exposed. As you near the top, shingles may need to be trimmed to fit the curvature of the gourd.

STEP EIGHT

Make a roof cap from the top of another gourd that is larger than the one selected for your birdhouse. If you like, cut a serrated edge on the cap and draw on shingles with a marker or wood-burning tool before gluing it to the top.

STEP NINE

The shingles and birdhouse bottom can be painted with wood stain or left in their natural color. Finally, waterproof your birdhouse with several thin coats of acrylic varnish.

CUT GOURD VASE

Anyone can have a cut glass vase. A cut gourd vase is considerably rarer, yet easier to make. It's best to select a round, symmetrical gourd with thick walls.

MATERIALS

Hard-shell gourd, cured
Soap
Water
Steel wool
Pencil
Sharp, pointed knife
Keyhole saw or jigsaw
Paintbrush
Brown leather dye
Clear liquid floor wax

A thin-walled specimen will probably break during sawing.

STEP ONE

Soak the gourd in soapy water for 20 minutes and use the steel wool to scrub off all dirt and mold. Allow to dry completely.

STEP TWO

Pencil in the cutting line to separate the top from the bottom. Draw a row of triangles above the cutting line, a row below, and a row at the bottom of the gourd. Then draw diamonds over the rest of the surface.

STEP THREE

Pierce the gourd with the knife on the line separating the top and bottom, creating a slit long enough for the saw blade to enter. Saw along the cutting line.

STEP FOUR

Remove all the pulp and seeds and clean the inside with soapy water and steel wool. Let the gourd dry completely.

STEP FIVE

Cut out all the triangles and diamonds, starting each cut with the knife and finishing it with the saw.

STEP SIX

Using the paintbrush, apply the dye to the outside of the gourd. Wash out the paintbrush and, when the dye is dry, use the paintbrush to apply a coat of floor wax.

CARVED GOURD PITCHER

For centuries, gourds have been used to hold water and other liquids. This interesting pitcher with a vine handle goes beyond the cut-a-hole-in-the-top level of craftsmanship.

STEP ONE

Soak the gourd and the gourd neck in soapy water for 20 minutes and use the steel wool to scrub off all dirt and mold. Allow to dry completely

STEP TWO

To make a stand for the pitcher, cut a ring from the gourd

MATERIALS

Bottle gourd, cured
Bottle gourd neck, cured
Soap
Water
Steel wool
Fine-toothed saw
Pocketknife or carving knife
White craft glue
Small spatula or putty knife
Wood dough
Sandpaper
Pencil
Brown permanent marker,
     with fine point
12-inch (30 cm) length
     of wisteria or other vine,
     1/2 inch to 1 inch (1.25
     to 2.5 cm) in diameter
Electric drill with 1/2-inch bit
Fresh leaves
Acrylic paints in yellow,
     orange, and brown
Paintbrush
Clear polyurethane

neck large enough to fit nicely on the bottom of the bottle gourd pitcher, using the fine-toothed saw. If necessary, carve the top of the ring with the pocketknife or carving knife until the bottom of the bottle gourd fits smoothly into it. Glue the ring to the bottom of the bottle gourd and allow to dry. Using the small spatula or putty knife, apply wood dough

to the joint between the pitcher and the stand. Scrape off any excess and sand smooth when dry.

STEP THREE

Using the pencil, draw a line around the bottom of gourd where you want the lower border of the design to be. To make a level line, put the gourd on a table, hold the pen-

cil with the point against the gourd (brace your little finger against the table), and turn the gourd. Go over the line with the permanent marker.

STEP FOUR

Draw the cutting line for the opening of the pitcher, slanting it from front to back. Pierce the gourd with the pocketknife or carving knife on the drawn line, creating a slit long enough for the saw blade to enter. Saw off the top.

STEP FIVE

Remove all the pulp and seeds and clean the inside with soapy water and steel wool. Let the gourd dry completely.

STEP SIX

Sand the rim of the pitcher smooth. Pencil a line below the rim, following the contour of the opening, to mark the top border of the design area. Go over the line with the

permanent marker.

STEP SEVEN

Pencil two circles where you want the vine handle to attach to the gourd. Measure the diameter of the vine and drill two holes large enough to accommodate the vine ends. Trim the vine, if necessary, to produce an attractively curved handle, and insert the ends into the holes. Glue the ends in place from the inside and allow to dry. As extra insurance, spread a thin layer of wood dough over the vine ends inside the gourd.

STEP EIGHT

Lay a leaf on the gourd and trace around it, using a pencil. Repeat the design as often as you like, perhaps varying the sizes of the leaves. Go over the lines with the permanent marker.

STEP NINE

With the pocketknife or carving knife, make shallow cuts around

the leaf outlines and just inside the top and bottom border lines, cutting just through the outer shell of the gourd. When possible, cut away from the design.

STEP TEN

Crosshatch squares about 1/16 inch (1 mm) wide in all the spaces between the leaves, by making vertical cuts about 1 inch long, then horizontal cuts the same length (see Figure 1). Holding the knife at a 45-degree angle, cut under the squares and peel off the outer layer of skin.

STEP ELEVEN

Paint the leaves yellow, shading them with orange toward the edges. Paint the stand and the handle brown, and paint a brown border around the pitcher's opening. When the paint is dry, brush a coat of polyurethane over the entire pitcher.

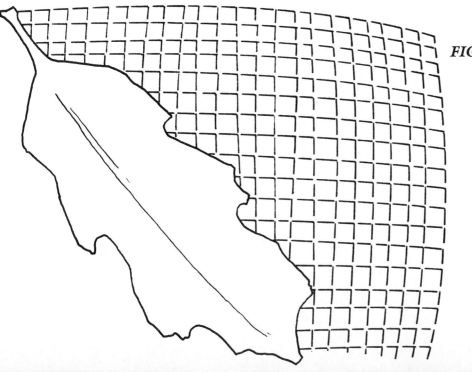

FIGURE 1

CARVED GOURD BOWL

This handsome bowl, with its tracery of curved, graceful lines, was carved with a simple U-shaped gouge. Its rich colors were added with leather dye and shoe polish.

STEP ONE

Soak the gourd in soapy water for 20 minutes and use the steel wool to scrub off all dirt and mold. Allow to dry completely.

STEP TWO

With the pencil, draw a line around the gourd where you want the top of the bowl to be.

STEP THREE

With the push drill, drill a hole on the cutting line large enough for the saw blade to enter. Saw off the top.

STEP FOUR

Remove all the pulp and seeds and clean the inside with soapy water and steel wool. Let dry completely.

STEP FIVE

Pencil a grid of squares on the gourd by drawing vertical and horizontal lines. On the gourd shown here, the vertical lines are 2 inches (5 cm) apart and the horizonal lines are 1-1/2 inches (4 cm) apart. Then draw diagonal lines through the grid to make a pattern of triangles.

STEP SIX

Select the triangles that will be darkest, and gouge a series of chips from inside them. To make clean cuts, first place the gouge at right angles to the gourd surface and make a stop cut. Then, holding the gouge at a low angle, scrape a chip out of the surface,

FIGURE 1

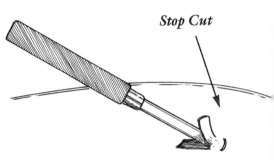

Stop Cut

aiming for the stop cut and stopping there (see Figure 1).

STEP SEVEN

Using a clean rag, wipe brown leather dye over the carved triangles, then wipe it off with a second rag. The dye will soak into the gouged areas, turning them dark brown. Allow to dry.

STEP EIGHT

Rub brown paste wax over the entire gourd and allow to dry. Then gouge out the remaining triangles as described in Step 6, revealing the lighter-colored material underneath.

MATERIALS

Hard-shell gourd, cured
Soap
Water
Steel wool
Pencil
Push drill
Keyhole saw
U-shaped wood-carving gouge
Clean rags
Brown leather dye
Brown paste wax shoe polish

CHEQUEREE

MATERIALS

Large gourd, 17 to 20 inches
(43 to 50 cm) tall and 1/4
to 3/8 inch (6 mm to 1 cm)
thick, cured
Soap
Water
Steel wool
Fine-toothed saw
Knife
#6 nylon rope
Candle
Cup hook
#12 braided nylon line
Coat hanger
1,500 to 12,000 beads
Turkey-tying pin

No Latin or African percussion section would be complete without the large, beaded gourd rattle known as the chequeree (sometimes spelled shakeree or shekere). Players shake the beads to the rhythm and accentuate the beat by tossing the flat end of the gourd against the hand to create a deep, dramatic *thump!*

STEP ONE

Select a symmetrical gourd with a rounded bottom that is still flat enough to stand on its own. The neck should rest comfortably in your hand. Soak the gourd in soapy water for 20 minutes and use steel wool to scrub off all dirt and mold. Let dry completely.

STEP TWO

Using the saw, cut off the stem end of the gourd about 2 inches (5 cm) down the neck. Remove all the pulp and seeds and clean the inside of the gourd with soapy water and steel wool. Let the gourd dry completely.

STEP THREE

Use a hot knife to cut a piece of #6 nylon rope long enough to fit around the circumference of the gourd where you want your beading to begin. Use a lit candle to "weld" the two nylon ends together to form a circle of rope. (You can knot the rope instead, if you like.) Slip the rope circle over the top of your gourd.

STEP FOUR

Screw a cup hook into the ceiling and attach a piece of line so it dangles in front of where you plan to work. Tie a loop in the line at eye level and trim the excess. Pull the bottom of the coat hanger down so you have a long loop, then bend the loop in half to form a large hook (see Figure 1). Insert the large hook into the gourd, and hang the gourd from the looped line.

STEP FIVE

Cut a piece of #12 nylon line four times the length of the portion of gourd to be covered with beads. Double the line and place the looped end behind the top rope on your gourd. Bring the two straight ends up over the rope and through the loop, and pull to secure the line to the rope (see Figure 2).

STEP SIX

Tie an overhand knot in the two lines. To make an overhand knot, place the index and middle fingers of one hand under the pair of lines, close to the rope. Wrap both lines around your two fingers, making a loop, and pull the ends of

the lines through the loop. Remove your fingers and insert the turkey-tying pin through the loop. Then use the pin to slide the knot up against the rope before tightening (see Figure 3). Add more strings in this manner until you have one every 3/8 inch (1 cm) around the top rope. You can always add or remove strings later.

STEP SEVEN

Beginning with two pairs of lines, slide a bead up the right line of the left pair until it touches the knot above it. Grasp the left line of the right pair and tie an overhand knot with the beaded line, using the pin to slide the knot up tight against the bead (see Figure 4). Working from left to right, move to the next two lines and tie

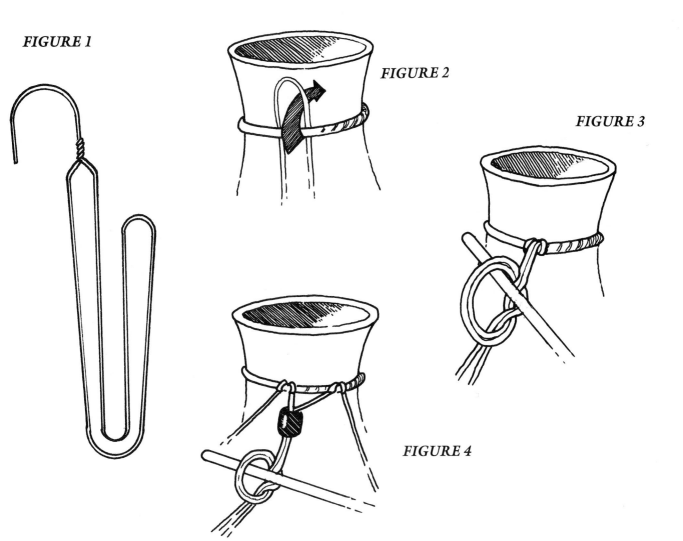

FIGURE 1

FIGURE 2

FIGURE 3

FIGURE 4

on a bead in the same manner. (In this case, they are the right line of the second pair and the left line of the third pair.)

STEP EIGHT

Keep tying on beads until you have completed an entire row around the gourd. Add additional rows in the same manner until the gourd is covered with beaded netting. The last row should be tied when the gourd begins to narrow toward the bottom. Do not make the net too tight. The first rows will be close together, but as your gourd gets wider it will be necessary to leave a little more line between the beads. If you tilt your chequeree on its side, there should be space between the net and the gourd.

STEP NINE

To connect the bottom rope, start with the first bead of the last row. Place the end of the #6 nylon rope under the knot holding the bead in place. Using the same pair of lines with which you tied this knot, put the lefthand string behind the rope and the righthand string in front of the rope. Now tie two overhand knots below the rope to hold it in place. Repeat this procedure all the way around the gourd.

STEP TEN

Cut the rope so that it is just long enough to prevent the net from slipping off the gourd if the chequeree is turned upside down. Weld it into a circle with the lit candle as described in Step 3. Trim

the excess strings and seal the ends with the candle.

STEP ELEVEN

To play your chequeree, balance it on your right palm and tilt the neck into your left hand. Raise the gourd onto your right fingertips and quickly drop your hand a few inches, allowing the gourd to fall onto the heel of your hand. As it falls, raise your right hand to its original level and toss the chequeree neck back to your left hand. As you toss the gourd back and forth, the beads will make a sharp clicking sound while your right hand adds a bass note when the chequeree strikes your palm. (Remember to let the gourd fall into your hand: Striking the chequeree too hard will break it.)

TAIL CHEQUEREE

MATERIALS

Bottle gourd, with walls 1/4 to 3/8 inch (6 mm to 1 cm) thick, cured
Soap
Water
Steel wool
Fine-toothed saw
Knife
#6 nylon rope
Candle
Cup hook
#18 braided nylon line
Turkey-tying pin
300 to 400 beads

This is a smaller variation of the regular chequeree and can be made from asymmetrical gourds. A curved gourd neck provides a natural handle. It is played by holding the neck in one hand and the tail in the other and pulling the tail so the beads click against the gourd.

STEP ONE

Soak the gourd in soapy water for 20 minutes and use the steel wool to scrub off all dirt and mold. Let the gourd dry completely.

STEP TWO

Using the saw, cut a hole (proportional to the gourd you

have chosen) about 3/4 to 2 inches (2 to 5 cm) in diameter just below the neck. Remove all the pulp and seeds, and clean the inside with soapy water and steel wool. Let the gourd dry completely.

STEP THREE

Use a hot knife to cut a piece of #6 nylon rope long enough to fit around the circumference of the gourd where you want your beading to begin. Use a lit candle to "weld" the two nylon ends together to form a circle of rope. (You can knot the rope instead, if you like.) Slip the rope circle over the top of your gourd.

STEP FOUR

Screw a cup hook into the ceiling and attach a piece of #18 nylon line so it dangles in front of where you plan to work. Tie the line around the neck of the gourd at about eye level.

STEP FIVE

Cut a piece of #18 line five times the length of the portion of gourd to be covered with beads. Double the line and place the looped end behind the top rope on your gourd. Bring the two straight ends up over the rope and through the loop, and pull to secure the line to the rope (see Figure 2 on page 153).

STEP SIX

Tie an overhand knot in the two lines. To make an overhand knot, place the index and middle fingers of one hand under the pair of lines, close to the rope. Wrap both lines around your two fingers, making a loop, and pull the ends of the lines through the loop. Remove your fingers and insert the turkey-tying pin through the loop. Then use the pin to slide the knot up against the rope before tightening (see Figure 3 on page 153). Add more lines in this manner until you have one every 1/2 inch (1.3 cm) around the top rope. You can always add or remove lines later.

STEP SEVEN

Beginning with two pairs of lines, slide a bead up the right line of the left pair until it touches the knot above it. Grasp the left line of the right pair and tie an overhand knot with the beaded line, using the pin to slide the knot up tight against the bead (see Figure 4

on page 153). Working from left to right, move to the next two lines and tie on another bead in the same manner. (In this case, they are the right line of the second pair and the left line of the third pair.)

STEP EIGHT

Keep tying on beads until you have completed an entire row around the gourd. Add additional rows in the same manner

until the gourd is covered with beaded netting. The last row should be tied when the gourd begins to narrow toward the bottom. Do not make the net too tight. The first rows will be close together, but as your gourd gets wider it will be necessary to leave a little more line between the beads. If you tilt your chequeree on its side, there should be space between the net and the gourd.

STEP NINE

Gather all the remaining lines together and tie them into one knot, leaving a tail. Be sure to tie the knot close enough to the gourd so the net cannot slide off the gourd when inverted.

STEP TEN

To play the tail chequeree, simply hold the neck with your left hand and pull on the tail with your right. The beads will click against the gourd. Relax your grip slightly on the tail and the net will fall away from the gourd.

GOURD DRUM

Because gourds trap large volumes of air in a resonant shell, they have been used as musical instruments since prehistoric times. Some of the earliest drums consisted of a piece of animal hide stretched across a cut and hollowed gourd in the same way the one shown in the photo was made. (This drum has a cowhide drumhead, which can be purchased from a music shop.) Gourds of all sizes and shapes can be used to make drums and, since no two gourds are exactly alike, each drum will have its own unique sound.

MATERIALS

14-inch (36 cm) diameter
   round, hard-shell basketball
   gourd, cured
Soap
Water
Steel wool
Pencil
Wood-burning tool
Electric drill with 1/8-inch bit
Fine-toothed saw
Sandpaper
Cowhide drumhead
Upholstery tacks
4 feet (1.2 m) of TV antenna
   wire
Semigloss stain

STEP ONE

Soak the gourd in soapy water for 20 minutes and use the steel wool to scrub off all dirt and mold. Allow to dry completely.

STEP TWO

Draw a pencil line around the gourd where you would like the top of the drum to be (about one-quarter of the way down from the top). Draw on designs to decorate your drum, starting about 1-1/2 inches (4 cm) below the line.

STEP THREE

Use the wood-burning tool to burn the design into the gourd.

STEP FOUR

Drill a hole into the gourd just above the line. Insert the saw blade and cut off the top of the gourd at the line. Sand the edge smooth.

STEP FIVE

Remove all the pulp and seeds and clean the inside with soapy water and steel wool. Let the gourd dry completely.

STEP SIX

Soak the drumhead in water for seven to eight hours.

STEP SEVEN

Lay the drumhead over the open end of the gourd and trim around the edges, leaving about 1-1/4 inches (3 cm) overlapping. Push a tack through the antenna wire near the end and push it through the drumhead and into the gourd. Wrap the wire around the rim so it holds the drumhead in place, and push another tack through the wire and drumhead, and into the gourd on the side opposite the first tack. Go another quarter of the way around the rim and tack again. Then tack on the opposite side. Continue tacking on opposite sides until you have one tack every inch around the drum. (Note: Do not stretch the drumhead too tightly across the gourd. It will tighten naturally as the cowhide dries.)

STEP EIGHT

Apply an even coat of semigloss stain to the gourd.

157

CHICKEN CONTAINER

Part of the charm of planting gourds is watching them take their unique shapes as they mature. The longer you stare at them, the more they begin to resemble animals. If you come upon a gourd in the shape of a chicken, use it to make this whimsical container.

STEP ONE

Soak the gourd in soapy water for 20 minutes and use the steel wool to scrub off all dirt and mold. Allow to dry completely.

STEP TWO

Find the area on the gourd where the chicken's neck would be and pencil in a sawtoothed

MATERIALS

Chicken-shaped gourd with
  a flat bottom, cured
Soap
Water
Steel wool
Pencil
Electric drill with 1/4-inch bit
Sharp, pointed knife
Fine-toothed saw
Paper or poster board
Cured gourd scraps
Utility knife (optional)
White craft glue
Small spatula or putty knife
Wood dough
Flat rock (optional)
Pocketknife or carving knife
1/4-inch (6 mm) diameter
  wooden dowel, 1 inch
  (2.5 cm) long
1-inch flat paintbrush
Acrylic paints in red, yellow,
  and black
Paintbrush with narrow,
  pointed tip

cutting line for the top of the box. Drill a hole for the bill on the front of the head, and cut a slot about 1-1/2 inches (3 cm) long and 1/4 inch (6 mm) wide on top of the head for the comb. Pierce the gourd with the sharp knife on the drawn line, creating a slit long enough for the saw blade to enter. Cut off the chicken's head.

STEP THREE

Remove all the pulp and seeds and clean the inside with soapy water and steel wool. Let the gourd dry completely.

STEP FOUR

Draw a pattern for the two tail pieces on paper or poster board (see Figure 1). Lay the patterns

on scraps of gourd and use a pencil to trace around the patterns. Using the saw or a utility

FIGURE 1

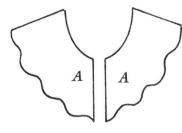

FIGURE 2

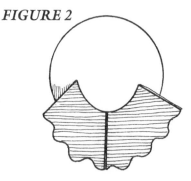

knife, cut out the two tail pieces. Glue them together, line A to line A, and allow to dry. Using the spatula or putty knife, apply a thin layer of wood dough over the joint and allow to dry. Glue the tail to the back of the chicken (see Figure 2).

Draw a pattern for the comb, trace it onto a gourd scrap, and cut it out. Insert it into the slot on the top of the head and glue in place. When dry, cover the junction with a thin layer of wood dough. Cut two wattles out of gourd scrap and set aside.

STEP FIVE

If the weight of the tail throws the chicken off balance, add extra weight to the front. Glue a small, flat rock (the size depends on how much weight you need) inside the chicken, at its lower breast, and allow to dry. Cover the area smoothly with wood dough and allow to dry.

STEP SIX

Using the pocketknife or carving knife, carve a point on one

end of the dowel, insert the other end in the hole for the beak, and glue in place. Glue the wattles underneath the beak.

STEP SEVEN

Using the flat paintbrush, paint the comb, tail, and wattles red, applying a heavy coat of acrylic paint. Brush a thin coat of red

paint over the head and wing areas, shading it lightly onto the breast. Paint the beak yellow. With the narrow-tipped brush and black paint, outline the eye, draw a line down the beak, and outline the tail feathers. Paint the eye yellow and the pupil black, and outline the wing feathers with red.

PAINTED SANTAS

St. Nicholas has taken on so many guises from decade to decade—and from culture to culture—that almost any gourd can be painted to resemble him. The tall Santa in the center of the photograph, who began life as an Indonesian bottle gourd, is 18 inches (46 cm) tall, while the small round one in front—at 4 inches (10 cm) tall and 4 inches wide—is a right chubby old elf. The copper-colored Santa is a bottle gourd; the two fat, red Santas are kettle gourds; the two small, elongated ones are ornamental "spoons."

STEP ONE

Soak the gourd in soapy water for 20 minutes and use the steel wool to scrub off all dirt and mold. Allow to dry completely.

STEP TWO

Pencil your design on the gourd.

STEP THREE

Paint the gourd, beginning with the larger expanses, allowing each color to dry before you add others.

STEP FOUR

When the painted gourd is

completely dry, spray it with the clear varnish.

MATERIALS

For one Santa:

Hard-shell gourd, cured
Soap
Water
Steel wool
Pencil
Acrylic paints
Brushes for use with acrylic
    paints
Clear varnish spray

Gourd Containers with Sea Lyme Grass

Far too distinguished to look like common gourds, these genuinely handsome containers will baffle houseguests who are seeing them for the first time. Anyone who identifies them on the first try gets to stay an extra night.

Step One

Soak the gourd in soapy water for 20 minutes and use the steel wool to scrub off all dirt and mold. Allow to dry completely.

Step Two

With the pencil, outline the opening you plan to make on the gourd. It can be level, slanted from back to front, or cut through both sides of a long-necked gourd (see the top left photo on the opposite page).

Step Three

Pierce the gourd with the knife on the drawn line, creating a slit long enough for the saw blade to enter. Saw around the opening and remove the cut shell.

Step Four

Remove all the pulp and seeds and clean the inside with soapy water and steel wool. Let the gourd dry completely.

Step Five

Use the wood rasp to shape and smooth the opening.

Step Six

Drill a row of holes around the opening approximately 1/4 inch (6 mm) from the edge and 1/2 inch (1.25 cm) apart.

Step Seven

Dye the inside of the gourd black, applying the dye with a paintbrush or the dauber that comes with the dye. When the inside is dry, dye the outside the desired color, again brushing or daubing it on. It's a good idea to experiment with the cut-out piece first, to help you judge what kind of result you'll get.

The long-necked gourd in the top left photograph was dyed red, then over-dyed chocolate brown. The gourd containing the dried flower arrangement was dyed navy blue. In the top right photograph, the multicolored gourd was dyed red and black, while its mate was dyed red.

After the dye has dried (about 24 hours), use the dauber or the paintbrush to apply a coat of the wax.

Step Eight

Thread the needle with the artificial sinew, rawhide, or waxed thread, knot the end, and pull the needle through one of the holes, from the inside out. Lay the three strands of sea lyme grass together and whipstitch them around the rim of the opening, wrapping the sinew over them.

Step Nine

To make the dried arrangement shown in the photo, cut the floral foam to fit snugly into the dish, and fit into place. Place the dish inside the gourd container.

Step Ten

Insert the hydrangeas into the foam, arranging them in a "high left to low right" configuration.

Step Eleven

Attach the ferns to the floral picks and insert them into the foam, filling in any openings.

MATERIALS

For one container:

Hard-shell gourd, cured
Soap
Water
Steel wool
Pencil
Sharp, pointed knife
Fine-toothed saw
Wood rasp
Electric drill with 1/16-inch bit
Black spirit dye for leather
Spirit dye for leather (color of your choice)
Paintbrush (optional)
Clear liquid floor wax
3 lengths of 1/16-inch-diameter sea lyme grass (enough to circle the gourd, with a few inches extra)
Large-eyed needle
Spool of artificial leather sinew, rawhide, or waxed heavy thread
Square of floral foam
Plastic or ceramic dish to fit inside gourd
10 dried pink hydrangeas, stems cut to various lengths
16 fronds of dried ferns, cut to various lengths
16 floral picks

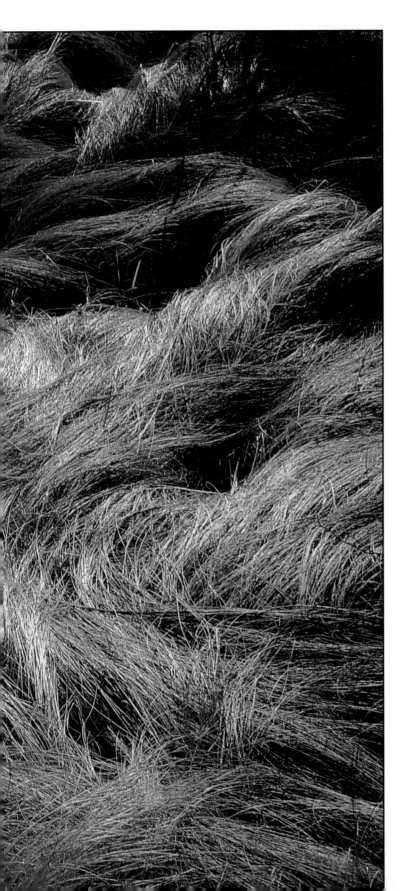

G raceful, pliable, and widely available, grasses are time-honored ingredients for both functional and decorative crafts. Although any attractive grass can be cut, dried, and used for a variety of projects, wheat is worthy of special note.

WHEAT WEAVING

The art of weaving grain has been practiced for at least 5,000 years by cultures throughout the world. Wheat weavings, or corn dollies, originated as fertility symbols made from the last sheaf of grain gathered at harvest time. It was believed that Ceres, the Roman goddess of the harvest, could be kept indoors in a corn dolly to protect her during the winter. In spring the corn dollies would be thrown into the field to help germinate the next crop.

Most weavings are done with wheat, although rye, oats, and other grains can also be used. The best wheat for weaving is long and flexible with a large

FIGURE 1

cavity in the stalk. If you live near a wheat field, ask the farmer if you can buy some and cut it off at the ground about two weeks before normal harvest time. Dry the stalks in the sun for a few days. Then gather the wheat into bundles and hang it upside down in a dry, well-ventilated place where it will be safe from mice and birds. Wheat for weaving can also be obtained by mail order.

Each stalk, or straw, consists of four parts that are important to wheat weaving (see Figure 1). The head, or ear, is the uppermost portion containing the seeds. The neck, or nubs, is where the head becomes a section of undeveloped seeds. The joint, or knee, is the section from which the leaf grows. The portion between the uppermost joint and the head is the part used for wheat weaving.

To prepare the straw for weaving, remove the leaves and soak the straw in warm water for between 15 minutes and four hours, depending on the variety. Commercial suppliers should offer a recommended soaking time; otherwise, you'll need to experiment. To determine whether you've soaked the straw enough, try pinching the very end of the straw. If it springs back to your touch, it's ready. If it seems stiff, soak it some more. Wrap your soaked straw in a moist towel during use. Freeze any leftover straw in a plastic bag rather than letting it dry out. Straw that has been dried and then resoaked will be brittle.

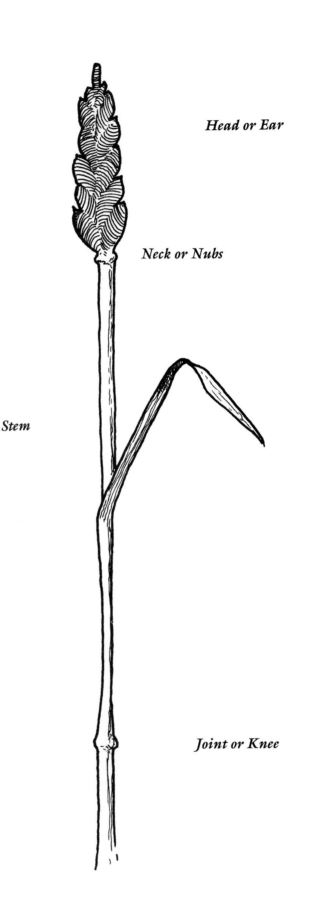

Head or Ear

Neck or Nubs

Stem

Joint or Knee

DRIED GRASS ARRANGEMENT

STEP FOUR

Hot-glue the mushroom to a floral pick and insert the pick into the foam at the front right of the arrangement.

STEP FIVE

Hot-glue each lotus pod to a floral pick, and insert the picks into the foam in front of and behind the grass and fern.

STEP SIX

Hot-glue four of the pomegranates to floral picks and insert the picks into the foam, clustering the pomegranates around the front lotus pod. Attach the fifth pomegranate to the outside of the container with rubber cement.

MATERIALS

1 sponge mushroom
Light blue spray paint
1 × 1-inch (2.5 × 2.5 cm) piece of floral clay
7 × 7-inch (17 × 17 cm) ceramic or plastic container
4 × 4-inch (10 × 10 cm) piece of floral foam
1-inch-diameter bundle of dried grasses about 2 feet (60 cm) high
13 pieces of horsetail fern, five trimmed to 4 inches, three trimmed to 6 inches (15 cm), two trimmed to 10 inches (25 cm), two trimmed to 14 inches (36 cm), and one trimmed to 2 feet
Glue gun
Floral picks
2 lotus pods
5 dried pomegranates
Rubber cement

This combination of grasses and ferns captures the wind-swept charm of wild materials.

STEP ONE

Mist the mushroom with the light blue paint and set it aside to dry.

STEP TWO

Press the floral clay into the bottom of the container, and press the foam on top of the clay, anchoring it firmly.

STEP THREE

Insert the grasses and pieces of horsetail fern directly into the foam, forming a crescent shape that curves from the upper left to the lower right corner.

THE CORIZON

This is a traditional design in Mexico, where it is sometimes known as the "house blessing." It is displayed in the home to bring the blessings of the field indoors and to enhance the fruits of a family's labors. It is also one of the most common wheat weavings in America.

MATERIALS

24 medium-width wheat
    straws
Cotton thread
Scissors

STEP ONE

Select 24 medium straws with evenly matched heads and stems (see page 164). Form an X shape with two straws so the heads and 1 inch (2.5 cm) of straw are above the intersection and the longer portion of the straw is below. The head of the straw on the top of the X should be on the right.

STEP TWO

Lay a third straw on top of the first straw and parallel to the second. Bend the stem of the third straw under the first straw and lay it across the second

straw parallel to the first (see Figure 1).

STEP THREE

Carefully pick up the weave and turn it over, making sure to maintain the position of all of the straws. As in Step 2, lay another straw across the X with its head to the right. Again bring the straw around and under, and lay it parallel to the heads on the left (see Figure 2).

STEP FOUR

Next you must lock these two new straws into position. To do this, grasp the straw end that

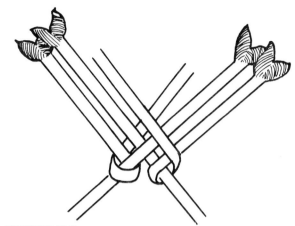

FIGURE 1

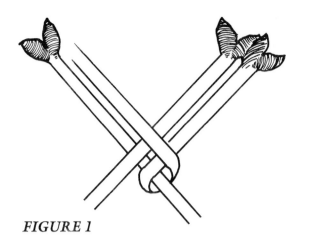

FIGURE 2

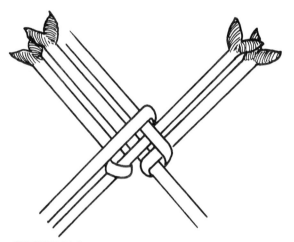

FIGURE 3

FIGURE 4

is lying parallel to the two right heads and bend it over to lie parallel to the lower left stem (see Figure 3). Turn the weave over and repeat this locking bend (see Figure 4). This completes one full round of weaving.

Step Five

Continue adding straws until all 24 have been woven and locked into place. You will notice that each time you add a straw and bend it around and up to the opposite side, you will be moving over an increasingly larger layer of straws. This is what gives the Corizon its character-

istic look. Also try to keep the heads from bunching up as you work around them. This will help prevent unwanted folds or creases in your straws.

Step Six

Because the last straw will not be locked into place by another one, you must tuck its end under the previous lock to secure it.

Step Seven

The hanger on this Corizon was made using a two-straw plait. Take the top two straws on one side and bend them at right angles to each other (as

if north and east). Bend the north straw over the other straw to point south, then bend the east straw over the first to point west and continue for about 4 inches (10 cm). You'll need to hold the base of the straws as you weave to keep them from twisting.

Step Eight

Repeat Step 7 using the top two straws on the other side to create another 4-inch plait. Wind the two plaits around each other to form the hanging loop, and tie at the ends with thread. Using scissors, trim the excess straws.

THE SWEETHEART

This is a traditional design of Welsh origin. It is one of the "love knots" and is associated with courting customs and marriage. The design requires only one type of straw plaiting called the hair braid. It is best made using large-eared wheat.

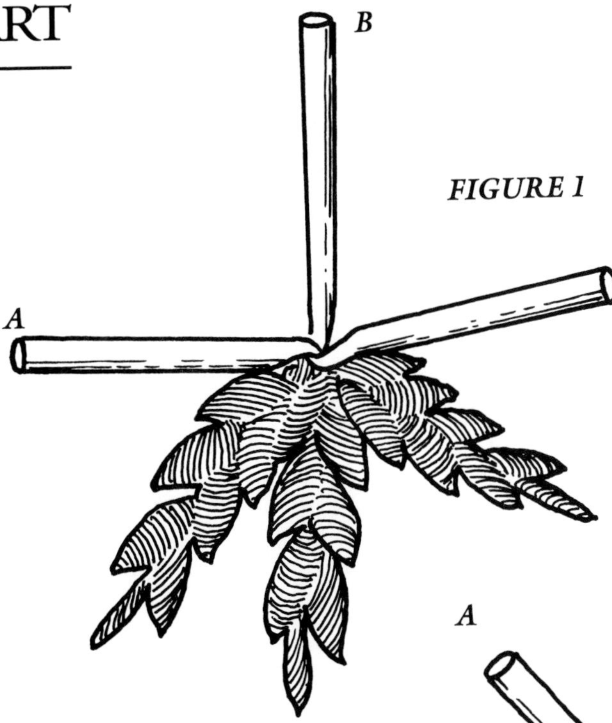

STEP ONE

Tie three thick wheat straws together with thread near the heads but below the necks (see page 164). With the heads toward you, spread the straws into an upside-down T shape (see Figure 1).

STEP TWO

Move straw C over the middle straw B to lie just inside straw A. Then move straw A over straw C (now the middle straw) to lie just inside straw B (see Figure 1).

STEP THREE

Continue alternately moving the outside straws over the inside to create the weave (see Figure 2). Work the straws at right angles to each other and try not to let the straws slip into a V shape. Also try to avoid gaps between straws. Weave a braid 7 inches (17 cm) long and tie it off with thread.

STEP FOUR

Repeat Steps 1 through 3 to create a second 7-inch hair braid.

STEP FIVE

Tie a bundle of 15 to 20 thick straws with thread at the necks and at a point 3 inches (7.5 cm) below.

STEP SIX

Use thread to tie the two hair braids to each side of the column at the upper tie. Bend them into a heart shape and attach the ends to the lower tie with thread.

STEP SEVEN

Tie together three small-headed stalks of medium width as in Step 1 and weave a 4-inch (10 cm) hair braid. Tie it off to form a loop and tie this at the point where the other braids join the top of the heart with the heads pointing down, as shown in the photo. Fan out the heads here and at the bottom.

STEP EIGHT

Tie a loop of 3/8-inch-wide ribbon around the upper junction at the top of the heart to make a hanger. Fasten a bow made from the 5/8-inch-wide ribbon over the lower junction at the bottom of the heart.

FIGURE 1

FIGURE 2

MATERIALS

26 thick wheat straws
Cotton thread
3 medium-width wheat straws
12 inches (30 cm) of 3/8-inch (1 cm) wide pink ribbon
24 inches (60 cm) of 5/8-inch (1.5 cm) wide pink ribbon

169

HOLIDAY WHEAT ARRANGEMENT

The tall lines of this winter arrangement show off the graceful elegance of the wheat straws, making it the perfect addition for a small end table or the corner of a room.

STEP ONE

Arrange the wheat around the wooden dowel and secure twice with floral tape, once about 2 inches (5 cm) up from the bottom and again about 14 inches (36 cm) up from the bottom.

STEP TWO

Trim the foam with a serrated knife to fit inside the clay pot, about an inch (2.5 cm) lower than the rim and 2 inches narrower than the pot. Fill in the space between the foam and the pot with stones to add stability. Press the bottoms of the wheat straws and dowel into the foam. Remove the

MATERIALS

24 straws of wheat, trimmed to 2 feet (60 cm)
1/4-inch (6 mm) wooden dowel, trimmed to 18 inches (46 cm)
Floral tape
Small block of foam
Serrated knife
Clay garden pot, 6 × 3 inches (15 × 7.5 cm)
Handful of stones
Glue gun
Several clumps of dried moss in two varieties
3 dried mushrooms
2 stems of canella berries, trimmed to 3 inches
6 lengths of raffia, trimmed to 12 inches (30 cm)

straws, fill the hole halfway with hot glue, and immediately reinsert the straws.

STEP THREE

Cover the foam with small clumps of moss and hot-glue in place. Arrange the dried mushrooms on one side of the arrangement and hot-glue in place. Hot-glue one stem of canella berries to the other side of the arrangement.

STEP FOUR

Holding all of the raffia strands together, tie them around the wheat straws to cover the floral tape in the middle of the arrangement. Hot-glue a small clump of moss to cover the knots in the raffia and finish by hot-gluing a stem of canella berries on top of the moss.

WHEAT AND ROSES WREATH

While wreaths made from either all wheat or all roses have been popular in the wreathmaking tradition, these materials work surprisingly well together.

STEP ONE

Arrange the straws of wheat into small bouquets of three to five stems each. Position the first bouquet against the wire base and secure by wrapping several times with floral wire. Position the next bouquet so that it covers the stems of the previous bouquet and secure

with floral wire. Continue wiring bouquets of wheat until the base is covered, tucking the stems of the last bouquet under the first bouquet to conceal the stems.

STEP TWO

Wire the bow to the top of the wreath and form loops and curves in the streamers as desired. Position the roses evenly around the wreath, and hot-glue them deep into the wheat. Last, hot-glue four love-in-a-mist seed heads around each rose.

MATERIALS

15-inch (37 cm) heavy-gauge wire wreath base
100 straws of wheat with heads, trimmed to 4 inches (10 cm)
Medium-gauge floral wire
Large French ribbon bow
Glue gun
3 dried roses
12 love-in-a-mist seed heads

STRAW MARQUETRY HEART

The art of straw marquetry has been practiced for hundreds of years. It involves using sheets of split straw as an appliqué. When flattened, the straw exhibits colors and textures that are not apparent when whole. Marquetry is also a fun way to make use of the leftover straw trimmed from your weaving projects. Hearts are a common folk motif in straw work. The design for this one comes from Norway, where making marquetry hearts is a family tradition.

STEP ONE

Soak the straws in a mixture of three parts warm water and one part vinegar. (Vinegar helps break down the starch in the straw.)

STEP TWO

Split each straw lengthwise and open it. Iron the straw from the inside until it is flat and dry. Make sure the iron is not so hot that it scorches or discolors the straw. (The permanent press setting should work well.)

Also, do your ironing on a fairly hard surface. Pressing the straw on a too-soft ironing board can split the wheat.

STEP THREE

Cut two shapes, like the one in Figure 1, out of sturdy paper with a sharp knife or scissors. Glue strips of straw side by side over the entire surface of both shapes with the shiny side up. Turn the shapes over and use scissors to trim the edges. Make two cuts in each as shown in Figure 1 to form the three tongues that will be woven to form the heart. Let the pieces dry completely.

STEP FOUR

Interlace the two shapes in an over-under basket weave to create the heart (see Figure 2). Add a few dabs of glue to secure the weave.

STEP FIVE

Bend a 6-inch (15 cm) split straw into a loop and glue the ends to the front and back of the heart to make a handle. Tuck the lower ends of two wheat heads under the front of the handle and glue into place.

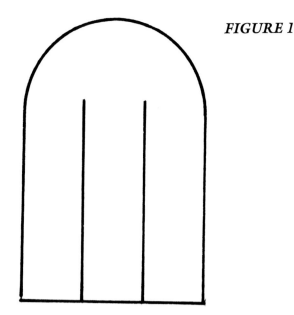

FIGURE 1

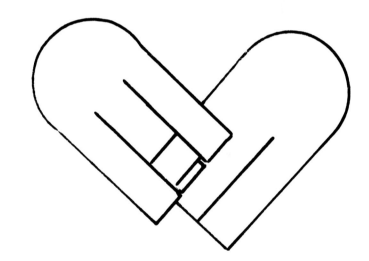

FIGURE 2

STRAW MARQUETRY STAR

Stars have long been used to represent hope for the future and the dawning of a new era. This traditional piece of straw marquetry is both pretty and easy to make. It can be used on its own as a Christmas ornament or with other small marquetry shapes in a mobile or other arrangement.

STEP ONE

Soak the straws in a mixture of three parts warm water and one part vinegar. (Vinegar helps break down the starch in the straw.)

STEP TWO

Split each straw lengthwise and open it. Iron the straw from

MATERIALS

12 to 14 wheat straws, with heads removed
Water
Vinegar
Graph paper
Sharp knife
White craft glue

173

the inside until it is flat and dry. Make sure the iron is not so hot that it scorches or discolors the straw. (The permanent press setting should work well.) Also, do your ironing on a fairly hard surface. Pressing the straw on a too-soft ironing board can split the wheat.

STEP THREE

Make a drawing of your star on graph paper (or trace the one in Figure 1 and transfer it to heavier paper).

STEP FOUR

Glue strips shiny-side-up to fill each of the eight diamond-shaped star points, and trim as necessary.

STEP FIVE

Split a 2-3/4-inch (7 cm) straw into four strips 3/32 inch (2.5 mm) wide. Glue these along the borderlines between the diamonds to intersect in the center of the star and create eight "rays" between the points.

FIGURE 1

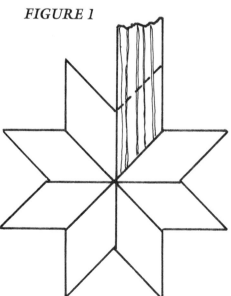

THE HORSESHOE

The horseshoe is a common weaving in many cultures. It is believed to be a symbol of good luck and is often presented to travelers in hopes of ensuring a safe journey. It employs a five-part spiral around a central core.

MATERIALS

70 medium-width wheat straws	Scissors
Wire clippers	8 delicate wheat straws with heads
Wire coat hanger	20 inches (25 cm) of 5/8-inch (1.6 cm) wide ribbon, the same color as the 3/8-inch ribbon
12 inches (30 cm) of 3/8-inch (1 cm) wide ribbon	
Cotton thread	

Step One

Cut enough medium-width wheat straws 14 inches long to make a bundle 1/2 inch (1.3 cm) thick. Using the wire clippers, cut a 14-inch (36 cm) long piece of wire from the coat hanger. Position the wire inside the bundle and insert one end of the 3/8-inch ribbon next to the wire. Tie with thread at the top (securing the ribbon), in the middle, and at the bottom.

Step Two

Tie five straws to the ribbon end of the core with about 1/4 inch (6 mm) against the core and the working ends protruding next to the ribbon. You should have one straw each on the north, east, and south sides of the core and two straws on the west side. Tie again around the five straws and the ribbon just below the core.

Step Three

Bend the five straws perpendicular to the core, with one straw pointing north, one east, one south, and two west (see Figure 1). Move the lower west straw over the upper and across the south straw at a 45-degree angle (see Figure 2). Next bend the south straw up and lay it at a 45-degree angle over the east straw. Continue bending the straws in this manner, making sure to maintain a square shape at each level without curving the straws around the core (see Figure 3).

Step Four

As your spiral progresses, you will need to add new straws. When you have used about two-thirds of a straw, it will begin to get thicker and coarser. Clip the working straw off with scissors at the point where the next straw will bend over it. Insert the thin end of a new straw into the old one (see Figure 4) and continue weaving. Make sure to replace your straws at different levels to avoid weakening the spiral.

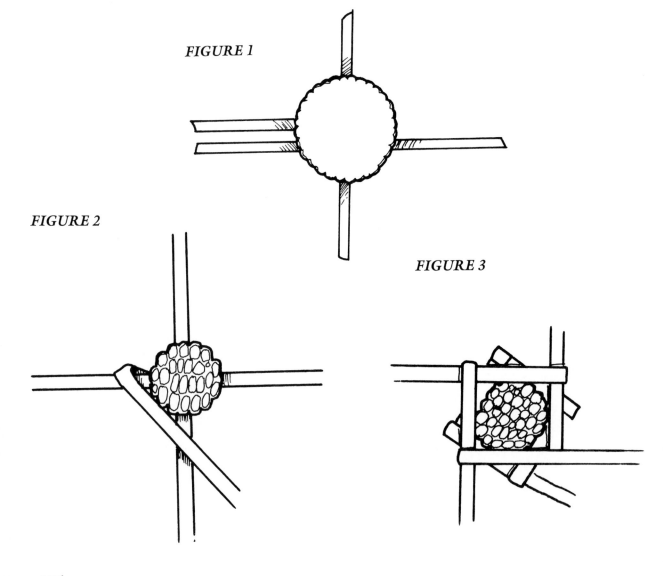

FIGURE 1

FIGURE 2

FIGURE 3

FIGURE 4

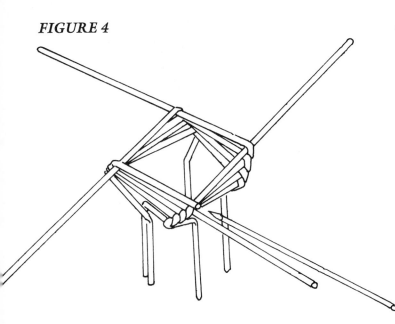

FIGURE 5

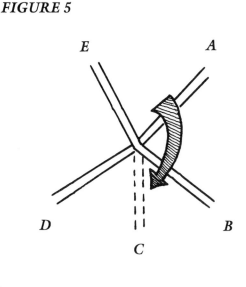

FIGURE 6

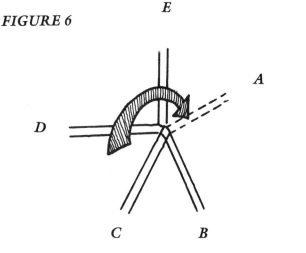

FIGURE 7

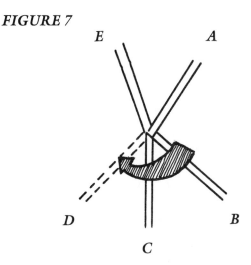

STEP FIVE

Continue your spiral until you have almost reached the end of the core. Bend the spiral into a horseshoe shape, and tie or stitch the free end of the ribbon securely to the inside of the core. Continue spiral weaving past the core and onto the ribbon. Finish weaving by tucking the last working straw under the previous round. Cut off all the straws.

STEP SIX

To make the favor embellishment, you will use the "fill the gap" plait. First bunch and tie four delicate straws together just below the heads. Bend the straws perpendicular to the heads and spread them radially as if they were four arms of a five-pointed star. The point that is left vacant is called the gap.

STEP SEVEN

Move straw A over straw B and into the gap to become straw C, leaving a gap at A (see Figure 5). Move straw D over straw E to fill the gap at A (see Figure 6). Move straw B over straw C to fill the gap at D (see Figure 7). Continue until you have about 4 inches (10 cm) of plait, and stretch this to about 5 to 6 inches (12 to 15 cm). Tie this plait into a loose knot and tie the end to the beginning with thread. Pull one side of the knot out farther than the other to create its distinctive shape.

STEP EIGHT

Repeat Steps 6 and 7 to make a second knot like the first, and tie the two knots side by side at one end of the horseshoe spiral. Add a bow of 5/8-inch ribbon to match the hanger.

COURTIER'S KNOT

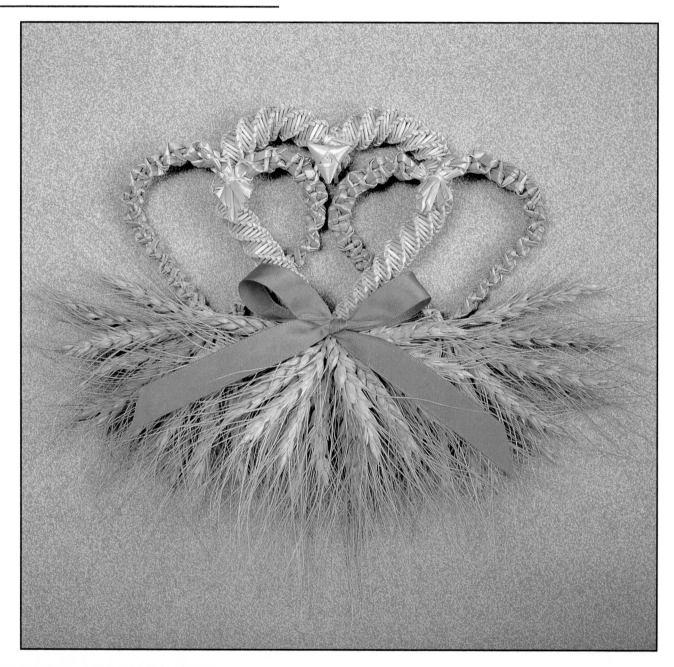

MATERIALS

60 delicate wheat straws
32 medium- to large-width
   wheat straws
Medium-gauge wire
Cotton thread
Scissors
Glue gun
18 inches (46 cm) of 5/8-inch
   (1.5 cm) wide ribbon

Legend has it that this weaving was developed as a way to chaperon young lovers. When a suitor would come courting, the girl's father would give him some wheat to plait. This would keep the young man's hands busy and allow him to demonstrate his talents for his sweetheart. Often these knots were hung in the home after marriage as a reminder of youthful romance.

STEP ONE

The central heart of this courtier's knot uses two lengths of five-part spiral weaving. Begin by making a 6-inch (15 cm) long core of 15 medium straws, or about 3/8 inch (1 cm) in diameter. Insert a length of wire in the center and tie the core with thread at the top, bottom, and middle.

FIGURE 1

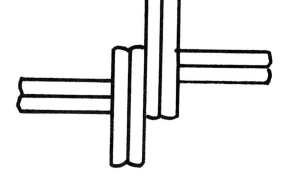

STEP TWO

To begin your spiral, tie five straws at the bottom of the bundle so that one straw points north, one east, and one south, and two straws point west (see Figure 1 on page 176). Move the lower west straw over the upper and across the south straw at a 45-degree angle (see Figure 2 on page 176). Next bend the south straw up and lay it at a 45-degree angle over the east straw. Continue bending the straws in this manner, making sure to maintain a square shape at each level without curving the straws around the core (see Figure 3 on page 176).

STEP THREE

As your spiral progresses, you will need to add new straws. When you have used about two-thirds of a straw, it will begin to get thicker and coarser. Clip the working straw off with scissors at the point where the next straw will bend over it. Insert the thin end of a new straw into the old one (see Figure 4 on page 177) and continue weaving. Make sure to replace your straws at different levels to avoid weakening the spiral.

STEP FOUR

Continue spiraling all the way to the top of the core and tie it off with thread. Cut off all but 1/2 inch (1.25 cm) of the remaining straw with scissors.

STEP FIVE

Repeat Steps 1 through 4 to make another 6-inch spiral. Bend the spirals to form one heart shape and tie at the top and bottom.

STEP SIX

The outer hearts use a compass weave. Cut a 5-1/2-inch (14 cm) piece of wire and insert it into a straw. Bunch and tie eight straws around this wire core near the heads but below the necks. Position two straws each on the north, south, east, and west sides and bend the straws perpendicular to the core so two straws point in each direction.

STEP SEVEN

Bend the north straws to the south and the south straws to the north on opposite sides of the core (see Figure 1 on page 179). Give the wheat a quarter turn and repeat. Continue turning and bending, keeping the weave square and leaving no gaps between straws, until you have woven 5 inches (12 cm). Tie off the end with thread.

STEP EIGHT

Repeat Steps 6 and 7 to make another 5-inch compass weave, and bend the two to form one heart shape. Tie at the bottom.

STEP NINE

Repeat Steps 6 through 8 to make another heart. Make sure the two hearts match in size, then link them into the larger spiral heart and tie at their tops. Fan out the wheat heads and let the piece dry on a screen or cake rack.

STEP TEN

To make the triangle at the top of the spiral heart, first split open a straw 10 inches (25 cm) long. While still wet, fold this straw at 90 degrees with the inside facing up (see Figure 2). Fold the right side to the left and around to form the first point of the triangle (see Figure 3). Place the downward end at the top of the right side and cut the short section of the straw at 60 degrees. Wrap the straw around this cut end to form the second point (see Figure 4). Wrap the remaining straw around to form the third point (see Figure 5). Continue wrapping until you get to the end of your straw. Cut the straw to a sharp point and slip it under the previous folds on the back. Allow the triangle to dry, and hot-glue into place.

STEP ELEVEN

Use the ribbon to tie a bow around the bottom of the spiral heart.

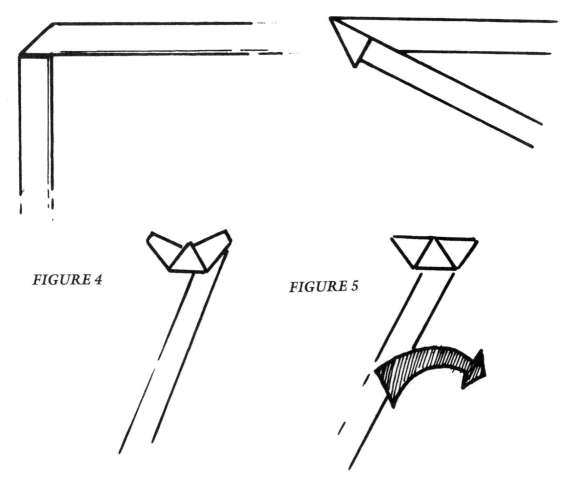

FIGURE 2

FIGURE 3

FIGURE 4

FIGURE 5

THE COUNTRY FAVOR

The country favor is the most traditional and diverse of all wheat weavings, so much so that it is considered more of a category than an individual design. It was originally developed as a courting gesture and was given to a sweetheart in hopes of eliciting a special favor; hence the name. Country favors are as varied as the wheat weavers who make them. This one is by Morgyn Geoffry Owens-Celli of Long Beach, California.

MATERIALS

26 medium-width wheat
    straws
Cotton thread
16 delicate wheat straws

STEP ONE

Bunch and tie together with thread 12 medium wheat straws near the heads but below the necks (see page 164). Lay the bunch on a table and spread the straws out, dividing them into two groups of six straws each.

STEP TWO

Beginning with the right-hand group, lift up the second straw from the outside and move the outside straw under it and over all the other straws on the right-hand side and lay it down to become the inside straw of the left-hand group (see Figure 1). Lift what is now the second straw from the outside of the right-hand group and again move the new outside straw under it and over the others to become the inside straw of the left-hand group. Repeat a third time, leaving three straws in the right-hand group and nine in the left.

STEP THREE

Now move to the left-hand group and lift the second straw from the outside and move the outside straw under it and over all the other straws on the left-hand side to become the inside straw of the right-hand group. Repeat two more times until you again have six straws on each side. This is called a diamond ribbon plait (see Figure 2).

STEP FOUR

Continue plaiting in this manner until you have a 6-inch (15 cm) ribbon of plaited straws. Loop the ribbon behind itself and tie with the thread to form the central loop of your country favor.

STEP FIVE

To make the side loops, bunch and tie together with thread seven medium-width straws and lay them on the table with four on the right and three on the left. As in the diamond ribbon plait, pass the outside straw on the right-hand side under the second straw and over the others on the right-hand side to become the inside straw of the left-hand group (see Figure 3).

FIGURE 1

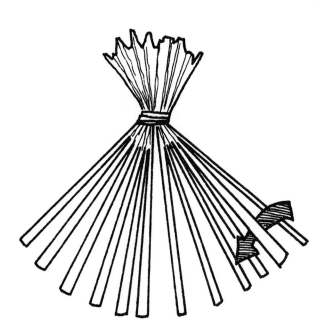

FIGURE 2

182

FIGURE 5

FIGURE 3

FIGURE 4

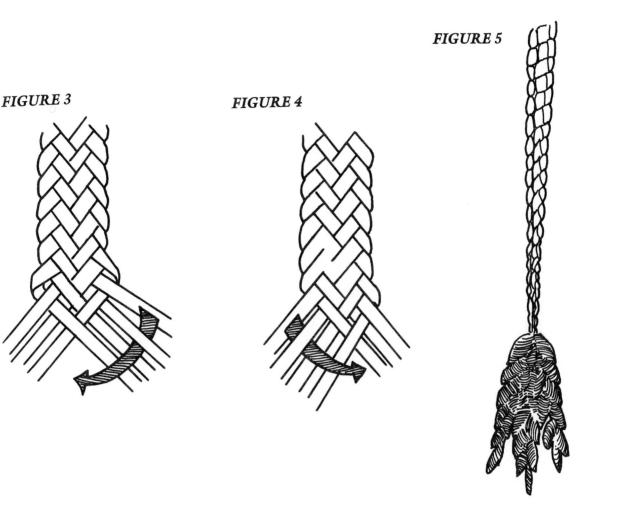

Repeat on the left-hand side by bringing the outside straw under one and over two to become the inside straw of the right-hand group (see Figure 4). This is called a seven-straw flat plait.

Step Six

Continue plaiting in this manner until you have a 5-inch (12 cm) ribbon of plaited straws. Again loop the plait and tie. Follow Step 5 to make a second plait and tie both with thread to the sides of the diamond plait.

Step Seven

The knots on the front of this favor are made using a weave called a fill-the-gap plait. To make it, first bunch and tie four delicate straws together at the heads. Pull all the straws perpendicular to the heads

and arrange as if each were four arms of a five-pointed star. There will be one arm missing, which is called the gap.

Step Eight

Move straw A over straw B and into the gap to become straw C, leaving a gap at A (see Figure 5 on page 177). Move straw D over straw E to fill the gap at A (see Figure 6 on page 177). Move straw B over straw C to fill the gap at D (see Figure 7 on page 177). Continue until you have about 4 inches (10 cm) of plait.

Step Nine

Loosely tie the plait into an overhand knot and tie the end to the beginning with thread. Open up the knotted plait and pull one side into a larger loop

than the other to create the elongated knot that is the distinctive part of this design.

Step Ten

Repeat Steps 7 through 9 to create another knotted plait and tie both to the front of the favor with thread.

Step Eleven

The final loops on the sides are each made with four delicate straws, using the fill-the-gap plait (repeat Steps 7 and 8). Weave each about 3 inches (7.5 cm) long, then pull and stretch the weave until you have about 4 inches (see Figure 5). This will give the weave a different look. Tie each loop into place with thread and spread out the heads of all of the wheat.

CONES, NUTS, SEEDS, AND PODS

Cones, seeds, nuts, and pods aren't as showy as flowers, herbs, or even leaves. Theirs is a less obvious beauty. Their colors range from beige to brown, their textures are prickly, and their shapes are subtle, yet they can yield handsome crafts.

There are no complex technicalities involved in gathering, drying, or preserving cones, seeds, nuts, and pods. They are there for the taking, ready to pick from the tree or retrieve from the ground. The only challenges are beating the squirrels to the nuts, rescuing the cones before they rot, and using the seeds before they germinate.

Since insects are just as fond of these items as crafters are, it's wise to wage a minor extermination campaign as your first step. Spread cones, seeds, or pods in a single layer on a baking sheet and bake them at 200°F for 25 minutes, to kill any eggs or larvae.

CONE KISSING BALL

The best-known kissing balls are made from mistletoe and hang from doorways throughout the Christmas holidays. But there's no reason to limit your materials or the season in which you get kissed. This cone-and-nut ball is topped with a romantic bouquet.

STEP ONE

Bake all cones, nuts, pods, and seeds at 200°F for 25 minutes, to kill any larvae or eggs.

STEP TWO

Color the foam ball with the shoe dye and allow to dry.

STEP THREE

Wrap the piece of medium-gauge wire with brown floral tape, and bend it double. Stick the ends into and through the ball, leaving a loop to serve as a hanger. Bend the straight ends of the wire back against the bottom of the ball.

STEP FOUR

Make cone flowers by cutting across each Douglas fir cone between two layers of petals, using wire cutters or pruning shears (see "Making Cone Flowers" below).

STEP FIVE

Drill through each seed and nut so that you have entrance and exit holes. Make sure the holes are on the part of the object that you want to end up against the ball.

STEP SIX

Insert a 4-inch (10 cm) piece of wire through each seed, pod, and nut, and twist the wire ends together, starting close to the object and continuing to the ends of the wire. Loop a 4-inch piece of wire around each cone and cone flower, and twist the wire ends together in a similar fashion.

STEP SEVEN

To attach an object to the foam ball, dip the end of its twisted wire in glue and insert it into the foam ball. Use any pattern you wish, but make sure the ball is covered.

STEP EIGHT

Spray the finished ball with clear varnish, and allow it to dry.

STEP NINE

Make the dried decoration by positioning the sprigs of peach canella berries with stems at the top of the ball and berries equidistant around the ball. Hot-glue the stems to the ball. Next, glue the bunches of caspia around the top of the ball. Hot-glue the bow to the top of the ball and hot-glue the dried roses among the loops of the bow.

DESIGNER'S TIP

MAKING CONE FLOWERS

Cone "flowers" are traditional modifications of whole cones. To make one, cut between two layers of "petals," using heavy scissors or pruning shears (see Figure 1). Most crafters leave four to eight layers of petals on their flowers, which can then be wired or glued onto craft projects (see Figure 2).

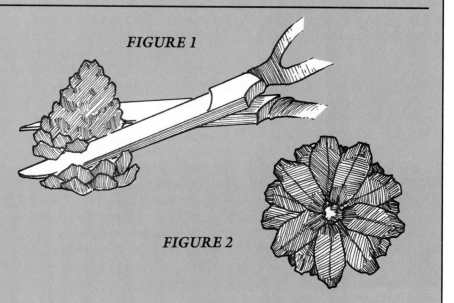

FIGURE 1

FIGURE 2

MATERIALS

18 pinecones, 1 to 2 inches
    (2.5 to 5 cm) in diameter
20 buckeyes
3 eucalyptus pods
15 peach seeds
20 sweet-gum balls
16 Douglas fir cones, about 2
    inches (5 cm) in diameter
6 to 12 small cones of any
    variety

5-inch (12 cm) diameter
    foam ball
Liquid brown shoe dye
16-inch (41 cm) length of
    medium-gauge wire
Brown floral tape
Wire cutters or pruning shears
Electric drill with 6/64-inch bit
92 4-inch (10 cm) lengths
    of fine-gauge wire

White craft glue
Clear varnish spray
4 sprigs of dried peach
    canella berries
Glue gun
12 small bunches of
    dried caspia
1 printed ribbon bow
5 dried red roses

CONE AND NUT WREATH

Whatever varieties of evergreens and nut-bearing trees abound in your region, you can combine the various shapes and colors of their cones and nuts into a handsome wreath that requires no further decoration.

MATERIALS

15 white-pine cones, 2 to 3 inches (5 to 7 cm) in diameter
10 white-pine cones, 1 to 1-1/2 inches (2.5 to 4 cm) in diameter
15 large pecans, about 1-1/2 inches (4 cm) long
15 small pecans, about 3/4 inch (2 cm) long
5 peach pits
5 buckeyes
5 Douglas fir cones, about 3 inches in diameter
5 sweet-gum balls
14 Virginia pine cones, about 2 inches long
22 Virginia pine cones, about 4 inches (10 cm) long
Jigsaw
15 × 15-inch (39 × 39 cm) piece of pegboard
Electric drill with 9/16- and 5/64-inch bits
Household bleach
Wire cutters or pruning shears
99 6-inch (15 cm) lengths of fine-gauge floral wire
Clear varnish spray
12 × 12 inch (30 × 30 cm) square of brown felt
White craft glue
6-inch length of heavy-gauge floral wire
Pliers

STEP ONE

Bake the cones and nuts at 200°F for 25 minutes, to kill any insect larvae or eggs.

STEP TWO

Using the jigsaw, cut a circular piece of pegboard 12 inches (30 cm) in diameter and cut an 8-inch (20 cm) diameter hole in the center, making a doughnut-shaped base.

STEP THREE

Using the drill and 9/16-inch bit, drill holes in the pegboard base, for wiring in the cones and nuts. Extra holes will be especially useful close to the outside and inside rims.

STEP FOUR

Soak the white-pine cones and pecans in household bleach for two to five minutes, until they reach the desired color.

STEP FIVE

Make "flowers" from the white-pine cones by cutting through the width of the cone, between two layers of "petals," using wire cutters or pruning shears. Leave four to five layers of petals on each flower.

STEP SIX

Using the drill and 5/64-inch bit, drill through all of the nuts and pits, making an entrance hole and an exit hole. Drill the holes on the part of the nut that will end up next to the base. Insert the 6-inch pieces of fine-gauge floral wire through the holes of all of the nuts and pits, and twist the wire ends together, right up against each item. Set aside.

STEP SEVEN

Wire each cone and flower by doubling a 6-inch piece of fine-gauge wire, looping it around the cone between two layers of petals, and twisting the wires together close to the cone.

STEP EIGHT

To make a loop for hanging, insert the heavy-gauge wire through two holes of the pegboard base and twist the ends together.

STEP NINE

Begin wiring material on the inside rim of the base. Insert the wires of two small Virginia pine cones into adjacent holes, lay the cones flat, and twist together the wire ends of both cones. (Pliers make this easier.) Continue wiring ton he small pinecones until the entire inside rim is covered. Take the larger Virginia pine cones and wire them to the outside rim by the same procedure.

STEP TEN

Lay the white-pine cones flat between the rims and wire them to the base. These merely add fullness to the wreath; other cones and nuts will be wired on top of them.

STEP ELEVEN

Wire the large cone flowers to the base in clusters of three, equidistant around the wreath, then wire on the remaining nuts, cones, and cone flowers.

STEP TWELVE

When the wreath is full, use pliers to make sure all wires are firmly secured on the back of the base. Clip any wire ends over 1 inch (2.5 cm) long, and bend wire ends flat against the back. Spray the wreath with clear varnish.

STEP THIRTEEN

Cut the brown felt into a circle 12 inches in diameter and cut an 8-inch-diameter hole in the middle. Make a slit for the hanger loop to fit through, and glue the felt onto the back of the wreath.

CONE SWAG

MATERIALS

7 Norway spruce cones, 4 to 6 inches (10 to 15 cm) long
7 Norway spruce cones, about 2 inches (5 cm) in diameter (length is not important)
3 seeds, about 1-1/2 inches (4 cm) long, from a large cone
11-inch (30 cm) length of heavy-gauge floral wire
17 9-inch (22 cm) lengths of fine-gauge floral wire
3 9-inch lengths of very fine-gauge floral wire
Brown floral tape
Pruning shears
Clear varnish spray
2 yards (1.8 m) green velvet ribbon 1-1/2 inches wide

Sometimes the simplest shapes are the most pleasing. This vertical swag combines cones, cone flowers, and large cone seeds for a year-round decoration.

STEP ONE

Bake the cones and seeds at 200°F for 25 minutes, to kill any insect larvae or eggs.

STEP TWO

Wrap all wires with floral tape. Make a loop in one end of the 12-inch piece of heavy-gauge wire to make a hanger. The remainder of the wire will serve as the base for the other materials.

STEP THREE

Using pruning shears, make cone "flowers" from the 2-inch-diameter cones by cutting across the width of the cone, between two layers of "petals." Leave five to six layers of petals on each flower.

STEP FOUR

Wire each cone and flower by doubling a 9-inch piece of fine-gauge wire, looping it around the cone between two layers of petals, and twisting the wires together close to the cone. Wrap a 9-inch piece of very fine-gauge wire around the narrow end of each large seed.

STEP FIVE

Wire a cone to the bottom of the base, so the cone fits snugly against the wire. Wire the rest of the cones to the base, alternating one flower with one cone, until the swag is filled. Wire the three large seeds to the top of the swag. When you wire the materials to the base, leave a wire "stem" of about 1 inch (2.5 cm) on each cone and flower except the bottom one, to allow flexibility in positioning.

STEP SIX

Retape all wires to hide the wire ends and help secure the cones. Make a bow from the ribbon, and tie it to the top of the swag, leaving 10-inch (25 cm) streamers.

CONE AND SUMAC WREATH

If you live in an area where pine trees are plentiful, you might try making this striking pinecone and sumac wreath. Gather the cones after they've fallen to the ground and allow them to dry thoroughly in paper bags or on a wire screen. Sumac bushes are easy to find in uncultivated fields or along roadsides. By late fall or winter the blossoms will dry naturally on the plant, turning a deep burgundy color. These can be picked and used immediately. Be sure to pick only red sumac blossoms—white blossoms belong to poison sumac.

STEP ONE

Bake the cones at 200°F for 25 minutes, to kill any insect larvae or eggs.

STEP TWO

Cut the wire into 6-inch (15 cm) long pieces. The length will vary depending on the diameter of your pinecones. After wrapping a cone, you'll need at least 2 inches of wire left to secure the cone to the base. Wrap a piece of wire around each cone between the lower rows of petals.

STEP THREE

Beginning on the outer edge of the wreath base, secure the cones to the base in a single layer. Continue adding layers of cones until the base is completely covered.

STEP FOUR

Glue the stems of the sumac blossoms to the cones at various points around the wreath, making sure that the points of attachment are hidden in the layers of pinecones.

MATERIALS

175 to 200 pinecones
Heavy wire
Wire cutters
24-inch (60 cm) diameter
  wire wreath base
Glue gun
50 dried sumac blossoms

TABLE TREE AND CANDLE HOLDERS

Very small cones make excellent craft materials, assuming you gather enough of them. This handsome set uses about a gallon of hemlock cones.

Table Tree

STEP ONE

Bake the cones at 200°F for 25 minutes, to kill any insect larvae or eggs.

STEP TWO

Using the drill and 1/2-inch bit, drill a hole in the center of the 3-inch piece of wood, and glue the dowel in the hole with craft glue. Allow it to dry.

STEP THREE

Spread a thin coat of craft glue on the top of the dowel, and insert it into the bottom of the foam cone.

STEP FOUR

Hot-glue the hemlock cones to the "tree," covering the surface completely. The foam is less likely to melt if you apply the glue to the hemlock cones, rather than to the foam. Using a warm glue gun will produce even less melting.

If your friends and family are particularly accident-prone, you might want to wire the cones to the foam tree. To do that, loop a piece of very fine-gauge floral wire around the base of each cone, twist the wires right next to the cone, and insert the wire ends into the foam tree. For normal wear and tear, however, a glue gun will produce satisfactory—and much faster—results.

STEP FIVE

Spray the tree with clear varnish.

MATERIALS

Table Tree

About 1/2 gallon (2 l) of hemlock cones or other very small cones, 3/8 to 3/4 inch (1 to 2 cm) long
1 piece of wood, 3 inches (7 cm) square and 1/2 inch (1.25 cm) thick
Electric drill with 1/2-inch bit
1/2-inch-diameter wooden dowel, 6 inches (15 cm) long
White craft glue
9-inch (22 cm) foam cone
Glue gun
Fine-gauge floral wire (optional)
Clear varnish spray

MATERIALS

Candle Holders

About 1/2 gallon (2 l) hemlock cones or other very small cones, about 1/2 inch (1.25 cm) long
Serrated knife
5-inch (12 cm) foam ball
2 metal candle cups
Glue gun
Clear varnish spray
2 5-inch-diameter circles of brown felt

Candle Holders

STEP ONE

Bake the cones at 200°F for 25 minutes, to kill any insect larvae or eggs.

STEP TWO

Using the serrated knife, cut the foam ball in half and cut out a 1-inch (2.5 cm) diameter hole in the top of each half, deep enough to hold the candle cup.

STEP THREE

Insert the candle cups in the holes.

STEP FOUR

Hot-glue the hemlock cones to the foam halves, covering the top surfaces completely. The foam is less likely to melt if you apply the glue to the cones, rather than to the foam. Using a warm glue will produce even less melting.

STEP FIVE

Spray the candle holders with clear varnish and allow to dry.

STEP SIX

Glue the felt circles to the bottoms of the holders.

SEED CHRISTMAS TREE ORNAMENTS

A fresh Christmas tree seems to call for ornaments made from nature's materials. Use interesting seeds of any variety to make these.

STEP ONE

Remove all the flesh from the pumpkin seeds. Wash them and allow them to dry.

STEP TWO

Bake all the seeds at 200°F for 25 minutes, to kill any insect larvae or eggs.

STEP THREE

Apply glue around the perimeter of the cardboard circle.

STEP FOUR

Place pumpkin seeds side by side on the glue around the circle, with about two-thirds of their length projecting off the cardboard (see Figure 1). Let dry.

STEP FIVE

Apply a circle of glue on the cardboard below the pumpkin seeds and add a second row of pumpkin seeds, overlapping the first. Let dry, then glue on a third row, overlapping the second.

STEP SIX

Squeeze a few drops of glue into the center of the ornament and add the rapeseeds or other small seeds to fill the space. Let dry.

STEP SEVEN

Seeds may be left their natural color. If desired, spray the ornament with white, red, or green paint, and allow to dry.

STEP EIGHT

Spray the ornament with clear varnish and allow to dry. Then apply a circle of glue around the back of the ornament. Fold the gold thread in half, to serve as a hanger, and lay the ends on the back with the loop extending off the ornament. Glue on the green felt.

MATERIALS

For each ornament:

About 22 pumpkin seeds
About 7 rapeseeds, white millet seeds (sold as wild bird seed), or other small seeds
White craft glue
1-1/2-inch (4 cm) diameter circle of thin cardboard or poster board
White, red, or green spray paint (optional)
Clear varnish spray
5-inch (12 cm) length of heavy gold thread
1-1/2-inch diameter circle of green felt

FIGURE 1

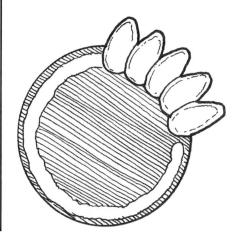

CHRISTMAS PINECONE BASKET

This festive cone basket makes the perfect container for spicy orange pomanders or your favorite holiday potpourri. After the holidays pass, remove the evergreens and replace the red bow with one of another color.

STEP ONE

Bake the cones at 200°F for 25 minutes, to kill any insect larvae or eggs.

STEP TWO

Build the basket's base by wiring the ends of the 12 straight twigs to the embroidery hoop. Trim the twigs flush with the hoop. Bend the fresh-cut twig to form the handle. Position each end against the hoop, nail in place, and reinforce by wrapping several times with wire.

MATERIALS

About 30 small pinecones
Medium-gauge wire
About 12 straight twigs, 1/3 inch (8 mm) in diameter, trimmed to 8 inches (20 cm)
6-1/2-inch (16.5 cm) diameter wooden embroidery hoop
22-inch (55 cm) fresh-cut twig, 1/3 inch diameter
Small nails
Tack hammer
Wire cutters
Glue gun
Clear varnish spray
10 dried strawflower blooms
6 strands of red raffia
Sprig of dried pepperberries
Small dried strawflower bloom
5 sprigs of fresh evergreens

STEP THREE

Attach the bottom row of pinecones to the basket by looping a length of wire around each cone, twisting the wire several times, and then wiring the cone to the embroidery hoop. Be sure each cone fits snugly against the hoop and against adjoining cones. (It's easier to work with longer lengths of wire so you don't have to cut the wire after each cone.)

STEP FOUR

Hot-glue the top row of cones onto the tips of the bottom cones, angling their tops slightly inward. Add sheen to the cones

with a coat of clear varnish and allow to dry completely.

STEP FIVE

Position the strawflowers randomly on the basket and hot-glue in place. Holding all of the raffia strands together, tie them into a bow. Trim off one side of the bow's streamers next to the bottom cones. Spiral the other streamers around the basket's handle, hot-gluing intermittently as needed. Hot-glue the sprig of pepperberries onto the center of the bow and hot-glue a small strawflower bloom on top of the pepperberries. Last, line the basket with the sprigs of fresh evergreens.

SEED FLOWERS

through the second hole. Twist the wires together.

STEP FOUR

Working on the side of the cardboard without the wire, apply a ring of glue around the circumference, close to the outside rim.

STEP FIVE

Press on the outer ring of seeds, laying them flat and close together, allowing their bottom halves to project off the cardboard. Let dry.

STEP SIX

Glue on the second and third rings of seeds, allowing each ring to overlap the previous one. Let dry.

STEP SEVEN

Apply a few drops of glue in the center and add the small seeds. Let dry, then spray the flower with clear varnish.

These decorative flowers look festive by themselves or as additions to other fresh or dried arrangements. The "petals" can be made from any attractive seed—pumpkin, watermelon, Indian corn, yellow corn. Any small seeds can serve as the centers—mustard, lettuce, or white proso millet (commonly sold as wild bird seed).

STEP ONE

Remove any flesh from the seeds. Wash all the seeds and allow them to dry, then bake at 200°F for 25 minutes, to kill

any insect larvae or eggs.

STEP TWO

Glue together the cardboard and felt circles and allow them to dry.

STEP THREE

With the ice pick or awl, punch two holes approximately 1/8 inch (3 mm) apart in the center of the circle. Going from the felt side to the cardboard side, insert the wire through one hole, bend back about 1 inch (2.5 cm) of it, and bring the bent end back

MATERIALS

For each flower:
1-1/2-inch diameter (4 cm) circle of stiff cardboard or poster board
1-1/2-inch diameter circle of green felt
White craft glue
Ice pick or awl
18-inch (46 cm) length of heavy-gauge floral wire
25 to 35 medium or large seeds
6 to 8 very small seeds
Clear varnish spray

CORNHUSKS

Cornhusks are good for making compost, bedding hogs, and creating good-looking traditional crafts. Many a child has played with cornhusk dolls, and many a homestead door has boasted a cornhusk wreath.

Most craft stores carry cornhusks in a variety of colors, usually in 4-ounce (10 g) packages. (Exercise some restraint while shopping; 4 ounces is a lot of cornhusks.) On the other hand, free husks abound in cornfields and grocery stores, temporarily wrapped around ears of corn.

Gather husks when the corn is mature and the husks are dry. Peel them off the ear as carefully as possible, to avoid tearing them. The bigger they are, the more versatile they will be at craft-making time. Lay the husks out to dry in a well-ventilated place, then store them in plastic bags.

To dye cornhusks, dissolve ordinary fabric dye in boiling water, according to the package directions. Remove the dye from the heat, add the corn-

199

husks, and leave them in the dye until they reach the desired color—anywhere from a few minutes to overnight, depending upon whether you want a subtle pastel shade or a deep, rich hue. Remove the husks from the dye and spread them in a single layer on newspaper to dry.

When making crafts, always work with wet cornhusks. Dry ones won't bend or twist; instead, they will rip and tear. Soak dry husks in a pan or a bucket of warm water until they are pliable—usually about 15 minutes. If you have trouble separating packaged husks, submerge the whole bundle for a few minutes, then peel them apart.

CORNHUSK ANGELS

No Christmas mantle is complete without caroling angels. This graceful trio will add a note of harmony to any home.

STEP ONE

Soak the cornhusks in the warm water for about 15 minutes, until they're pliable.

STEP TWO

Make a "fish hook" in one end of the 3-inch piece of heavy-gauge wire, and insert the other end in the foam ball. (Don't pull it all the way through yet.)

STEP THREE

Take a piece of husk approximately 2-1/2 inches (6 cm) wide and 6 inches (15 cm) long and use your fingers to gather it in the middle. Position the husk on top of the ball and pull the heavy-gauge wire until the hook is in the foam, catching the gathered center of the husk and fastening it to the ball. Spread the husk across the ball to cover the "head" and twist a piece of fine-gauge wire around the "neck," right below the ball (see Figure 1).

STEP FOUR

To make the arms, place the 7-1/2-inch piece of medium-gauge wire lengthwise along one side of a cornhusk approximately 8 inches (20 cm) long and 3-1/2 inches (8 cm) wide. Roll the husk tightly around the wire to form a cylinder. Tie the center with a piece of fine-gauge wire. Trim the husk ends so the cylinder is 7-1/2 inches (19 cm) long (see Figure 2).

STEP FIVE

Gather a 3 × 3-1/2-inch (7 × 8 cm) piece of husk around one arm about 3/4 inch (2 cm) from one end of the cylinder. Tie it with fine-gauge wire. Turn the husk inside out, back toward the center of the cylinder, to make the "sleeve" puff at the angel's wrist. Tie the sleeve at the center of the arm with fine-gauge wire (see Figure 3). Repeat on the other arm to form the other sleeve.

STEP SIX

Fit the arms between the neck pieces and tie them all together below the "bust."

STEP SEVEN

Cut two pieces of husk 1-1/4 inches (3 cm) wide and 3 inches (7 cm) long for the bodice. To avoid raw edges, fold each long side to the center, so that both strips are 3/4 inch wide. Lay the middle of each strip on a "shoulder" and bring its ends down the front and back, crossing the two strips at the waist, both in front and in back. Twist a piece of fine wire around the waist.

STEP EIGHT

Bend the arms upward, out of the way before making the skirt. Then, using your largest and prettiest husks first, position four to six large husks evenly around the doll's chest and head, overlapping the waist by about 1/2 inch (1.3 cm). Wrap a piece of fine-gauge wire around the waist (you'll be able to feel the other waist wire underneath) and gently fold the skirt down (see Figure 4).

STEP NINE

While the husks are still wet, reposition the arms. Allow the doll to dry thoroughly, about three days.

STEP TEN

Spread glue on the head and wrap the corn silk around the head to make hair. Glue down any wayward silks.

STEP ELEVEN

With white craft glue, glue two husks together to make one thick one and allow to dry. Cut out a pair of wings and a hymnal, and hot-glue them to the angel. Twist masking tape around the 4-inch piece of heavy-gauge wire, bend it into a halo shape, and insert it into the back of the head.

FIGURE 1

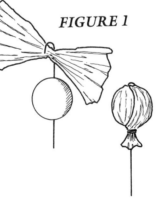

FIGURE 4

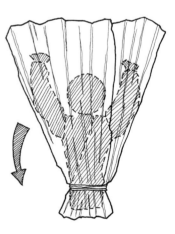

FIGURE 2

FIGURE 3

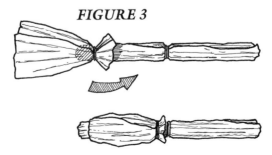

CORNHUSK WREATH WITH POINSETTIAS

Cornhusks left in their natural color provide a perfect backdrop for "poinsettia flowers" and "leaves" made from husks and dyed bright red and green.

Wreath

STEP ONE

Soak the cornhusks in the warm water until they're pliable, about 15 minutes.

STEP TWO

Using cornhusks of any size, cover the wreath base by wrapping husks around it and gluing them on with craft glue.

STEP THREE

To make a hanger for the wreath, wrap the piece of floral wire around the base and twist the ends together next to the base. Bend the wire ends into a loop and twist them together.

MATERIALS

Wreath

1 pound (0.45 kg) of natural-colored cornhusks
Bucket full of warm water
12-inch (30 cm) straw wreath base
White craft glue
12-inch length of heavy-gauge floral wire
About 160 floral pins
Scissors or craft knife
7-inch (17 cm) diameter bow made from plaid ribbon 1 inch (2.5 cm) wide
Fine-gauge floral wire
3 cornhusk poinsettia flowers (see opposite page)
18 to 20 cornhusk poinsettia leaves (see opposite page)

STEP FOUR

Cut 960 strips of cornhusk approximately 7 inches (17 cm) long and 1 inch wide. Cut 160 strips 2 inches (5 cm) long and 1/4 inch (6 mm) wide.

STEP FIVE

Fold six of the 7-inch strips in half end to end, group them in a bundle, and tie them around the middle with a piece of the 1/4-inch-wide cornhusk (see Figure 1). Trim the ends of the tie close to the bundle. Make approximately 160 bundles.

STEP SIX

With scissors or a craft knife, shred the lower part of each bundle by cutting the husk ends below the tie into strips about 1/8-inch (3 mm) wide.

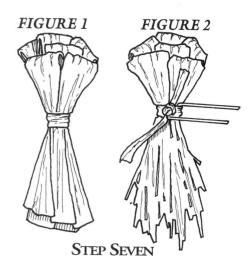

FIGURE 1   **FIGURE 2**

STEP SEVEN

Insert a floral pin into each bundle, so that the pin's end is hidden (see Figure 2).

STEP EIGHT

Pin a row of bundles around the outside of the base, placing them very close together so the base is covered (see Figure 3).

FIGURE 3

STEP NINE

Pin a row of bundles around the inside of the base, again placing them very close together.

STEP TEN

For the front face of the wreath, cut the bundles off below their ties and pin them close together on the base, covering it completely.

STEP ELEVEN

Position three poinsettia flowers around the wreath. Push each stem wire through the base, bend it over, and push the bent end back through. Form bunches of three to five leaves and wrap fine-gauge floral wire around their ends, leaving a stem about 3 inches long. Add groups of leaves on both sides of each flower, pushing the wired ends into the base.

STEP TWELVE

Attach the bow to the wreath with a floral pin.

Poinsettia Flowers and Leaves

STEP ONE

To make the center of the flower, lay the pale green cornhusks on top of each other and wrap them around one end of the heavy-gauge wire "stem." Using the fine-gauge wire, wire the husks to the stem (see Figure 4). Shred the husks with the craft knife.

STEP TWO

Using the scissors, cut each red husk into the shape of a petal—pointed on one end, about 1 inch (2.5 cm) wide at its widest part, and tapered to about 1/4 inch (6 mm) at the other end (see Figure 5). The pointed end is the outside of the petal.

STEP THREE

With the fine-gauge wire, wire three petals equidistantly around the center of the flower (see Figure 6). Wire a second row of three underneath the first, spacing these petals between the ones in the first row. Continue to add rows until you have used all 21 petals.

STEP FOUR

Wrap the base of the flower with masking tape, overlapping about 1/4 inch of the stem. Wrap over the masking tape with green floral tape, spiraling the floral tape down the length of the stem.

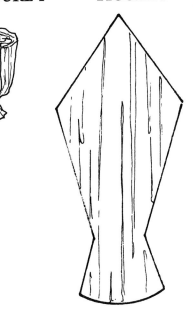

FIGURE 4   **FIGURE 5**

STEP FIVE

Using the scissors, cut the green cornhusk into a leaf shape, using the petal pattern in Figure 5.

MATERIALS

Poinsettia Flowers and Leaves

For each flower:
6 1-1/2-inch × 2-inch (4 × 5 cm) pieces of pale green cornhusk
15-inch (39 cm) length of heavy-gauge floral wire
Fine-gauge floral wire
Craft knife
Scissors
21 1-1/2-inch × 3-inch (4 × 7 cm) pieces of red cornhusk
Masking tape
Green floral tape

For each leaf:
1-1/2-inch × 3-inch piece of green cornhusk
Scissors
Fine-gauge floral wire

FIGURE 6

203

CORNHUSK HOEDOWN

MATERIALS

For each doll:

About 1/2 ounce (15.5 g) of
  cornhusks, half of them
  dyed for clothing, half left
  their natural color
Bucket full of warm water
#20 crochet thread, or other
  heavy thread
6-inch (15 cm) length of
  medium-gauge floral wire
13-inch (33 cm) length of
  medium-gauge floral wire
Black felt-tip pen, with fine
  point
Red felt-tip pen, with fine
  point (optional)
18-inch (46 cm) length of
  heavy-gauge floral wire
Floral tape
White craft glue
Darning needle
1 × 4-inch (2.5 × 10 cm) piece
  of cornstalk
Knife or scissors

With this trio around the
house, you may find yourself
stepping to a square-dance
rhythm. To make them, you'll
need undyed husks for the
head and hands, but the colors
of the clothing can vary with
your tastes and available husks.
Contrasting coats and pants
work especially well.

STEP ONE

Soak the cornhusks in the
warm water for about 15 minutes, until they're pliable.

STEP TWO

Select three natural-colored
husks 7 to 8 inches (17 to 20
cm) long and 2 to 3 inches (5
to 7 cm) wide at the bottom
(the widest part). Lay them on
top of each other, with the narrow ends at the top. Treating
the three husks as one, fold the
top over about 3/4 inch (2
cm), then fold again by the
same amount. Roll the husks

lengthwise, making a long
cylinder for the head and the
body (see Figure 1). Tie the
cylinder with crochet thread at
the "neck," about 1 inch (2.5
cm) from the top.

STEP THREE

Twist the 6-inch piece of medium-gauge wire around the
body about 1/2 inch (1.3 cm)
below the neck to make the
arms (see Figure 2). Tear the
body husks vertically into strips
about 1/2 inch wide. Bring
these strips out along the arms
and fold them back toward the
body at each end of the wire, to
form the hands.

About 1/4 inch (6 mm)
from the end of one hand,
begin wrapping a 1/2-inch-
wide colored cornhusk around
an arm until you reach the
body. Tie this "sleeve" on near
the body with crochet thread,
and repeat for the other arm.

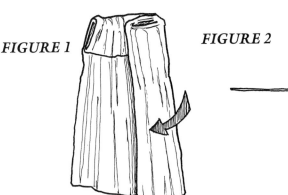

FIGURE 1

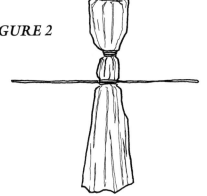

FIGURE 2

FIGURE 3

STEP FOUR

Fold the 13-inch piece of medium-gauge wire in half, and push the folded end into the head to make the legs. Bend the bottom inch or so of each wire to form a foot. Wrap a 1/2-inch-wide dark husk around each foot to make a shoe, and continue about an inch up the leg.

Using a 1-inch-wide husk in a contrasting color, wrap each leg up to the "waist" to make pants. Tie at the waist with crochet thread.

STEP FIVE

Wrap a 1-inch-wide colored husk around the "chest" and tie at the waist with crochet thread.

STEP SIX

Cut a piece of husk about 2-1/2 inches (6 cm) long and 3-1/2 inches wide to make the coat. In one of the long sides, cut two 1-inch slits, positioning each slit 1/2 inch in from the edge (see Figure 3). Using those slits as armholes, wrap the husk around the body and tie it at the neck with crochet thread.

STEP SEVEN

To make the hat, cut a 1-1/2 × 2-inch (4 × 5 cm) piece of husk and fold one end into a circle. Tie it about 1/8 inch from the

end with crochet thread (see Figure 4). Turn the circle inside out; the tied end is now the top of the hat (see Figure 5). Place the hat on the head and tie it on with crochet thread, about 1/4 inch from the top of the head, leaving enough room for the face. Roll the brim up.

Using a husk that matches the coat or pants, cut a hatband about 1/8 inch (3 mm) wide and 2 inches long, and tie it on the hat, covering the crochet thread. Trim the ends closely.

STEP EIGHT

Using the black felt-tip pen, draw the face. If desired, add rosy cheeks with the red felt-tip pen.

STEP NINE

Use the 18-inch length of heavy-gauge wire to make a

FIGURE 4

FIGURE 5

stool frame with four 1-3/4-inch (4.5 cm) legs and four 1-inch crossbars for the seat. Start by bending 1-3/4 inches of one end of the wire back against itself to make the first leg. Then bend a 1-inch piece perpendicular to the leg, to form one side of the seat. Bend the next 1-3/4 inches down and back up for the second leg, continuing in this fashion until you've finished the frame (see Figure 6). Wrap it in floral tape.

Wrap 1/2- to 1-inch-wide cornhusks around the frame and across the seat. Secure with a dab of glue.

STEP TEN

Bend the doll's legs into a sitting position and set it on the stool. Cut a 1/4-inch-wide and 4- to 5-inch (10 to 13 cm) long piece of cornhusk the color of the pants, and thread it through

FIGURE 6

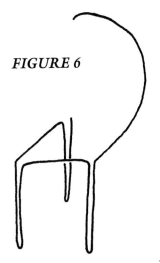

the darning needle. Bring the needle up through the bottom of the seat and over one of the doll's thighs, then back down through the seat. Repeat for the other thigh, and tie the ends of the husk in a knot on the underside of the seat.

STEP ELEVEN

Using a knife or scissors, cut a piece of cornstalk into the shape of a musical instrument: guitar, banjo, or fiddle. Position the arms correctly to hold the instrument, and tie the instrument to the doll's wrists with crochet thread. For optimum harmony, make a different instrument for each of the three dolls.

CORNHUSK FLOWERS

These well-shaped flowers can be made with natural-colored husks or with ones that have been dyed. With slight variations of technique, they can resemble roses, chrysanthemums, or carnations.

STEP ONE

Soak the husks in the warm water for approximately 15 minutes, until they're pliable.

STEP TWO

Fold a husk in half end to end. Still holding the first husk, fold a second husk the same way, overlapping the first one (see Figure 1).

MATERIALS

For each flower:

About 7 cornhusks, 8 to 9 inches (20 to 22 cm) long and 3 to 4 inches (7 to 10 cm) wide at the middle
Bucket full of warm water
4-inch (10 cm) length of fine-gauge floral wire
Wire cutters or heavy shears
18-inch (46 cm) length of heavy-gauge floral wire
Masking tape
Green floral tape

STEP THREE

Roll the overlapped husks lengthwise, jelly-roll style, to create a rose effect (see Figure 2). Add additional overlapping husks until the "flower" is the size you want.

STEP FOUR

Wrap the fine-gauge floral wire around the base of the flower, twist it together tightly, and trim the wire ends with the wire cutters.

STEP FIVE

Trim the excess husk below the wire, tapering the base instead of cutting straight across.

STEP SIX

Make a "fishhook" in one end of the heavy-gauge floral wire and insert the other end down through the center of the flower to make the stem (see Figure 3).

FIGURE 1

STEP SEVEN

Wrap the tapered base of the flower and about 1 inch (2.5 cm) of the stem with masking tape. Wrap over the masking tape with green floral tape, spiraling the floral tape down the length of the stem.

FIGURE 2

VARIATIONS

To make a chrysanthemum, use your fingers to tear the folded husks into strips about 1/2 inch (4 cm) wide (see Figure 4). To make a carnation, use shears to cut the folded petals open (see Figure 5).

FIGURE 3

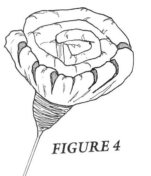

FIGURE 4

FIGURE 5

WRAPPED WREATH WITH FLOWERS

On this husk-covered wreath, the grain of the cornhusks follows the circular curve of the base, for a smooth, molded look. Dyed cornhusk flowers in jewel tones and green horsetail ferns add interest.

STEP ONE

Soak the cornhusks in the warm water for 15 minutes, or until they are pliable.

MATERIALS

30 to 35 cornhusks, 6 to 8
   inches (15 to 20 cm) wide
   at the widest point
Bucket full of warm water
18-inch (46 cm) diameter
   straw wreath base
Straight pins
White craft glue
6 cornhusk flowers
   (see opposite page)
6 6-inch (15 cm) floral picks
6 to 8 12-inch (30 cm)
   lengths of horsetail fern
3-1/2 yards (3.2 m) of
   3-inch (7.5 cm) wide
   printed ribbon
Fine-gauge floral wire
Sharp, pointed knife
6 to 8 12-inch lengths of
   medium-gauge floral wire

STEP TWO

Wrap the husks around the wreath base so that the lengths of the husks follow the curve of the base, and attach them with straight pins, pushing the pin into the base at an angle. Overlap the husks so that the base is well covered. Let dry overnight, then glue the edges of the husks down for a smooth base.

STEP THREE

Make a bow with the printed ribbon and wire it to the base with the fine-gauge floral wire.

STEP FOUR

Attach the cornhusk flowers to floral picks and pick them into the base, arranging them in a staircase pattern. If any stems of the cornhusk flowers are unattractively visible, slit a piece of horsetail fern down its length, cutting only one

wall of the fern, not all the way through it. Wrap the fern around the flower stem and hot-glue it in place if necessary.

STEP FIVE

To stiffen the remaining ferns, insert a piece of medium-gauge floral wire into the base of each one and thread it up through the center, almost to the top. Carefully bend the wired ferns into attractive curves and hot-glue them to the base.

LITTLE GIRLS AT PLAY

Children have played these games for centuries. One athletic girl is jumping rope while the other keeps an eye on her doll. Except for minor variations in color and props, the two dolls are identical.

MATERIALS

Girl with Doll

About 1 ounce (31 g) of
    natural-colored cornhusks
Bucket full of warm water
#20 crochet thread, or other
    heavy thread
5-inch (12 cm) length of
    medium-gauge floral wire
Large pink cornhusk, 8 to 9
    inches (20 to 22.5 cm) long
    and wide
12-inch (30 cm) length of
    medium-gauge floral wire
Small blue cornhusk
3 inches (7 cm) of corn silk
White craft glue
Black felt-tip pen, with fine
    point
Red felt-tip pen, with fine
    point (optional)

Girl with Doll

STEP ONE

Soak the cornhusks in the warm water for about 15 minutes, until they're pliable.

STEP TWO

Select three natural-colored husks 7 to 8 inches (17 to 20 cm) long and 2 to 3 inches (5 to 7 cm) wide at the bottom (the widest part). Lay them on top of each other, with the narrow ends at the top. Treating the three husks as one, fold the top over about 3/4 inch (2 cm), then fold again by the same amount. Roll the husks lengthwise, making a long cylinder for the head and body (see Figure 1 on page 205). Tie the cylinder with crochet thread at the "neck," about 1 inch (2.5 cm) from the top.

STEP THREE

Twist the 5-inch piece of medium-gauge wire around the body about 1/2 inch (1.3 cm) below the neck to make the arms (see Figure 2 on page 205). Tear the body husks vertically into strips about 1/2 inch wide. Bring these strips out along the arms and fold them back toward the body at each end of the wire, to form the hands. Tie with crochet thread.

About 1/4 inch (6 mm) from the end of one hand, begin wrapping a 1/2-inch-wide husk around an arm until you reach the body. Tie it on with crochet thread, and repeat for the other arm.

Using a piece of pink husk about 1/2 inch wide, wrap the arms to form short sleeves, starting at the center of the body and wrapping down the arm about 1 inch.

STEP FOUR

Fold the 12-inch (30 cm) piece of wire in half and push the folded end into the head to make the legs. Bend the bottom inch or so of each wire to form a foot, with 1/2 inch in front of the leg and 1/2 inch behind. Wrap a 1/2-inch-wide blue husk around each foot to make a shoe, and continue about an inch up the leg.

Using a 1-inch-wide natural-colored husk, wrap each leg up to the waist. Tie at the waist with crochet thread.

STEP FIVE

Wrap a pink husk 7 to 8 inches wide and 3 inches long around the doll to make the dress, cutting slits to accommodate the arms (see Figure 3 on page 205). Tie at the neck and waist with crochet thread. Cut a waistband 1/4 inch wide and 4 inches (10 cm) long, and tie it around the waist. Cut a pink neckband 1/4 inch wide and 2 inches long, and tie it around the neck.

STEP SIX

Arrange the corn silk on top of the head for hair, going from front to back. Glue it to the head, and twist the silks around the face to form curls. Cut a blue cornhusk headband 1/8 inch (3 mm) wide and 2 inches long, tie it around the head, and tie a bow in front.

STEP SEVEN

Using the black felt-tip pen, draw the face. If desired, add rosy cheeks with a red felt-tip pen.

Baby Doll

STEP ONE

Soak the cornhusks in the warm water for about 15 minutes, until they're pliable.

STEP TWO

Cut off the narrow end of the husk to make a piece about 3 inches (7 cm) long, 1/3 inch (8 mm) wide on one end, and about 1-1/4 inches (3.1 cm) wide on the other. Fold over the narrow end about 3/4 inch (2 cm), then over again by the same amount. Roll the husk lengthwise, making a cylinder for the head and body. Tie the cylinder with crochet thread at the "neck," about 1/4 inch (6 mm) from the top.

STEP THREE

Starting at the bottom, cut the body lengthwise into four pieces. Just below the neck, pull one of the body pieces straight out to the side and wrap a second body piece around it. Tie at the shoulder with thread, and repeat for the other arm.

STEP FOUR

Glue the corn silk to the top of

MATERIALS

Baby Doll

2 7 × 4-inch (18 × 10 cm) natural-colored cornhusks
Bucket full of warm water
Scissors
#20 crochet thread, or other heavy thread
White craft glue
1 inch of corn silk
Black felt-tip pen, with fine point

the head for hair. Cut a 1-1/2 × 1/2-inch (4 × 1.3 cm) piece of husk and wrap it over the head to make a hood, crossing the ends at the back of the neck. Tie it around the neck.

STEP FIVE

Cut a 1-1/2 × 2-1/2 inch (4 × 6 cm) piece of husk and wrap it around the doll for a dress, cutting slits in the top to accom-modate the arms. Tie at the neck with crochet thread.

STEP SIX

Using the felt-tip pen, draw the face.

CHRISTMAS TREE ORNAMENTS

Small cornhusk figures look particularly good on a real tree. Their rustic simplicity and cheerful attitude are perfect for the Christmas season.

Snowman

STEP ONE

Soak the cornhusks in the warm water for about 15 minutes, until they're pliable.

MATERIALS

Snowman

1/2 ounce (15.5 g) of natural-colored cornhusks
Bucket full of warm water
#20 crochet thread, or other heavy thread
4-inch (10 cm) length of heavy-gauge floral wire
Handful of loose polyester fiberfill
1/8-inch × 8-inch (3 mm × 20 cm) piece of black cornhusk
1-1/2-inch × 4-inch (4 × 10 cm) piece of red cornhusk
4-inch length of red thread
Black felt-tip pen, with fine point
1-3/4-inch (4.5 cm) length of heavy-gauge floral wire
Masking tape
Red felt-tip pen, with fine point

STEP TWO

Select four natural-colored husks 7 to 8 inches (17 to 20 cm) long and 2 to 3 inches (5 to 8 cm) wide at the bottom (the widest part). Lay them on top of each other, with the narrow ends at the top. Treating the four husks as one, fold the top over about 3/4 inch (2 cm), then fold again by the same amount. Roll the husks lengthwise, making a long cylinder for the head and body (see Figure 1 on page 205). Tie the cylinder with crochet thread at the "neck," about 1 inch (2.5 cm) from the top.

STEP THREE

Twist a 4-inch piece of heavy-gauge wire around the body about 1/2 inch (1.3 cm) below the neck to make the arms (see Figure 2 on page 205). Tear the body husks vertically into strips about 1/2 inch wide. Bring these strips out along the arms and fold them back toward the body at each end of the wire, to form the hands. Tie at the wrists with crochet thread.

About 1/4-inch (6 mm) from the end of one hand, begin wrapping a 1/2-inch-wide husk around an arm until you reach the body. Tie the husk on with crochet thread, and repeat for the other arm.

STEP FOUR

Select a husk approximately 7 inches (18 cm) wide. Gather it into a circle at the wide end and tie it with crochet thread about 1/4 inch from the end. Turn the husk inside out (see Figures 4 and 5 on page 205). Stuff the cavity with polyester fiberfill and tie the open end around the doll's neck, positioning the opening in the back and trimming the stuffed husk so that the body is about 3 inches tall. Add stuffing as needed to make a full body. Overlap the edges of the opening, and tie the snowman around the waist with crochet thread. Cut a piece of black husk 1/8 inch wide and 6 inches (15 cm) long, and tie it around the waist to hide the thread. Cut another piece of red husk 1/8 inch wide and 4 inches long, and tie it around the neck. Tie the red thread around the neck to use as a hanger.

STEP FIVE

To make the hat, fold one end of the red husk into a circle. Tie it about 1/4 inch from the end with crochet thread. Turn the circle inside out; the tied end is now the top of the hat. Place the hat on the head and tie it on with crochet thread, about 1/4 inch from the top of

the head, leaving enough room for the face. Roll the brim up.

Cut a black husk hatband about 1/8 inch wide and 2 inches long and tie it on the hat, covering the crochet thread. Trim the ends closely.

Step Six

Using the black felt-tip pen, draw the face.

Step Seven

Cover the 1-3/4-inch piece of heavy-gauge wire with masking tape to make the broomstick. Using the red felt-tip pen, draw a candy cane pattern around the stick. Tie a 3/4-inch-long piece of husk on the end with crochet thread and shred the husk to make the broom head. With crochet thread, tie the broom to the snowman's hand.

Santa Claus

Step One

Soak the cornhusks in the warm water for about 15 minutes, until they're pliable.

Step Two

Lay the natural-colored husks on top of each other, with the narrow ends at the top. Treating the three husks as one, fold the top over about 3/4 inch (2 cm), then fold again by the same amount. Roll the husks lengthwise, making a long cylinder for the head and body (see Figure 1 on page 205). Tie the cylinder with crochet thread at the "neck," about 3/4 inch from the top.

Step Three

Twist the 4-inch piece of medium-gauge wire around the body about 1/4 inch (6 mm)

MATERIALS

Santa Claus

3 natural-colored cornhusks, 7 to 8 inches (17 to 20 cm) long and 2 to 3 inches (5 to 8 cm) wide at the bottom (the widest part)

Bucket full of warm water

About 1/2 ounce (15.5 g) of red cornhusks

2 3 × 1/2-inch (7 × 1.3 cm) black cornhusks

#20 crochet thread, or other heavy thread

4-inch (10 cm) length of medium-gauge floral wire

6-inch (15 cm) length of medium-gauge floral wire

3-inch length of red string

1 inch of dried corn silk

White craft glue

Black felt-tip pen, with fine point

Red felt-tip pen, with fine point (optional)

below the neck to make the arms (see Figure 2 on page 205). Tear the body husks vertically into strips about 1/2 inch wide. Bring these strips out along the arms and fold them back toward the body at each end of the wire, to form the hands.

About 1/4-inch from the end of one hand, begin wrapping a 1/2-inch-wide red husk around an arm until you reach the body. Tie this "sleeve" on with crochet thread, and repeat for the other arm.

STEP FOUR

Fold the 6-inch piece of medium-gauge wire in half, and push the folded end into the head to make the legs. Wrap a black husk around the bottom of each leg to make a boot, and tie with crochet thread. Wrap the rest of the way up the legs with 1/2-inch-wide red husks, and tie at the waist.

STEP FIVE

Cut a 2-1/2 × 3-inch (6 × 7 cm) piece of red husk to make the

MATERIALS

Angel

1/2 ounce (15.5 g) of natural-colored cornhusks
Bucket full of warm water
#20 crochet thread, or other heavy thread
4-inch (10 cm) length of medium-gauge floral wire
4 inches of dried corn silk
White craft glue
Black felt-tip pen, with fine point
Red felt-tip pen, with fine point
5-inch (12 cm) piece of raffia or string

coat. Wrap the husk around the body, cutting two slits into the top to accommodate the arms (see Figure 3 on page 205). Tie it at the neck with crochet thread.

STEP SIX

Position the corn silk around the face to make a beard and glue it on.

STEP SEVEN

Cut a 2-1/2 × 1-1/2-inch (6 × 4 cm) piece of red husk for the stocking cap. Wrap one end around the head, with the opening in the back, and tie it on the head with crochet thread. Tie the other end of the husk into a loose knot and drape the cap down the back. Cut a piece of natural-colored husk 1/8 inch (6 mm) wide and 2-1/2 inches long, and tie it around the forehead.

STEP EIGHT

Using the black felt-tip pen, draw the face. If desired, add rosy cheeks with the red felt-tip pen.

Angel

STEP ONE

Soak the cornhusks in the warm water for about 15 minutes, until they're pliable.

STEP TWO

Select three husks 7 to 8 inches (17 to 20 cm) long and 2 to 3 inches (5 to 8 cm) wide at the bottom (the widest part). Lay the husks on top of each other, with the narrow ends at the top. Treating the three husks as one, fold the top over about 3/4 inch (2 cm), then fold again by the same amount. Roll the husks lengthwise, making a long cylinder for the head and body (see Figure 1 on page

205). Tie the cylinder with the crochet thread at the "neck," about 3/4 inch from the top.

STEP THREE

Twist a 4-inch piece of medium-gauge wire around the body about 1/4 inch (6 mm) below the neck to make the arms (see Figure 2 on page 205). Tear the body husks vertically into strips about 1/2 inch (1.3 cm) wide. Bring these strips out along the arms and fold them back toward the body at each end of the wire to form the hands.

About 1/4-inch from the end of one hand, begin wrapping a 1/2-inch-wide husk around an arm until you reach the body. Tie the husk on with crochet thread, and repeat for the other arm.

STEP FOUR

Wrap two 2-1/2 × 4-inch (5 × 10 cm) husks around the body for underskirts, and tie at the neck with thread. Cut the husks into 1/2-inch-wide vertical strips to add fullness to the skirt

STEP FIVE

Cut a 2-3/4 × 5-inch (6 × 12 cm) piece of husk for the dress and wrap it around the doll. Cut two slits for the arms (see Figure 3 on page 205). Tie at the neck with thread.

STEP SIX

Glue the corn silk to the top of the head for hair, and let it drape down the back. Using the black felt-tip pen, draw the face. If desired, add rosy cheeks with the red felt-tip pen.

STEP SEVEN

Cut a pair of wings from a cornhusk and glue them on the angel's back. Tie a piece of raffia around the neck and knot the end, to use as a hanger.

LITTLE RED RIDING HOOD AND WOLF

With only a few defining characteristics, cornhusk dolls can become storybook characters. The red cape and hood and the large gray wolf make these characters unmistakable.

Red Riding Hood

STEP ONE

Soak the cornhusks in the warm water for 15 minutes, until they are pliable.

STEP TWO

Select three natural-colored husks 7 to 8 inches (17 to 20 cm) long and 2 to 3 inches (5 to 7 cm) wide at the bottom (the widest part). Lay them on top of each other, with the narrow ends at the top. Treating the three husks as one, fold the top over about 3/4 inch (2 cm), then fold again by the same amount. Roll the husks lengthwise, making a long cylinder for the head and body (see Figure 1 on page 205). Tie the cylinder with the crochet thread at the "neck," about 1 inch (2.5 cm) from the top.

STEP THREE

Twist the 5-inch (12 cm) piece of medium-gauge wire around the body about 1/2 inch (1.3 cm) below the neck to make the arms (see Figure 2 on page 205). Tear the body husks vertically into strips about 1/2 inch wide. Bring these strips out along the arms and fold them back toward the body at each end of the wire, to form the hands. Tie with crochet threads.

About 1/4-inch (6 mm) from the end of one hand, begin wrapping a 1/2-inch-wide husk around an arm until you reach the body. Tie this "sleeve" on with crochet thread, and repeat for the other arm.

STEP FOUR

Fold the 12-inch (30 cm) piece of wire in half and push the folded end into the head to make the legs. Bend the bottom inch or so of each wire to form a foot, with 1/2 inch in front of the leg and 1/2 inch behind. Wrap a 1/2-inch red husk around each foot to make a shoe, and continue about an inch up the leg.

Using a 1-inch-wide natural-colored husk, wrap each leg up to the waist. Tie at the waist with crochet thread.

STEP FIVE

Wrap a husk 7 to 8 inches wide and 3 inches long around the doll to make the dress, cutting slits to accommodate the arms (see Figure 3 on page 205). Tie at the neck and waist with crochet thread. Cut a waistband 1/4 inch wide and 4 inches (10 cm) long, and tie it around the waist.

STEP SIX

Position the corn silk on top of the head for hair and glue in place. Cut a piece of red husk 1 inch wide and 4 inches long and fold it over the head for the hood, with the pieces crossing at the back. Cut a 2-1/2 × 7-inch (6 × 17 cm) piece of red husk for the cape. Wrap it around the doll and tie it at the neck. Cut a red neckband 1/8 inch (3 mm) wide and tie it around the neck.

MATERIALS

Red Riding Hood

About 1/2 ounce (15.5 g) of natural-colored cornhusks
3 red cornhusks
Bucket full of warm water
#20 crochet thread, or other heavy thread
5-inch (12 cm) length of medium-gauge floral wire
12-inch (30 cm) length of medium-gauge floral wire
1 inch (2.5 cm) of corn silk
White craft glue
Black felt-tip pen, with fine point
Red felt-tip pen, with fine point (optional)
A purchased woven-raffia basket about 1/2 inch (1.3 cm) square

STEP SEVEN

Using the black felt-tip pen, draw the face. If desired, add rosy cheeks with a red felt-tip pen.

STEP EIGHT

Tie the basket to the wrists with crochet thread.

Wolf

STEP ONE

Soak the cornhusks in the warm water for 15 minutes, until they are pliable.

STEP TWO

Using the scissors, cut a piece of gray cornhusk about 9 inch-

es (22 cm) long and 1/4 inch wide. Twist it along its length and fold back about 1 inch of one end, to form a loop. Lay the piece of red husk on the loop so that about 1/8 inch (3 mm) extends beyond the end of the loop, for the tongue (see Figure 1). Form the twisted husk into a second loop, lay the second loop on top of the tongue, and tie both loops and tongue together with crochet thread, to make the nose (see Figure 2).

STEP THREE

Fold the 5-inch piece of wire in half. Wrap a 1/4-inch-wide piece of gray husk around the folded area of the wire and tie

the wrapped wire onto the nose with crochet thread, leaving about 1/2 inch (1.3 cm) extending above the nose, for the top of the head (see Figure 3). The remainder of the wire forms the front legs.

STEP FOUR

Fold the 7-inch piece of wire in half and place the folded end around the front legs, about 1/2 inch below the nose. Fold the last 1-1/2 inch of each wire down, for the back legs, leaving about 2 inches (5 cm) for the body (see Figure 4).

STEP FIVE

Cut a strip of gray husk 1/4 inch wide and 1 inch long and

trim each end into a V shape. Place the center of the gray husk under the nose, bring the ends up on the sides of the head for the ears, and tie in place with crochet thread.

STEP SIX

Using strips of husk about 1/4 inch wide, wrap around the nose and neck. Tie with thread. Fold a small husk over each foot, then wrap around the legs and body until the wolf is as large as you wish.

STEP SEVEN

Using a husk about 1/2 inch wide, wrap the 1-1/2-inch piece of wire, dip one end in glue, and insert it into the wolf for the tail.

FIGURE 1

FIGURE 2

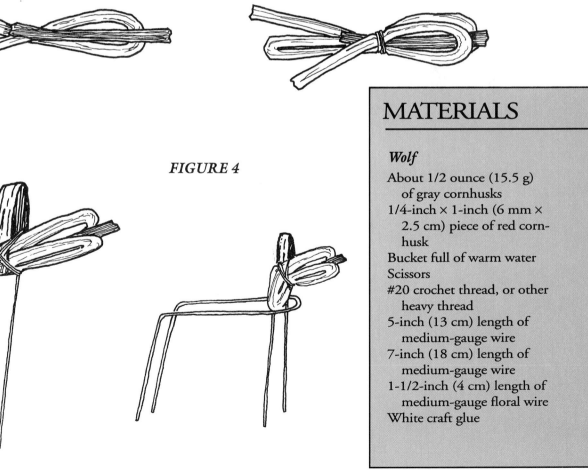

FIGURE 3

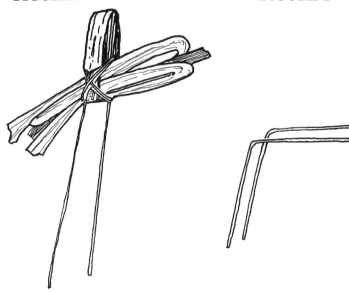

FIGURE 4

MATERIALS

Wolf
About 1/2 ounce (15.5 g)
    of gray cornhusks
1/4-inch × 1-inch (6 mm ×
    2.5 cm) piece of red corn-
    husk
Bucket full of warm water
Scissors
#20 crochet thread, or other
    heavy thread
5-inch (13 cm) length of
    medium-gauge wire
7-inch (18 cm) length of
    medium-gauge wire
1-1/2-inch (4 cm) length of
    medium-gauge floral wire
White craft glue

PINE NEEDLES

Crafting with pine needles dates back to prediscovered America, when Indians from the Seminole tribe made pine needle baskets and then treated the baskets with pine resin so they could be used to carry water. When the Pilgrims came to America, the Indians shared their knowledge of basket making and working with natural materials.

Subsequent generations of pine needle crafters have developed new patterns, functions, and designs, although the basic coiling method invented by the Indians is still in use today. The aesthetics of the craft, however, have improved over the years with the use of sliced nuts, dyes, and different colors and thicknesses of thread and raffia. If pine trees are not indigenous to your area, you can order pine needles and peripheral materials from one of the suppliers listed on page 253.

There are several varieties of pine trees that have needles

long enough for crafting. The longleaf pine tree *(Pinus palustris)*, the slash pine tree *(Pinus caribaea)*, loblolly pine *(Pinus taeda)*, ponderosa pine *(Pinus ponderosa)*, Jeffrey pine *(Pinus jeffreyi)*, and the digger pine *(Pinus sabiniana)* all have long needles. Their average length ranges from 8 to 12 inches (20 to 30 cm).

GATHERING AND PREPARING NEEDLES

Collect needles after they have matured, turned brown, and fallen from the tree, usually from midsummer to late fall. Look for needles that have recently fallen; they are usually a lighter brown than needles that have been on the ground for a while, and are easier to work with. Choose only whole pine needle clusters that are straight and thoroughly dry, and discard ones with broken or dead ends.

Soften and sterilize the needles by placing them in a large pan and pouring enough boiling water over the needles to cover them. Allow them to sit for at least one hour and then shake off the excess water. Wrap the needles in an old terry-cloth towel for two to three hours. Be sure you don't leave the damp needles wrapped up any longer than this or they will mildew and rot! Soak only the amount of needles you will be using in the next two to three days.

Check the materials list for the project you plan to make to see if it calls for the caps to be removed or left on. The caps can be pulled off with your fingers or popped off with a dull-edged knife.

BASIC TECHNIQUES AND STITCHES

The Three-Step Basic Starting Procedure

This procedure is used for all projects that start around a nut slice, a leather circle, or a wooden base. To start, you will need four whole pine needle clusters, scissors, and thread. Raffia was the favored thread for centuries and it adds a lovely contrasting color to projects, but the life of the project can be extended by using nylon upholstery thread.

Step 1: Remove the caps of the pine needle clusters.

Step 2: Tie on approximately 1 yard (0.9 m) of thread and wrap about every 1/2-inch (1.3 cm), working down from the previously capped end of the pine needles. Use two double overhand knots to secure (see Figure 1). The double loop of this knot locks the knot in place.

Step 3: Cut off the short end of the thread and trim the pine needles as close to the knot as possible.

Working with Nuts

Black walnuts and hickory nuts can be thinly sliced to form a decorative center in the bottom of a project or can be woven into the coils that form the sides of a project. To start around a nut slice, place the pine needle bundle on the edge of the nut, keeping the loose pine needles to the left. Insert a threaded needle from the back through the first small hole in the nut and come out

FIGURE 1

FIGURE 2

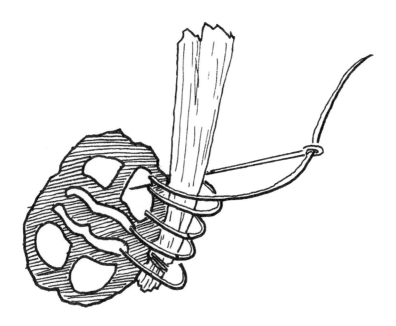

To form the second row, pull the free end of the pine needle coil up slightly and slide the gauge over it. Add several pine needle clusters to the gauge so that it is full but not difficult to slide. You will need to add pine needles one at a time as you work to keep a continual coil. Add a new pine needle cluster every two or three stitches or as needed to keep the gauge full.

Plain Stitch

For the beginning pine needle crafter, the plain stitch is recommended. The plain stitch is a simple back-to-front looping circular stitch in one direction. On the second row you will follow the stitching pattern set by the first row around the nut. Always work from back to front, inserting the darning needle at the top of the previous coil, adjacent to and to the right of the stitch directly below. Go through the previous coil about 1/8 inch (3 mm) to the left, and guide your needle out of the coil adjacent to and on the left side of the stitch directly below. Then bring the needle up and over the topmost coil and take the next stitch in the same manner, inserting the needle from back to front. Study the illustrations on page 221 and practice to master additional stitches once you feel comfortable with this one.

Adding Thread

As you approach the end of the your thread, stop when there's still 3 or 4 inches (7 or 10 cm) left to tie your new thread onto. For easier handling, use only 1-yard (0.9 m) lengths of thread. Using a double overhand knot, tie the knot close enough to the work so that it

through the nut's front side. Almost any needle will work, but many crafters prefer cotton darning needles because their eyes are large enough to accommodate just about any thread and the needle has a good, sharp point. If the nut doesn't have small holes, or if the small holes are too small for your needle to pass through, make your two attaching stitches through the large holes in the nut (see Figure 2).

Overlap both the pine needle bundle and the nut with thread and run the sewing needle through the second small hole, working again from back to front. Continue around the nut, making three or four stitches in each large opening in the nut. As you work your way back to the beginning, try to hide the knot and the trimmed ends of the pine nee-

dles by separating the bundle and tucking the knot and trimmed ends into the middle of the coil. Take a few more stitches to secure, leaving the ends of the coil loose. The first row is finished. Now you must add the gauge to the coil.

The gauge is a 1-inch (2-1/2 cm) long piece of metal tubing (copper or aluminum tubing also works) that the pine needles are inserted through to keep the pine needles in place while you work and to ensure a uniform thickness in the coils (see Figure 3 on page 220). The gauge's diameter can vary from 5/16 to 1/4 of an inch (1/5 to 6 mm). As you work, you move the gauge ahead and add more needles. Flaring the end of the gauge into which you insert additional pine needles can make adding the pine needles easier.

FIGURE 3

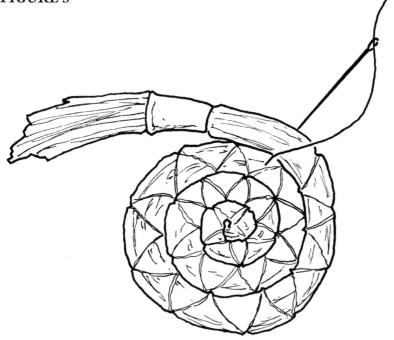

can be pulled to the outside of the coil. The next coil will hide the knot.

Leave the two short ends of thread attached and positioned on top of the coil until the next stitch is made. Hold the loose ends of the thread along with the pine needle bundles. Lap the next stitch over the loose ends of the thread along with the pine needle bundle. Lap another stitch over the loose ends of the thread to secure, and trim off the excess thread close to the stitch. This method will help keep the knot from pulling loose. When adding thread on the last row of the basket, the knot must be pulled into the middle of a coil to conceal it. Trim off the thread ends.

Adding Extra Stitches

If you are working on a large piece, you may need to add extra stitches as the diameter of the work gets larger. Either make new stitches between the established stitches as needed; or, if you want to keep an even

stitching pattern, add a new stitch between every pair of existing stitches.

Ending the Coil

As you approach the end of the last coil of your project, stop adding pine needles to the gauge. Continue working until there are just a few pine needles left in the gauge. You may need to cut the pine needles from the center of the coil in order to have a smooth finish with only a single layer of pine needles. Trim the remaining pine needle ends close to the last stitch. Leave the thread and needle attached for backstitching.

Backstitching

This stitch is used as a finishing stitch on the last row of any project. After ending the coil with the thread still attached, start stitching backward, crossing the thread over the last stitch to form an X. Insert the needle into the same hole as the stitch below, going in from the back side of the work and coming out in the same hole as the

stitch below on the front side of the work. End the thread by running stitches back through the previous stitches in your project.

Footers

The footer is an added coil of pine needles attached to the bottom of larger baskets. It serves as a base for the piece to sit on. To begin, follow the three-step basic starting procedure (see page 218). To make the footer coil, stitch the coil to the bottom of the basket on the last outside row. Using the gauge and the same plain stitch and following the same stitching pattern as was used for the rest of the basket, add extra pine needles as needed to keep an even coil.

As you return to the starting point, remove the gauge and spread the coil, then conceal the knot and the trimmed pine needle ends in the middle of the spread coil. Cut out pine needles from the middle of the coil to splice the coil together. Take a few extra stitches to conceal the starting point. End the coil, trim off the pine needle ends, and backstitch around the footer.

Protective Coatings

Clear shellac or acrylic spray will protect and strengthen your finished projects. Be sure your project is completely dry before applying the finishing coat. A good-quality shellac hardens the pine needles, protects the threads, waterproofs the item, and enhances the natural wood hue of the pine needles. Apply the shellac to both sides of the project with a small paintbrush. Acrylic spray makes a convenient alternative, especially for small projects.

THE STITCHES

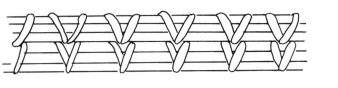

CHAIN STITCH

FERN STITCH

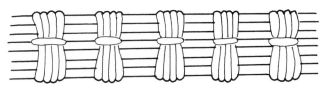

TI STITCH

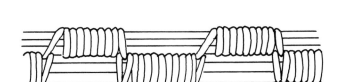

INDIAN WRAP

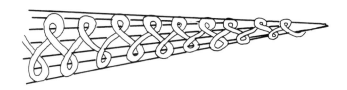

POPCORN STITCH

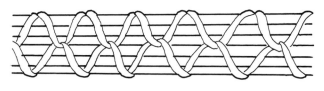

WHEAT STITCH

FAGOTING STITCH

DIAMOND STITCH

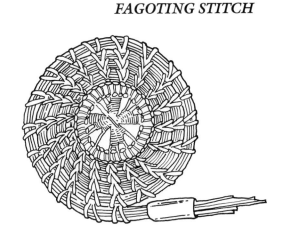

OVERCASTING or FEATHER STITCH

BACKSTITCH

EMBELLISHING

Making Braids

Soften and sterilize the needles by soaking them in a large pan of boiling water for a total of at least two-and-a-half hours so they'll be flexible enough to braid. Tie together three pine needle clusters, with their caps left on, with a strong thread. Separate the needles into three equal sections and begin to braid (see Figure 4). Braid six times and then add a pine needle with its cap on to the left of the braid. Continue adding new pine needle clusters as needed, always adding the new cluster to the left side of the braid. The cap of the pine needle should stick out of the braid about 1/4 of an inch.

Continue braiding until you approach the desired length (you'll need about 2 yards [1.8 m] to tie a large braid bow). As you approach the desired length, stop adding pine needles, but continue to braid. Tie off with strong thread and cut the needle ends close to the tie.

To tie the braid into a bow, cut away all ends that are sticking out. Tie the bow as you normally would, and stitch it in the middle to secure. Let the bow dry overnight and then shellac both sides and allow to dry at least 24 hours. Pine cones or other natural materials can be glued to the bow's streamers.

Making Bells

Begin with six single needles that have been tied together at the top with strong thread and trimmed close to the knot. Starting with the knotted end, roll the bundle of needles into a tight, flat circle, stitching as necessary to secure. Continue rolling until the circle is 1 inch (2.5 cm) in diameter; this forms the top of the bell. Add a gauge to your work and slope the next eight rows downward and outward to form the sides of the bell. Be sure to keep adding single pine needles as you work.

Gently slope the last three or four rows outward to form the bell's final shape. Stop adding pine needles as you approach the stopping point and start cutting away the middle of the last coil so you can taper down to a single needle. Backstitch a few times to secure the thread. Shellac and let dry. Last, attach small cones to a thread and sew them through the top of the bell to form the bell's clapper.

FIGURE 4

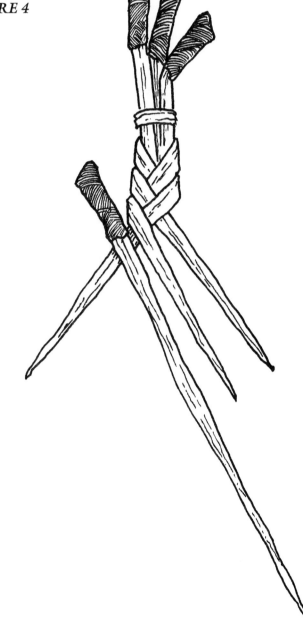

223

PINE NEEDLE COASTERS

These attractive, yet functional, coasters use simple stitches formed around a sliced walnut and make an ideal first pine needle project. Matching hot pads can be made by simply adding rows of pine needles.

STEP ONE

Prepare the pine needles by soaking as directed in the basic instructions on page 218. Begin the coaster around the halved black walnut with the three-step basic starting procedure described and illustrated on page 218.

STEP TWO

Continue adding needle clusters through the gauge and securing with a plain stitch (see page 219) until the coaster is the size of the 4-inch round. You can finish here or add one or two side rows. To make a side row, continue to plain stitch, but stitch the next coil on top of the outer half of the previous coil. This will give the coaster a small lip. Add a second side row on top of the first if you want a higher lip.

STEP THREE

Taper the size of the coil down to finish the project and back-stitch (see page 221) around the entire edge of the project.

STEP FOUR

Add a protective coating to the coaster by applying clear shellac or acrylic spray. Allow the coating to dry completely before handling the coaster.

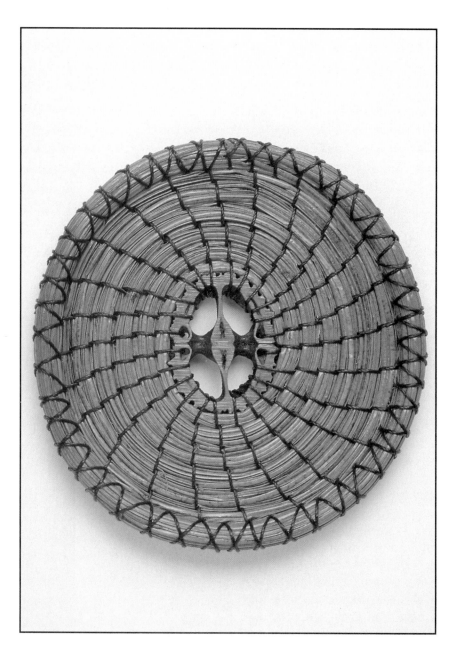

MATERIALS

For one coaster:

About 20 pine needle clusters, caps removed
Cotton darning needle
Nylon upholstery thread
5/8-inch (1.5 cm) gauge
Black walnut, thinly sliced
4-inch (10 cm) diameter wood round
Clear shellac or acrylic spray

OLD-FASHIONED HANGING BASKET

This plant basket makes an ideal first project, even for children, and the basket can be displayed outdoors if you apply a good protective coating of clear shellac or acrylic spray.

STEP ONE

Prepare the pine needles by soaking as directed in the basic instructions on page 218. Cut the cardboard container so it's slightly shorter than the length of the pine needles. Remove the outer paper from the container so it won't show through the pine needles. If the paper won't come off or if the container was printed with a company's logo, spray the box with brown paint and allow to dry completely.

STEP TWO

Thread the darning needle with the upholstery thread. Position a bundle of five to seven pine needle clusters vertically on the outside of the container so that their caps are above the rim of the container. Use a cross-stitch to sew them to the container about 1 inch below their caps. Continue sewing small bundles around the entire circumference, keeping the caps even and close together so the container does not show. End with the thread on the inside of the container and tie off with a knot.

STEP THREE

Gather the clusters just below the bottom of the box. Hold the clusters in place with a rubber band while you tie them with the nylon thread. Wrap the thread around several more times, keeping it tight, and then tie off with several knots. Use the scissors to trim the needle ends on a slant.

STEP FOUR

Make a length of pine needle braid long enough to hide the stitches around the top of the basket. (See basic braid-making instructions on page 223.) Arrange small cones, nuts, and/or pods in a small cluster and glue them in place on the front center of the basket.

STEP FIVE

To make one side of the handle, tie ten pine needle clusters together just below their caps with a 6-foot (1.8 m) length of thread. Insert a 9-inch length of the medium-gauge wire through the middle to add strength and help reinforce the shape. Wrap the bundle of pine needles every 1/2-inch (1.3 cm) down from the capped end and then wrap

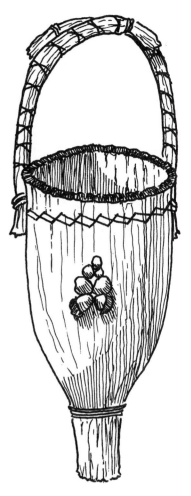

FIGURE 1

back up again. Repeat the process again to form the other side of the handle.

STEP SIX

Securely stitch one end of each side of the handle with an overlapping stitch to opposite sides of the basket. Slant-cut the ends of the handles to trim. Wrap the two loose ends of the handles around each other and stitch them together (see Figure 1).

STEP SEVEN

Add a protective coating to the basket by applying clear shellac or acrylic spray. Allow the coating to dry completely before handling the basket.

MATERIALS

Approximately 100 pine needle clusters, caps on
Round cardboard container (an oatmeal or salt box works well)
Brown spray paint (optional)
Cotton darning needle
Nylon upholstery thread
Scissors
Rubber bands
Several small cones, nuts, and/or pods
White craft glue
2 9-inch (22 cm) lengths of medium-gauge floral wire
Clear shellac or acrylic spray

Decorative Basket

Compare the stitches in this basket with the stitches on other projects in this chapter and you'll quickly realize how the different color and thickness of raffia can influence a project's finished look.

Step One

Prepare the pine needles by soaking as directed in the basic instructions on page 218. Fold back the ends of a single pine needle bundle onto itself about 1/4 inch (6 mm), keeping the loose needles on the left side of the bundle. Wrap the raffia around the fold twice.

Step Two

Thread the raffia through the needle and stitch through the fold to hold it in place. Continue winding and stretching the pine needles into a circle using a plain stitch (see page 219) in 1/4-inch intervals until you've formed a 1-inch (2.5 cm) circle. Add the gauge to your work.

Step Three

Add more pine needles through the gauge after every two or three stitches to keep the gauge full, and follow the stitching pattern established in Step 2.

Step Four

When you are satisfied with the diameter of the basket (the basket shown here measures 10 inches [25 cm]), begin working the sides of the basket by slightly raising the pine needles and gauge to overlap the top of the outside row.

Step Five

Create the shape of the basket's sides by gently sloping the first six side rows of pine needles outward. Place the seventh side row directly on top of the sixth, and gently slope the last six side rows inward.

Step Six

Stop adding pine needles as you approach the top of the basket and taper the last bundles down to a few single needles. Remove the gauge and cut the remaining needles at an angle with the scissors. Backstitch over the ending point several times to secure, or continue backstitching all the way around the rim if you prefer that look.

Step Seven

To make the basket's lid, repeat Steps 1 through 3, taking care to check the lid for correct fit after every row. Make a small handle for the basket with a 6-inch (15 cm) length of braided pine needles. (See page 223 for basic instructions and illustrations on making pine needle braids.) Tuck both ends of the braid through the center top of the lid and sew in place.

Step Eight

Add a protective coating to the basket by applying clear shellac or acrylic spray. Allow the coating to dry completely before handling the basket.

MATERIALS

Approximately 150 to 200 pine needle clusters, caps removed
Cotton darning needle
Raffia
5/8-inch (1.5 cm) gauge
Sharp scissors
Clear shellac or acrylic spray

PINE NEEDLE WREATH

Dress up this pine needle wreath for the holidays with a red bow and some greenery to create a warm, traditional Christmas look.

STEP ONE

Prepare the pine needles by soaking as directed in the basic instructions on page 218. Place the wire ring in the middle of a bundle of ten pine needle clusters without caps and secure the clusters to the ring with a double overhand knot (see Figure 1 on page 218).

STEP TWO

Thread the needle with 1 yard (0.9 m) of the upholstery thread and form the first row by wrapping the thread around the pine needle coil, with the metal ring hidden on the inside of the coil. Wrap the thread around both the needles and the wire ring in 1/2-inch (1.3 cm) intervals to establish the stitching pattern for the following rows, and use the clothespin to hold the thread taut as you add new pine needle clusters.

STEP THREE

After three or four wraps, add four more pine needle clusters evenly around the wire ring. Hide the light-colored ends of the pine needles by tucking them into the middle of a bundle. Continue around the ring until you reach the starting point. Stop and cut off the light-colored ends of the beginning pine needles close to the tied thread.

STEP FOUR

Continue over the starting point, adding three or four more wraps to cover the cut ends. Separate the pine needle coil underneath the ring and pull it to the top of the ring to form the second row. Add the 5/8-inch gauge to the work, and continue around the ring, adding pine needle clusters and upholstery thread as needed and following the stitching pattern you established in the first row. Continue working until you're satisfied with the finished size of the wreath. (The wreath shown in the photo has six rows.)

STEP FIVE

To make the decorative outer coil shown in the photo, stop adding pine needle clusters on the last plain row about ten stitches from the finish. Taper down to a stopping point so you end with three to five single needles. You may need to cut away a few needles from the middle of a bundle to reach this point. Trim the last few needles off close to the last stitch but do not cut the thread. All of the pine needles used from this point on should have their caps intact.

STEP SIX

Place three pine needles on top of the last row and continue stitching 1/2-inch from the capped end of each pine needle. Add three more pine needles at every stitch. As the bundle gets thicker, cut into the middle to eliminate bulk. As you add three needless, cut three needles away from the coil.

STEP SEVEN

Continue around the ring until you reach the beginning three clusters. Taper the pine needle bundle down to a single layer of needles. Backstitch over the needles with three stitches to secure the end of the thread. Stitch the bells and bows to the wreath.

STEP EIGHT

Add a protective coating to the wreath by applying clear shellac or acrylic spray. Allow the coating to dry completely before handling the wreath.

MATERIALS

About 200 pine needle clusters, caps removed
About 40 to 50 pine needle clusters, caps on
10-inch (25 cm) diameter wire ring
3 yards (2.7 m) of nylon upholstery thread
Cotton darning needle
Clothespin
5/8-inch (1.5 cm) gauge
2 pine needle bells (see instructions on page 223)
2 pine needle braid bows (see instructions on page 223)
Clear shellac or acrylic spray

PINE NEEDLE CRACKER BASKET

This long, narrow basket makes a good project for a beginning pine needle crafter, and the basket looks at home in almost any decor.

STEP ONE

Prepare the pine needles by soaking as directed in the basic instructions on page 218. Use the band saw to round off the corners of the piece of plywood. Using the electric drill and 1/16-inch bit, drill holes all the way around the base 1/4 inch from the edge and 1/4 inch apart.

STEP TWO

Begin the basket with the three-step basic starting procedure explained and illustrated on page 218. Then start creating the coil on the left side of the wood base about 2 inches (5 cm) from the short end. Insert the darning needle from the bottom of the base up through the holes in the wood, overlapping pine needle coils with each stitch. You will need to add extra pine needle clusters as you go around the base. Use the clothespin to hold the thread taut as you add extra pine needle clusters.

STEP THREE

Try to hide the knot and trimmed ends of the pine needles as you work your way back to the beginning point by separating a bundle and tucking the knot and ends of the needles into the middle of the coil. This step finishes the first row of the basket.

STEP FOUR

Pull the pine needle coil up to form the second row. Add the gauge to the coil. Following the same stitching pattern, continue around the basket two times to form the side rows. Work the walnuts into the next row (see Figure 1 and the basic instructions on page 218) at each end and then finish with three more rows of coiling.

STEP FIVE

Add a protective coating to the basket by applying clear shellac or acrylic spray. Allow the coating to dry completely before handling the basket.

MATERIALS

About 200 pine needle clusters, caps on
1/4-inch (6 mm) plywood, cut to 10-1/2 inches (26 cm) long by 2-1/2 inches (6 cm) wide
Band saw
Electric drill with 1/16-inch bit
Cotton darning needle
Nylon upholstery thread
Clothespin
5/8-inch (1.5 cm) gauge
Black walnut, thinly sliced
Clear shellac or acrylic spray

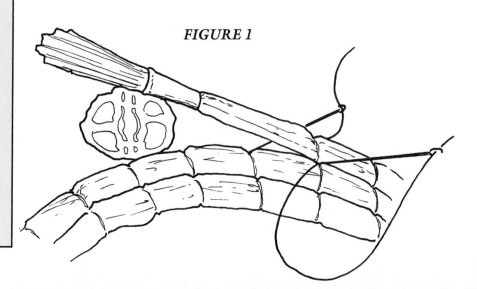

FIGURE 1

These simple tree ornaments make a great project for weekend campers. Once the needles have been softened, they are easy to braid, and the braiding made during an evening of stories around the campfire may well yield enough ornaments to decorate an entire tree.

STEP ONE

Prepare the pine needles by soaking as directed in the basic instructions on page 218. Tie six of the pine needle bunches together with thread just below their caps and divide them into three equal sections. Slip one end of the floral wire through the center of the pine needles until it protrudes 4 inches below the free ends of the needles. Keep the wire with the center section as you braid.

STEP TWO

Braid the pine needles twice and then add another bundle of pine needles to the braid by placing it against the braid on the left side of the braid with its cap protruding about 1/4 inch (6 mm). (See Figure 4 on page 223.) Continue adding new bundles to the left side after every two braids until you've braided all 18 bundles.

STEP THREE

Secure the braid by wrapping the end of the floral wire several times around the stopping point. Cut the leftover floral wire with the wire cutters. Use the scissors to cut off any pine needles that stick out along the braid and to cut the pine needles at the end of the braid on a slant.

MATERIALS

For either ornament:

18 longleaf pine needle bunches, caps on
Spool of brown quilting thread
Medium-gauge floral wire, 4 inches (10 cm) longer than the pine needles
Wire cutters
Sharp scissors
Phone book or other heavy object

Glue gun
1-foot (30 cm) length of narrow velvet ribbon
10 evergreen sprigs, trimmed to 2 inches (5 cm)
3 sprigs of dried German statice, trimmed to 2 inches
2 miniature hemlock cones
Clear shellac or acrylic spray

STEP FOUR

Bend the braid into a wreath or candy-cane shape and place it under a heavy object to flatten and dry overnight. (If you're making the wreath, hot-glue the overlapping braid ends together before placing the ornament under a heavy object.) Add a protective coating to the ornaments by applying clear shellac or acrylic spray. Allow the coating to dry completely before decorating.

STEP FIVE

To decorate, form several loops in the middle of the velvet ribbon, position them on the ornament, and hot-glue in place. Hot-glue the evergreen and German statice sprigs over the center of the loops. Finish by hot-gluing the hemlock cones over the center of the evergreen and statice sprigs.

SEASIDE MATERIALS

Finding and collecting mementos along the beach is certainly one of the greatest pleasures for coastal vacationers. What to do with those seashells and pieces of driftwood once you return home, though, has always been a mystery. They're just too pretty and usually hold too many special memories to throw them away, so instead they end up in the back of a junk drawer.

This chapter includes a variety of inspirational ways to use seashells, driftwood, and even sand. You may be surprised to find these materials spray-painted, gilded, hot-glued, and mixed with dried flowers and herbs. If you don't have your own stash of seashells, avoid the temptation to purchase them in bulk from seaside shops or mail-order suppliers. Many, if not all, of these shells are harvested by a process known as dredging, which is detrimental to ocean life. A few phone calls to neighbors will usually yield more seashells than you can possibly use, and your neighbors will be happy to see their treasures finally put to good use.

SAND CANDLE

MATERIALS

Cooking spoon or garden
  trowel
24 × 18 × 10 inch (60 × 46 ×
  25 cm) box filled with sand
1 to 2 pieces of driftwood,
  3 to 5 inches (7 to 12 cm)
  long
3 small shells, 2 to 4 inches
  (5 to 10 cm) long
12-inch (15 cm) length of
  candle wicking
Candle wick tab
8- to 12-inch (20 to 30 cm)
  long stick, 7/16 inch
  (1 cm) in diameter
Double boiler or thermo-
  statically controlled electric
  skillet
3 pounds (1-1/2 kg) of
  paraffin
Serrated knife

With gritty sand on the outside
and glassy-smooth wax on the
inside, a sand candle is a study
in contrasting textures.

STEP ONE

Using the cooking spoon or
garden trowel, dig a hole in the
middle of the box of sand.
Make the hole about 6 inches
(15 cm) deep in the center and
increasingly shallow toward the
sides, until it's about 6 to 8
inches (15 to 20 cm) wide.

STEP TWO

Just inside the rim of the hole,
place the driftwood pieces and
shells on one side of the hole,
with about 1-1/2 inches (4 cm)
of the materials protruding
above the rim. Hold them in
place by pushing them gently
into the sand.

STEP THREE

Thread the wicking through
the wick tab and place the tab
in the center of the hole. Do
not cover it with sand. Lay the
stick across the top of the hole
and wrap the wick around it, to
hold the wick straight.

STEP FOUR

In the double boiler or thermostatically controlled skillet
set at 150°F, heat the paraffin
until it liquefies. *Caution: Never
melt paraffin in a pan placed
directly on a stove burner, or over
an open flame, or in an electric
pan with only an on/off switch.
Paraffin may catch fire if it is
overheated.*

STEP FIVE

Pour 1/4 inch (6 mm) of wax

into the hole. Make sure the wick is centered, and allow the wax to harden. Reheat the remaining wax and pour it into the hole, filling the hole. The wax should cover at least 1-1/2 inches of the shells and drift-

wood. Make sure the wick is centered, and allow the wax to harden.

STEP SIX

Using your hands, gently scoop the candle out of the sand. Use

the serrated knife to slice a small piece off the bottom to flatten the candle, and trim the wick to 1 inch (2.5 cm).

SAND PAINTING

The technique of sand painting is extraordinarily simple. The creativity lies in combining colors and patterns in pleasing ways.

STEP ONE

Mix the colors of sand you want to use. To do so, place 1/2 to 1 cup (125 to 250 ml) of sand in each 1-cup container, spoon in tempera paint, and stir until you are pleased with the color. Start gradually; even 1/4 teaspoon (1.25 ml) of paint adds significant color. To create additional colors, add more than one color paint to the same container of sand,

or combine the colored sands. If you use powdered tempera, the colored sand will be ready for immediate use. If you use liquid tempera, allow the sand to dry (two to three days).

STEP TWO

Pour or spoon a layer of sand into the bottom of the jar. Either smooth it out so that it is level, or create a pattern of waves and undulations with the spoon, the plastic drink stirrer, or a small piece of cardboard. Continue adding different colored layers of sand and creating patterns until the jar is filled. Screw the lid onto the jar.

MATERIALS

4 pounds (2 kg) of clean, white sand
1-cup (250 ml) container for each color sand you plan to make
Teaspoon
Powdered or liquid tempera paints in various colors
1-pint (500 ml) clear glass or plastic jar with lid
Plastic drink stirrer or small piece of cardboard (optional)

Driftwood Mobile

Picking up attractive driftwood along a beach is almost irresistible, but what do you do with it once you get home? One answer is to construct a mobile that will sway gracefully in the breeze.

Step One

Using the soft scrub brush or old paintbrush, brush the sand off the driftwood pieces. If necessary, rinse them under running water and allow to dry. Brush on a coat of shellac or water-proofing sealer with the paintbrush.

Step Two

Lay the pieces of driftwood on the floor, arranging them in various positions until you are pleased with the result. Aim for balance—the weight, both physical and visual, on the left and right halves of the mobile should be roughly equal.

Step Three

Using the pencil, mark the places where the pieces of wood

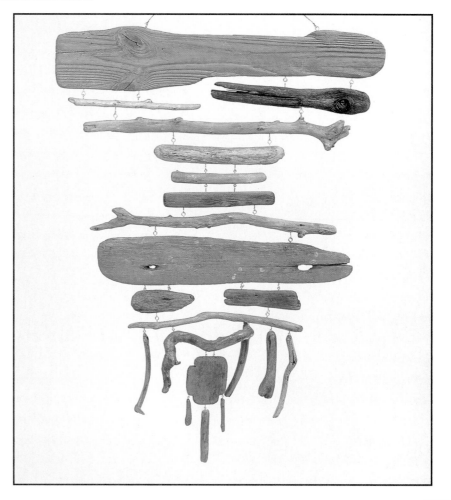

Materials

Soft scrub brush or old paint-
    brush
Driftwood pieces of various
    sizes and shapes
Shellac or water-proofing
    sealer
Paintbrush
Pencil
Screw eyes of various sizes
Electric drill with 1/16- and
    1/8-inch bits
Needle-nosed pliers
30- to 40-inch (75 to 100 cm)
    length of #12-gauge steel or
    copper wire

will be attached to each other. All attachments will be top to bottom, not side to side. You'll need screw eyes on the bottom of the piece above and on top of the piece below. Also decide on the size screw eye needed for each connection. The larger the piece of wood that a screw eye is supporting, the bigger the screw eye needs to be.

Step Four

Drill starter holes for the screw eyes in the wood at the locations you've marked, using the smaller or larger bit for smaller or larger screws. With the needle-nosed pliers, open one eye of each upper-lower connecting pair. Screw the screw eyes into the wood, link one with

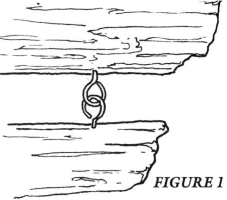

FIGURE 1

the other, and close the opened eye with the pliers (see Figure 1).

Step Five

Drill two holes at either end of the top of the uppermost piece of wood and attach two large screw eyes. Connect the piece of wire to them, to use as a hanger.

COPPER SHELL PRINT

The intricate shapes and textures of your favorite seashells can be displayed in small copper wall hangings.

STEP ONE

Roll out the clay to an even thickness at least 1/4 inch (6 mm). With the outside of the shell faceup, gently press the shell into the clay to hold it in place.

STEP TWO

Center the sheet of copper over the shell. Impress the shell's shape into the copper by gently rubbing the copper with the burnisher. Sign your name in the bottom right corner with the pen.

STEP THREE

Position the sheet of copper in the center of the mat's opening and glue in place. Glue the backing in place and display after all the glue has dried.

MATERIALS

Modeling clay or adhesive floral clay
Rolling pin
Scallop shell large enough to almost fill the area of the frame opening, or several smaller shells
Sheet of copper at least 1/2 inch (1.3 cm) larger than the frame opening
Plastic burnisher
Fine-tip pen, ink cartridge removed
Picture mat set
White craft glue

NAUTILUS ARRANGEMENT

The chambered nautilus is so arresting a shell that it needs only a simple arrangement.

STEP ONE

Hot-glue the oyster shells to the cardboard, piling them up in a mound; cover the cardboard completely. Glue the nautilus shell on top of the center of the mound.

STEP TWO

Run a line of glue across one narrow side of the floral foam and stand it up inside the shell, glued-side-down.

MATERIALS

24 oyster half shells
Glue gun
Oval piece of cardboard
    5 inches (12 cm) wide
    and 7 inches (17 cm) long
Nautilus shell about 6 inches
    (15 cm) wide at its widest
    point
4 × 4 × 2-inch (10 × 10 × 5
    cm) block of floral foam
12 pieces of dried brown
    grass, in various lengths
    from 12 to 24 inches (30
    to 60 cm)
4 40-inch (100 cm) pieces
    of split rattan
Hammer
4 1/2-inch (1.3 cm) tacks
    with heads
Medium-gauge floral wire
Brown floral tape
36 small shells of various types
Floral picks
6 stems of cockscomb,
    trimmed to 3 inches (7 cm)

STEP THREE

Insert the grass into the foam so that it curls toward the center on each side of the arrangement.

STEP FOUR

Using your fingers, curl one end of each piece of split rattan. Drive a tack from the center of the curl through all the layers of rattan, and bend the protruding end of the tack back against the rattan. Insert two of the rattan pieces into the foam, with the curls toward the center of the arrangement.

STEP FIVE

Cut the floral wire into lengths ranging from 6 to 14 inches (15 to 36 cm) and wrap them with the floral tape. Glue the small shells to the ends of the covered wires and insert the wires into the foam in the center of the arrangement, as shown in the photo. Allow some shells to spill over the front.

STEP SIX

Attach floral picks to the cockscomb stems and pick the cockscomb into the foam, filling in the empty spaces below and between the small shells.

STEP SEVEN

Glue the two remaining rattan curls horizontally to the oyster shell base, with the curls toward the arrangement.

PINK SHELL WREATH

STEP SIX

Glue the sprigs of baby's-breath to the base, spacing them evenly among the shells.

STEP SEVEN

Bend the chenille stem into an inverted U-shape and glue it to the back of the wreath at top center, to serve as a hanger.

STEP EIGHT

With the remaining piece of ribbon, tie a four-loop bow with 11-inch (27 cm) streamers, and wire it to the bottom of the base. Hot-glue the third starfish to the center of the bow.

MATERIALS

Pink spray paint
14-inch (36 cm) diameter vine wreath base
6 sprigs of eucalyptus, 2 trimmed to 7 inches (17 cm), 2 trimmed to 9 inches (22 cm), and 2 trimmed to 10 inches (25 cm)
Burgundy spray paint
Glue gun
1 sea biscuit, 4 to 5 inches (10 to 12 cm) wide
8 flat shells, 2 to 3 inches (5 to 7 cm) wide, preferably with a pink cast
3 starfish, approximately 1 inch (2.5 cm) wide
10 sprigs of dried baby's-breath, trimmed to 2 inches
2 yards (1.8 m) of 1-inch-wide white iridescent ribbon, cut into two equal pieces
4-inch length of pink chenille stem
Fine-gauge floral wire

Many of the shells that wash up on the beach have a pink cast. Highlight their color with materials that echo that hue, and make a delicate wreath to grace a bedroom or bath.

STEP ONE

Spray the wreath base and the two 7-inch sprigs of eucalyptus pink. Spray the remaining eucalyptus burgundy.

STEP TWO

Glue the sea biscuit to the base at the bottom center of the wreath.

STEP THREE

Lay four flat shells on each side of the sea biscuit, overlapping them. Rearrange them until you're pleased with the result, then glue the shells to the base. The edges of the two shells closest to the sea biscuit should lie under the edges of the sea biscuit. Glue one starfish near the top of each shell arrangement.

STEP FOUR

Place glue on the stem ends of the eucalyptus and insert into the base under the sea biscuit, in a fan shape with the two 10-inch sprigs of burgundy on the outside, then the pink sprigs, then the 7-inch burgundy sprigs.

STEP FIVE

Glue one end of one piece of ribbon to the back of the wreath, behind the top shell on the left. Wrap the ribbon around the base three or four times, and glue it to the back of the wreath behind the top shell on the right.

Seashore Jewelry

Shell jewelry can be made as classical or as funky as you like, and the materials are usually inexpensive.

Necklace

Step One

Drill a hole in each shell on the opposite side of the shell's natural opening. Use the pliers to gently undo and remove the clasp on one end of the necklace and set aside. Thread the chain through the needle.

Step Two

Thread the shells onto the chain by guiding the needle in through the natural opening in the shell and out through the drilled hole. When all the shells are on the necklace, remove the needle and reassemble the clasp.

MATERIALS

Necklace

Electric drill with 1/16-inch bit
30 to 45 sea snail shells
Simple gold or silver chain necklace
Small pair of pliers
Sewing needle, with eye wide enough for necklace chain to fit through

MATERIALS

Lace Jewelry Pin

Scissors
The back of a writing pad or other piece of cardboard
Jewelry pin backing or large safety pin
Glue gun
1 foot (30 cm) of narrow lace
Straight pin
Pencil
Small shell
2 small pearl buttons

Lace Jewelry Pin

Step One

Cut two pieces of cardboard into rectangles that are just big enough to cover the pin backing or large safety pin. Hot-glue the two pieces of cardboard together and then hot-glue the doubled cardboard to the top of the jewelry pin backing. If you're using a safety pin, hot-glue the doubled cardboard to the side of the large safety pin that doesn't open. (Be sure not to glue the pointed side of the safety pin to the cardboard.)

Step Two

Cut two 1-inch (2.5 cm) lengths of lace and set aside. Loop the remaining lace back and forth to cover the cardboard, decreasing the length of the loops slightly with each one as shown in the photo. Hold the lace in place with a straight pin. Hot-glue the 1-inch streamers under the top loop. Carefully remove the sewing pin and hot-glue the lace in place. (Use an unsharpened pencil or pencil eraser to press the lace into the hot glue to prevent burning yourself.)

Step Three

Hot-glue the small shell in the center of the lace bow and then hot-glue a pearl button near the bottom of each streamer.

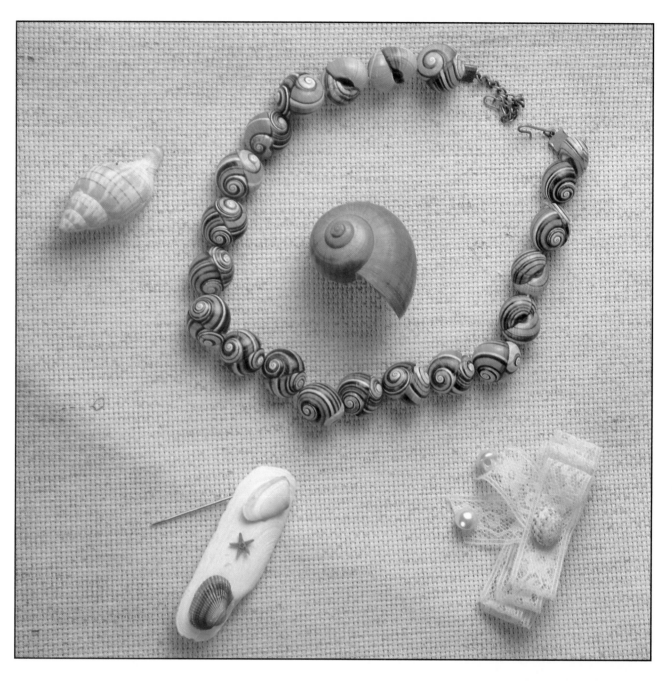

Shell Jewelry Pin

STEP ONE

Cut two pieces of cardboard into rectangles that are just big enough to cover the pin backing or large safety pin. Hot-glue the two pieces of cardboard together and then hot-glue the doubled cardboard to the top of the jewelry pin backing. If you're using a safety pin, hot-glue the doubled cardboard to the side of the large safety pin that doesn't open. (Be sure not to glue the pointed side of the safety pin to the cardboard.)

STEP TWO

Hot-glue the long, narrow shell on top of the cardboard. Arrange the smaller shells on top of the larger one and hot-glue them in place.

MATERIALS

Shell Jewelry Pin

Scissors
The back of a writing pad or other piece of cardboard
Jewelry pin backing or large safety pin
Glue gun
Narrow shell slightly longer than the pin
2 small shells
1 small starfish

245

SHELL CHRISTMAS TREE ORNAMENTS

When decorated with dried herbs and flowers, seashells can become intriguing ornaments for the Christmas tree.

Wine Shell Ornament

STEP ONE

Hot-glue one end of the 2-1/2-inch shell to the center of the wine-colored shell so that it is standing upright.

STEP TWO

Hot-glue the foliage and flowers inside the flat wine-colored shell in the order given in the materials list, creating a fan shape. Hot-glue the 1-inch shell at the base of the arrangement so that it covers the stems of the foliage and flowers.

STEP THREE

Fold the ribbon in half and cross it in the center. Hot-glue it to the back of the ornament, leaving a loop at the top of the shell about 2 inches long to serve as a hanger, and allowing the crossed ends to dangle beneath the ornament.

Orange Shell Ornament

STEP ONE

Hot-glue the foliage and flowers to the outside of the orange shell in the order given in the materials list, creating a fan shape.

STEP TWO

Hot-glue three of the white shells among the sprigs of foliage, and glue the fourth shell at the base of the arrangement so that it covers the stems of the foliage and flowers. Hot-glue the starfish to the orange shell.

STEP THREE

Fold the ribbon in half and cross it in the center. Hot-glue it to the inside of the orange shell, leaving a loop at the top of the shell about 2 inches long to serve as a hanger, and allowing the crossed ends to dangle beneath the ornament.

MATERIALS

Orange Shell Ornament

Glue gun
3 sprigs of sweet Annie, trimmed to 3 inches (7 cm)
3 sprigs of German statice, trimmed to 2 inches (5 cm)
3 sprigs of yellow yarrow, trimmed to 2 inches
Orange shell, about 3-1/2 inches (8 cm) in diameter
4 white shells of various shapes, 1 to 2 inches (2.5 to 5 cm) long
1 starfish, about 1 inch in diameter
1 orange strawflower
19-inch (48 cm) length of white velvet ribbon, 1/2 inch (1.3 cm) wide

White Shell Ornament

STEP ONE

Hot-glue the coral, foliage, and flowers inside the flat white shell in the order given in the materials list, creating a fan shape.

STEP TWO

Hot-glue the three small white shells in the spaces between the materials, and glue the lavender shell at the base of the arrangement so that it covers the stems of the foliage and flowers.

STEP THREE

Fold the ribbon in half and cross it in the center. Hot-glue it to the back of the shell, leav-
(continued on page 248)

MATERIALS

Wine Shell Ornament

Glue gun
1 long, narrow shell, about 2-1/2 inches (6 cm) long
Flat, wine-colored shell, about 3-1/2 inches (8 cm) in diameter
2 bay leaves, 1 inch (2.5 cm) long
5 stems of blue sage, trimmed to 2 inches (5 cm)

3 stems of pearly everlasting, trimmed to 2 inches
3 stems of magenta globe amaranth, trimmed to 1 inch
1 flat, round shell, about 1 inch in diameter
19-inch (48 cm) length of wine-colored velvet ribbon, 1/2 inch (1.3 cm) wide

White Shell Ornament
(continued from page 246)

ing a loop at the top of the shell about 2 inches long to serve as a hanger, and allowing the crossed ends to dangle beneath the ornament.

MATERIALS

White Shell Ornament

Glue gun
2 pieces of purple coral, about 2 inches (5 cm) long
2 sprigs of rosemary, trimmed to 3 inches (7 cm)
2 stems of lavender, trimmed to 2 inches
2 stems of purple annual statice, trimmed to 1 inch (2.5 cm)

1 flat white shell, about 4-1/2 inches (11 cm) in diameter
3 white shells, about 3/4 inch (2 cm) long
1 shell with lavender markings, 1 inch long
19-inch (48 cm) length of lavender velvet ribbon, 1/4 inch (6 mm) wide

SHELL TISSUE BOX

MATERIALS

40 to 50 shells in various sizes
Plastic tissue box
Glue gun

Seashells are a popular motif on towels, soaps, and even shower curtains. This simple tissue box fits nicely into the seashore theme.

STEP ONE

Separate the shells into three piles based on size: small, medium, and large. Arrange several of the largest shells on the top and sides of the tissue box and hot-glue in place.

STEP TWO

Continue gluing shells onto the box until it's just about covered, working with the large and medium-size shells. Last, fill in the bare spots with the smallest shells.

DRIFTWOOD TABLE ARRANGEMENT

A small block of hidden foam converts a large piece of driftwood into a base for a wonderful, natural arrangement.

STEP ONE

Examine your piece of driftwood and determine which side will form the front of your arrangement. Hot-glue the block of foam to the back side

of the driftwood and use floral pins to cover the foam with Spanish moss. Set aside four or five small pieces of moss for later use.

STEP TWO

Insert the cattail stems in the top of the foam, staggering their height as shown in the photo on page 000. Next,

insert the wild grass among the cattails. Then insert the birch branches and the silver dollar eucalyptus.

STEP THREE

Decorate the front of the driftwood by hot-gluing on the silk succulents and the small pieces of moss.

MATERIALS

Large piece of driftwood
(or several smaller pieces
hot-glued together)
Glue gun
Block of floral foam, 5 inches
(12 cm) square
Floral pins
Spanish moss
5 cattails, trimmed to 18
inches (46 cm), 16 inches
(41 cm), 14 inches (36 cm),
12 inches (30 cm), and
10 inches (25 cm)
10 stems of dried wild grass,
trimmed to 14 inches
3 birch branches, trimmed
to 14 inches
3 stems of dried silver dollar
eucalyptus, 2 trimmed to
8 inches (20 cm) and
1 trimmed to 5 inches
(12 cm)
4 silk succulents

SHELL CANDLE ON ROPE BASE

A length of rope and a seashell add up to a very nautical-looking candle. Use any shell that will hold liquid wax—for example, a murex, whelk, conch, or clam.

STEP ONE

Working on a flat surface protected with newspaper, coil the rope into a circle about 3 inches (8 cm) in diameter and three rows high. Hot-glue the coils together between the rows, and glue the ends inside the circle. Allow to dry.

STEP TWO

Place the shell on top of the coiled rope, making sure it is as level as possible. To prevent the hot, liquid wax from running out when you pour it into the shell, make sure the tip of the shell does not point down. Hot-glue the shell to the coiled rope.

MATERIALS

Old newspaper
1/2-inch (1.25) diameter rope, 18 inches (46 cm) long
Glue gun
Shell, 4 to 5 inches (10 to 12 cm) wide
6-inch (15 cm) length of candle wicking
Candle wick tab
1 pound (1-1/2 kg) of paraffin
Double boiler or thermostatically controlled electric skillet
Red crayon
Pencil or knife

STEP THREE

Thread the wicking through the wick tab, and place the tab in the center of the shell.

STEP FOUR

In the double boiler or thermostatically controlled skillet set at 150°F, heat the paraffin until it liquefies. *Caution: Never melt paraffin in a pan placed directly on a stove burner, or over an open flame, or in an electric pan with only an on/off switch. Paraffin may catch fire if it is overheated.*

STEP FIVE

Remove the paper from the crayon, break the crayon into pieces, and add a piece at a time to the wax, allowing it to melt. Keep adding pieces of crayon until the desired color is reached.

STEP SIX

Pour 1/4 inch (6 mm) of wax into the shell. Make sure the wick is centered, and allow the wax to harden. Reheat the remaining wax, and add it to the shell until it reaches 1/4 to 1/2 inch (6 mm to 1.25 cm) below the top. Keep the wick centered in the wax. Lay a pencil or knife across the shell and wrap the excess wick around it to keep it out of the wax. Allow the wax to harden, and trim the wick to about 1 inch (2.5 cm).

GOLD AND WHITE WREATH

This pale, delicate wreath adds
an interesting focal point to a
bedroom or bath.

STEP ONE

Spray the vine wreath base
lightly with the metallic gold
paint. Spray the shells so that
they are well covered. Let dry.

STEP TWO

Hot-glue the large, flat shell to
the bottom center of the base.
Glue the ten assorted shells
around the base, spacing them
equidistantly.

STEP THREE

Hot-glue the bunches of baby's-
breath around the front of the
wreath, filling in all the spaces
between the shells. Hot-glue
the stems of peppergrass
among the baby's-breath.

STEP FOUR

Wire one end of the pearl garland to the bottom of the vine
base and wrap it all the way
around the wreath, as shown in
the photo. Wire the other end
to the base.

MATERIALS

Metallic gold spray paint
12-inch (30 cm) diameter vine
   wreath base
Flat shell, about 7 inches
   (17 cm) in diameter
10 assorted shells, 1-1/2 to
   3 inches (4 to 7 cm) long
Glue gun
25 2-inch-diameter (5 cm)
   bunches of baby's-breath
11 stems of peppergrass,
   trimmed to 2 inches
2 6-inch (15 cm) lengths of
   fine-gauge floral wire
1-1/2 yards (1.4 m) of pearl
   garland

CONTRIBUTING DESIGNERS

NORA BLOSE AND MICHELLE WEST create and market herbal crafts in Enka, North Carolina. (Pages 41, 49, 52, 53, 82, 191, and 251.)

PHYLLIS COMBS's family boasts four generations of cornhusk crafters. She markets her work under the name Shuckery and Wood Pretties, in Weber City, Virginia. (Pages 204, 208, 210, and 213.)

DOUG ELLIOTT is a naturalist, craftsman, and storyteller from Union Mills, North Carolina. His latest book is *Wildwoods Wisdom* (Paragon House, 1992). (Projects: Pages 88, 96, 99, 104, 112, and 122. Designer's Tips and information: Pages 86, 87, 89, and 97.)

JANET FRYE is a floral designer and the proprietor of The Enchanted Florist, in Arden, North Carolina. (Pages 62, 94, 126, 132, 165, 207, 215, and 242.)

CYNTHIA GILLOOLEY is a floral designer and proprietor of The Golden Cricket in Asheville, North Carolina. (Pages 34, 46, 55, 58, 66, 76, 83, 127, and 170.)

JEANETTE HAFNER grows her craft herbs and flowers in her gardens in Orange, Connecticut. She teaches flower and herb drying, as well as design, and markets her wreaths and arrangements at craft fairs. (Pages 27, 38, 40, 48, 56, 64, 70, 71, and 80.

WANA HENRY specializes in crafts made from cones, nuts, seeds, and pods, in Church Hill, Tennessee, and markets her work at craft fairs. (Pages 186, 188, 190, and 192.)

JUDY HORN teaches cornhusk crafts and sells her wreaths, dolls, and arrangements at her store, The Corn Husk Shoppe, in Weaverville, North Carolina. (Pages 200 and 206.)

SALLY ANN KNUCKLES is the proprietor of Sea Candles in Powells Point, North Carolina. (Pages 238 and 250.)

CHRISTINE LEVIN specializes in gourds and beadwork in Cheshire, Oregon. (Pages 152 and 154.)

AILEEN LOVELACE uses various seeds to make crafts in Nickelsville, Virginia. (Pages 194 and 197.)

DAN MACK makes and markets rustic furniture in Warwick, New York. He is the author of *Making Rustic Furniture* (Sterling, 1992). (Page 119.)

JUDY MALLOW specializes in pine needle crafts in Carthage, North Carolina, and markets her work at craft fairs. (Pages 224, 226,230, 232, and 234.)

BILL "VASSILI" MARINOS is a gourd grower and crafter from Dearborn, Michigan. (Pages 140, 142, and 157.)

BETTY JEAN MARSHALL makes cornhusk wreaths and dolls in Big Stone Gap, Virginia. (Pages 202 and 210.)

ALYCE NADEAU grows 200 different herbs for her business, Goldenrod Mountain Herbs, in Deep Gap, North Carolina, where she makes and markets wreaths, arrangements, and other herbal crafts. (Pages 25, 28, 29, 30, 42, 54, 59, 60, 63, 68, 78, and 246.)

ETHEL OWEN is a gourd crafter from Birmingham, Alabama. (Page 138.)

MORGYN GEOFFRY OWENS-CELLI is an internationally recognized wheat weaver from Long Beach, California. His work has been displayed at the Smithsonian Institution in Washington, D.C. (Pages 166, 168, 172, 174, 175, 178, and 181.)

MARILYN REHM is a gourd crafter from Big Prairie, Ohio. (Page 151.)

MARY ANN ROOD is a gourd crafter from Apex, North Carolina. (Pages 136 and 137.)

REX SHEPPERD is the proprietor of Shepperd Woodworks in Creede, Colorado. (Page 102.)

LYN SILER is a well-known basket maker and teacher, whose shop, The Weavery, is in Waynesville, North Carolina. She is the author of *The Basket Book* and *Handmade Baskets* (Sterling, 1988 and 1991). (Page 115.)

MARY WOJECK is a gourd crafter from Marietta, South Carolina. The carving on the gourds was done by Frank Wojeck. (Pages 139, 141, 146, 148, and 158.)

AND THANKS TO...

Elizabeth Albrecht (51, 74, 81, 130), Lewis Applebaum (160), Julianne Bronder (248), Joseph Dwyer (240), Blanch Foster (229), Rood Friday (144), Fred Gaylor (67), Michael Gillooley (111), Harold Hall (145), Clodine Hamilton (159), Earline Hoffmann (106), Jim Hoffmann (110), Clyde Hollifield (128), Tina Kelley (249), Claudette Mautor (44), Sally Pfaff (36), Rob Pulleyn (131), Dot Rosenstengel (107), Vince Vangeau (239), Diane Weaver (93), Tom Wolfe (92, 124, 171, 196, 241, and 244), and Kay Zaia (243).

LOCATION PHOTOGRAPHY

The Claddach Inn
    Hendersonville, North Carolina
    Dennis and Vicki Tacilio, owners

The Waverly Inn
    Hendersonville, North Carolina
    John and Diane Sheiry, owners

ADDITIONAL PHOTOGRAPHY

Jim Colando
    East Lansing, Michigan
    (Pages 216 and 236).

Tim Barnwell
    Asheville, North Carolina
    (Pages 8, 20, 22, 72, 84, 108, 134, 162, 184, and 198.)

MAIL-ORDER SOURCES

FLOWERS AND HERBS

Capriland's Herb Farm
Silver St.
North Coventry, CT 06238

Heart's Ease
4101 Burton Dr.
Cambria, CA 93428-3003

Pequea Trading Co.
10 East Main St.
Strasburg, PA 17579

Rasland Farm
N.C. 82 at U.S. 13
Godwin, NC 28344

The Sassafrass Hutch
11880 Sandy Bottom, NE
Greenville, MI 48838

Sinking Springs Herb Farm
234 Blair Shore Rd.
Elkton, MD 21921

Smile Herb Shop
4908 Berwyn Rd.
College Park, MD 20740

Stillridge Herb Farm
10370 Rt. 99
Woodstock, MD 21163

Tom Thumb Workshops
P.O. Box 322
Chincoteague, VA 23336

Well-Sweep Herb Farm
317 Mt. Bethel Rd.
Port Murray, NJ 07865

PINE NEEDLES

Judy Mallow
Route 4 Box 100-B
Carthage, NC 28327

WHEAT WEAVING

American Foundation for the Straw Arts (AFSA)
5326 County Route 125
Campbell, NY 14821

Campus Granary
Bethel College Women's Association
North Newton, KS 67117

Morgan Geoffry Owens-Celli
P.O. Box 6398
Long Beach, CA 90806-6398

BIBLIOGRAPHY

Bailey, L.H. *Hortus Third.* New York: Macmillan Publishing Co., 1976.

Butcher, Mary. *Willow Work.* London, Britain: Dryad Press, Ltd, 1986.

Coats, Alice M. *Flowers and Their Histories.* New York: Pitman Publishing Co., 1956.

Cusick, Dawn. *Potpourri Crafts.* New York: Sterling Publishing Co., 1992.

Darnell, Jane, and Hawkes, Patricia. *Pods and Odd Bodikins.* Chester, Connecticut: The Globe Pequot Press, 1979.

Mallow, Judy. *Pine Needle and Nut Crafting.* Carthage, NC: Judy Mallow, 1984.

Mautor, Claudette and Pulleyn, Rob. *Everlasting Floral Gifts.* New York: Sterling Publishing Co., 1990.

Prawat, Carolyn Mordecai. *Gourd Craft.* Mount Gilead, Ohio: American Gourd Society, 1978.

Pulleyn, Rob. *The Wreath Book.* New York: Sterling Publishing Co., 1988.

Taylor, Carol. *Herbal Wreaths.* New York: Sterling Publishing Co., 1992.

INDEX